# Teaching Outside the Box

## HOW TO GRAB YOUR STUDENTS
## BY THEIR BRAINS

**Second Edition**

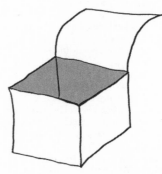

## LouAnne Johnson

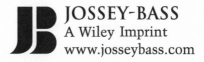

JOSSEY-BASS
A Wiley Imprint
www.josseybass.com

Published by Jossey-Bass
A Wiley Imprint
989 Market Street, San Francisco, CA 94103–1741—www.josseybass.com

**Library of Congress Cataloging-in-Publication Data**

Johnson, LouAnne.
  Teaching outside the box : how to grab your students by their brains / LouAnne Johnson.—2nd ed.
    p. cm.
  Includes index.
  ISBN 978-0-470-90374-2 (pbk.)
  1. Teaching. I. Title.
  LB1025.3.J6395 2011
  371.102—dc22                                                          2010049580

Printed in the United States of America
SECOND EDITION
*PB Printing*   10 9 8 7 6 5 4 3 2

# CONTENTS

## ACKNOWLEDGMENTS

This book would not have been possible without the teachers who taught me to believe in myself and follow my heart: Mary Ellen Boyling, Evelyn Hodak, Eleanora Sandblade, Caroline DeSalvo, Jerry Novelli, James Miller, Mary Ann Greggan, Jane Allen, and Kenneth Brodeur.

A shout out to my "posse"—the unforgettable, lovable, "unteachable" Carlmont Academy students who taught me how to teach.

*Muchas gracias y abrazos fuerzas a los estudiantes en mi primer clase de* Limited English. Their English may have been limited, but their desire to learn was unlimited.

Special thanks to all the teachers who tested the techniques from this book in their own classrooms and reported their results, to Kathy Chappel for providing an elementary school perspective, and to Lesley Iura and Kate Gagnon for their unwavering support of my work and writing.

# THE AUTHOR

**LouAnne Johnson,** author of the *New York Times* best-seller *Dangerous Minds,* is a former U.S. Navy journalist, Marine Corps officer, and high school teacher. Johnson is the author of seven nonfiction books and the novel *Muchacho*. At present, she is an assistant professor of teacher education at Santa Fe Community College in New Mexico.

A native of rural northwestern Pennsylvania, Johnson served nine years on active military duty, achieving the rank of Journalist First Class in the Navy and 2nd Lieutenant in the Marine Corps. She holds a BS in psychology and a master's degree in teaching English.

In 1989, Johnson began teaching as an intern at a northern California high school. Two years later, she was appointed department chair of a special program for at-risk teens. During the government evaluation of ten similar pilot programs, Johnson's group was rated first in academic achievement, increased self-esteem, and student retention. Her memoir about that experience, *My Posse Don't Do Homework,* was adapted for the 1995 hit movie *Dangerous Minds,* starring Michele Pfeiffer. *My Posse Don't Do Homework* also was condensed in *Reader's Digest* magazine, and, under the title *Dangerous Minds,* has been published in eight languages, including Italian, German, Japanese, and French.

Following publication of *My Posse Don't Do Homework,* Johnson continued to teach high school English for eight years, then left teaching full-time to return to college for more graduate studies in writing. Subsequently, she served as lead ESL instructor at Lexington Community College in North Carolina and as an adjunct instructor of developmental reading and writing for Western New Mexico University. She has also designed and presented workshops in classroom management and motivation for teachers across the country. A staunch advocate of school reform and a popular keynote speaker, she has presented addresses to over one hundred organizations, including the National School Boards Association, the National Council on Curriculum Development, the Association of Texas Professional Educators, National Hispanic University, and the European Council of International Schools. She has appeared on several television shows, including *Oprah, CBS Eye to Eye, NBC Weekend Today, Maury Povich,* and *CNN Talkback Live.*

## INTRODUCTION

**W**henever I finish writing a book and face the task of writing an introduction, my childhood comes back to haunt me. "Don't toot your own horn," Grandma Lucy Johnson used to warn me. "People will think you have a big head."

I honestly don't believe my head is exceptionally big. I know that I'm not the best teacher in the world. There are thousands of teachers in this country who do the same things I do in my classroom, but they don't have the time or energy to go home at night and write books. And though I'm not the world's best teacher, I am an excellent teacher and I know that my approach works. My philosophy, briefly, is this:

> When students believe that success is possible, they will try.
> So my first priority in any class is to help my students
> believe in themselves and their ability to learn.

During the past two and a half decades, I have taught adult English-language learners and college seniors, high school remedial readers and honors-level university freshmen, advanced placement high school juniors, developmental readers, GED students, and—most recently—alternative-licensure education students who decided at age thirty or forty or fifty that what they really want to do is teach school. I have also presented over one hundred keynote speeches and workshops around the world, which gave me the opportunity to meet thousands of gifted teachers. I took copious notes. And I spent many hours out of those twenty-five years asking questions, reading research about brain-based learning and nutrition and classroom lighting, corresponding with teachers and education students via e-mail, observing veteran teachers in action, sharing best (and worst) practices with other teachers, advising new teachers who approach me with classroom management problems—and trying to design a way to incorporate all of that information into one book.

The first chapter is a letter I wrote for all teachers, thanking them for teaching. I don't think it is possible to thank teachers too often for the work that they do. Next, I asked myself, what if I could sit down for a few hours with a new teacher and share all the things I wish I had known before I started teaching? That imaginary conversation became the first six chapters. And judging by the feedback I have received from readers, some veterans also enjoy those chapters—some for the nostalgia of recalling their own starry-eyed optimism or for some tip or strategy that they found helpful. Chapters Seven through Nine contain a collection of strategies that I have created, borrowed, or tweaked from my experience, observations, conversations, and research. Nothing world-shaking here. A few unusual suggestions, such as studying successful horse wranglers to gain insight into teaching rowdy students or adjusting student attitudes by pointing out that there are only five things we *have* to do in order to stay alive (and going to school is not on the list). But the middle chapters are primarily meant to provide a buffet of side dishes for teachers to pick and choose from, depending upon their tastes and appetites, as well as those of their students.

Chapters Nine and Ten contain information about the effects of essential fatty acids on brain function and light sensitivity—the two most popular topics from my workshops and speeches. This information originally appeared in my book *The Queen of Education* (Jossey-Bass, 1994) and has been revised and updated for its inclusion here.

Chapter Eleven gives an update on my "posse" from the movie *Dangerous Minds,* and Chapter Twelve offers a positive view of our profession which gets more than its share of bad press.

That brings me up to date on my notes so far. I'll have to buy a new notebook for my new job. I'm sure the new teachers in my classes will have much to teach me.

Sometimes I receive an e-mail asking if I could please add more suggestions for elementary school teachers in my books. I have done my best in this new edition, but my contribution in this area is still limited. I have successfully tutored several young children at their parents' request, but I have no training in early childhood or elementary education other than helping to raise four stepchildren for a few years. But I truly believe that most successful teaching strategies can be tweaked to fit students across a wide range of ages and abilities.

Human beings are human, and students are students. Regardless of their age, almost all students have the same concerns: Will I be able to learn the material? Will the teacher like me? Will I like the teacher? Will my classmates like me? And regardless of the subject or age level we teach, most effective teaching strategies can be modified to fit our students.

Here's an example of a grade 2 activity that I applied, with a few modifications, for a student in his mid-sixties.

In preparation for one of the courses I teach, I watched a video clip where a teacher created a "circle of friends" in her elementary school classroom. She asked six youngsters to sit in a circle and discuss all the good things they had seen each other do in school that day. The object of the exercise was to change the children's perception of their classmate, Matt, who always seemed to be in trouble. The teacher believed that if everybody, including the teacher and Matt himself, thought of Matt as a troublemaker, he would continue to live up to his label. When the other children complimented Matt for staying in his chair, not hitting people, and listening to instructions, he beamed. And, just as the teacher had hoped, Matt started repeating the positive behaviors. She stopped thinking of him as a troublemaker, and his classmates changed their opinions of him as well.

While I was viewing that video clip, I found myself thinking, "That boy reminds me of Joe," the oldest student in one of my classes—and the least popular, judging by the sighs and eye rolling of his classmates whenever he raised his hand during class. Joe had a tendency to ramble off-topic, and the more impatient his classmates became, the longer he rambled. Nobody wanted to sit with Joe during small-group activities. And eventually I found myself sighing when I saw his hand waving in the air.

I realized that if I allowed my impatience to show, it would give tacit approval to Joe's classmates to dislike and disrespect him. So I started looking for any small positive contribution that Joe made to the class and I made a point of thanking him in front of the other students. I removed the extra chairs from the classroom so that Joe couldn't be excluded when the students formed small groups, and I joined the group that contained Joe so I could engage him in the evening's activities. Before long I noticed a few classmates talking to Joe during the break, swapping stories about their recent public school classroom observations. I would not characterize the relationship between Joe and his classmates as friends, but they no longer ostracized him. And, most important, I stopped thinking of his questions as interruptions, which in turn changed my attitude. Surprisingly, once everybody started acting more interested in what he had to say, Joe seemed to have less to say. Or perhaps he no longer felt a need to demand attention once people stopped ignoring him.

I still have much to learn as a teacher. (I'm sure teachers who read the first edition of this book, especially reading teachers, will appreciate how much less I know now than I did when I wrote that first edition!) Every class of students brings new lessons to learn. The lessons aren't really new, but a lesson may be new to me, or it may be a reminder of something I learned previously, something that didn't take hold because it wasn't connected with a personal experience.

The title of this book, *Teaching Outside the Box,* isn't meant to imply that this book contains completely new or unique teaching strategies—there really is nothing new when it comes to teaching. Create a unique and unusual way to teach something, and you will find that somewhere along the line somebody else has already tried your method. Plato, perhaps, or Maria Montessori. What I mean to imply by the title is that I encourage teachers to step outside of the box that so often delineates teaching, where the focus is on changing student behavior to meet our expectations instead of changing our own behavior to evoke a different student response.

For example, chewing gum is a sticky problem (sorry, I couldn't resist) for many schools. Kids love chewing gum. And millions of students are threatened and warned and punished for chewing gum every day, even if they don't stick it under their seats or between the pages of their textbooks. It's an endless battle—as long as you continue to try to stop kids from chewing gum. One resourceful principal at a school where the custodial staff complained daily about having to spend so much time trying to remove dried gum from the floors and under the desks and chairs stepped outside the box and decided that since it was impossible to police all of the students all of the time, his school would no longer be a gum-free zone. Instead, his entire teaching staff taught their students how to chew gum politely and dispose of it properly. The result? No more complaints from the custodians. No more sticky floors and desks. Happy students.

That's what I mean by teaching outside the box. Shifting our focus so that we can see ourselves and our students from a different perspective. Fixing ourselves instead of fixing our students. Sending positive notes home to parents of students who misbehave, instead of sending negative news. Saying, "I really like you and it would make me so happy if you would do this assignment that I created because

I wanted to help you learn this new skill," instead of "If you don't do that assignment, you'll be sorry, Buster." Asking all your students to stand up and wriggle like worms instead of demanding that they sit down and fold their hands in their laps when they clearly have too much energy to focus quietly. Requiring everybody in your class to make a mistake instead of seeking perfection. Instead of constantly focusing on test scores, declaring the third week of each month as a test-free week. And so on.

There are literally hundreds of very good books about how to teach this or that. *Teaching Outside the Box* does not address the particulars of instruction so much as it focuses on what I believe is the key factor in any classroom: the student-teacher connection. My goal with this book is to help make teaching more enjoyable for both teachers and students. It breaks my heart to see so many frustrated teachers who truly care about their students but seem unable to reach them, just as it breaks my heart to see so many children who truly hate school.

On the other hand, my heart sings when I receive a letter such as this one from Laura Hauser, who sent me an e-mail asking for advice about taking over another teacher's class of "difficult" students.

31 August 2004

Ms. Johnson:

This is the end of my third week of teaching. I was given 125 "remedial" students. The other teachers told me they wouldn't show up to class. If they did, they would either sleep or disrupt the class; they wouldn't do homework and they didn't care if they passed or failed and I'd have to throw most of them out at some point or another.

I took a lot of your advice to heart. I went in on day one and told them all that I could guarantee they would have the best year in school they had ever had. I asked if that interested any of them, and they all admitted it did. I told them I only asked for three things, and I would do the rest. They had to show up every day; they had to come in with the attitude that they could and would learn something; and they had to try. I told them the story of Edison taking ten thousand tries to invent the light bulb and told them that I was only asking that they try three or four times. I asked how many had been told they were stupid or couldn't do math. Every hand went up. I told them it wasn't true; they just hadn't been taught math in a way they could understand it. I told them there were two words I would not tolerate in my class—"I can't"—because they all could and there wasn't a stupid one in the bunch.

Three weeks later, my students show up on time. The few who skipped in the beginning don't skip anymore, and no one skips on Friday, because it's cookie day. They do logic problems every day that require them to think, and now they ask for more. They do their homework; and if they get a low grade, they ask to fix it and turn it back in. I've told them I only care that they learn it and that if they're willing to do their homework or tests again, I am certainly willing to grade them again. I cut them some slack in the discipline department, but when I speak they stop and listen; and when I take someone outside and ask them to settle down, they do. I'm having a blast, and so are my students. Students tell me it's the first time a math teacher has actually cared about them and made them feel like they could succeed. Students that have on-the-job training in the afternoon come and hang out in math instead of leaving—some show up three periods a day—and participate in each class.

I can't thank you enough. If I had listened to those other teachers and not to you, I would be having a miserable year. But it's more rewarding than I could have imagined!

I know you're very busy finishing up your book, but thought you would like to know how much fun I'm having!

Laura Hauser

My fondest hope is that this book will help many more teachers define their own effective teaching philosophies, develop their own positive discipline policies, and experience the joy of teaching, just as Laura has.

I truly believe that teaching children is the noblest profession. Yes, the pay is sometimes insultingly low, and working conditions can be appallingly shabby. But we don't teach for the money or the glamour—we do it for the love.

Teaching Outside the Box

# Dear Teacher:
# An Open Letter

Dear Teacher:

Thank you.

Thank you for being a teacher.

And thank you for choosing to use your time and talents teaching students when you had so many other career options, most of which offer better pay, more comfortable working conditions, and much more respect from the general public than the teaching profession does.

Thank you for taking yet another exam to prove your competence, although you have already completed five or more years of college and hundreds of dollars' worth of standardized tests.

Thank you for continuing to teach higher-level thinking skills and advanced academics, in spite of having test after test after test added to your curriculum requirements, without any additional instruction time.

Thank you for getting up at 5 or 6 a.m. every day to go to a graceless room bathed in artificial light, a windowless closet, or a dilapidated trailer and for coping with the malfunctioning or nonexistent air conditioning and heating.

Thank you for eating your lunch out of a paper bag on a folding chair in a sparsely furnished lounge where a working coffee maker is a treat and a functioning microwave oven is a luxury.

For spending your so-called time off grading papers; making lesson plans; and attending professional development conferences, committee meetings, restructuring meetings, parent-teacher conferences, school board meetings, and continuing education classes.

Thank you for working countless hours of unpaid overtime because it is the only way to do your job well and because you cannot do less.

And for not reminding people constantly that if you were paid for your overtime, you could retire tomorrow and never have to work again.

Thank you for consistently giving respect to children who don't know what to do with it and don't realize what a valuable gift you are offering.

And for caring about children whose own families don't care—or don't know how to show that they do.

Thank you for spending your own money on pens and pencils, erasers and chalk, paper, tissues, bandages, birthday gifts, treats, clothing, shoes, eyeglasses—and a hundred other things that your students need but don't have.

For spending sleepless nights worrying about a struggling student, wondering what else you might do to help overcome the obstacles that life has placed in his or her path.

Thank you for raiding your own children's closets to find a pair of shoes or a sweater for a child who has none.

For putting your own family on hold while you meet with the family of a struggling student.

For believing in the life-changing power of education.

For maintaining your belief that all students can learn if we can learn how to teach them.

For putting up with the aching back, creaky knees, tired legs, and sore feet that go with the teaching territory.

Thank you.

Thank you for giving hopeless children enough hope to continue struggling against the poverty, prejudice, abuse, alcoholism, hunger, and apathy that are a daily part of so many tender young lives.

For risking your job to give a child a much-needed hug.

For biting your tongue and counting to a million while a parent lists the reasons why your incompetence is responsible for the misbehavior of his or her undisciplined, spoiled, obnoxious child.

For taking on one of the most difficult, challenging, frustrating, emotionally exhausting, mentally draining, satisfying, wonderful, important, and precious jobs in the world.

Thank you for being a teacher.

You truly are an unsung American hero.

You have my respect and my gratitude,

LouAnne Johnson

# Are You Teacher Material?

"How can I tell if I'm really teacher material?" a teacher candidate asked me in an e-mail. "Can I learn to be a good teacher? Or is it something you have to be born with?" She went on to explain that she had recently abandoned a well-paid position in advertising in order to pursue her dream of becoming a teacher.

"I know I will make a lot less money as a teacher," she wrote, "and I have accepted that reality, but now I'm wondering what will happen if I get my degree and get a job, and then I hate teaching. What if I find out that I just can't do it? I have a feeling that teaching is going to be very different from being a student teacher or observing experienced teachers. I guess what I'm asking is: Do you have any advice that might help me make the right decision about becoming a teacher?"

"To teach or not to teach?" is a question that stumps many people. Far too many of us know bright, energetic people who spent five or more years earning a bachelor's degree and teaching credential only to quit after one or two years in the classroom. New teachers give up for a long laundry list of reasons, but the most common complaints include disrespectful and disruptive students, apathetic administrators, overwhelming stacks of paperwork, lunchroom politics, parental pressure and pestering, and mental or emotional exhaustion.

Those complaints are valid. I have to say that I have worked with some excellent administrators, and their support enabled me to be a better teacher. But even with good support, teaching is very demanding and difficult work. Children today suffer from a host of emotional, mental, and physical challenges that affect their behavior and ability to learn. And unfortunately, many of their role models encourage them to treat themselves and others with extreme disrespect. Dealing with children requires abundant reserves of patience and tact. An indestructible sense of humor also helps. Government regulations have created a testing and accountability monster that consumes mountains of money, paperwork, time, and energy—and teachers have the task of feeding the monster. The monster is fickle, too, so if last-minute changes upset you, teaching will tax you to the limits of your flexibility. If you don't bend, you will definitely break. Of course, you already know that the pay is atrocious, primarily because people outside of education view teaching as babysitting with books. Thus, if wealth and prestige are important to you, teaching will be a disappointment. And teaching can be physically painful: hours of standing on your feet, bending over to read small print on small desks, and lugging boxes of books and papers to and fro can send you home with tired feet, an aching back, and a headache.

And then there are the students. It might seem facetious to say that you should like children if you plan to teach school, but apparently many people overlook this obvious fact. Every staff lunchroom has at least a few (and most have a large handful of) complainers and groaners who spend their breaks and lunch hours plotting against "the enemy," sharing their strategies for revenge, nursing their wounds, and displaying their battle scars. These are not necessarily bad people, but they are people who grew up and immediately forgot their own childhoods. Like people who fall in love with the idea of owning a dog, dreaming of the unconditional love a dog will offer, forgetting that puppies pee on the carpet, vomit on the bath mat, chew your slippers, and poop on the lawn, some would-be teachers envision themselves standing in front of a quiet, orderly classroom, facing a sea of silent, adoring, obedient, angelic little faces. When those angelic faces turn out to belong to noisy, messy, occasionally ill-mannered, selfish, and obstinate little stinkers, those teachers go into shock. Some fail to recover. They become bitter, humorless, and overly strict; and they spend the rest of their years in the classroom making themselves and their students miserable by trying to make reality fit their impossible fantasies.

All right, that's the downside of teaching. If you're still reading, still thinking you might like to be a teacher, then you are persistent and optimistic—two very helpful attributes for would-be teachers. And you are right to be hopeful, because the upside of teaching is so much bigger and so much more important than the downside.

Teaching is the most wonderful profession in the world. As a teacher, you make a direct, tangible contribution to the future of our country and the world by helping young people acquire knowledge and skills. You know that you are spending your life in an honorable pursuit and that your life has a purpose. Teaching provides endless challenges and opportunities for growth. Every day, teaching tests your interpersonal communications skills, your academic knowledge, or your leadership ability. On a good day, you'll be tested in all three areas, and you'll pass all three tests. You have the opportunity as a teacher to share your passion for learning with young people. If you are a good teacher, you will also inspire, motivate, and challenge those youngsters to develop their individual strengths and talents; and you will feel the incomparable joy when one of them (usually far more than one) realizes how much you have given and makes his or her way back to your classroom to give you a hug and a teary thank-you. And you will cry your own tears. And when you go home, you will share that student's thank-you with your family and friends, and they will all cry a few tears. When you go to bed that night, the last thing you will think before you go to sleep is, I did a fine thing. I helped a child become a successful adult. And that night, you will dream the sweetest dreams.

## SUPER, EXCELLENT, OR GOOD?

Teachers come in three basic flavors—super, excellent, and good. (Of course, there are mediocre teachers and, sadly, terrible teachers. But teaching poorly is not acceptable or excusable, so such practices are not included in this discussion.) Which flavor of teacher you decide to become depends on your personal strengths, intimate relationships, professional goals, and individual priorities. Before you begin teaching, seriously consider how much time and emotional energy you can afford to spend on your work outside the home. Take a long look at your life, your relationships, your financial and emotional obligations, your personal and career goals. If you find it hard to view your own life objectively, discussing your situation with a friend or close relative may improve your perspective. If your sister points out that you like expensive clothes and your husband reminds you that you become impatient and overly critical under stress, for example, you will need to decide whether you are willing to trim your wardrobe and do the hard work required to develop more patience.

Decide what is important to you and which aspects of your life should take priority. Will your children, parents, spouse, or partner feel neglected if you spend some of your free time creating lesson plans or counseling students? How much emotional energy will you need to conserve during the day in order to have enough left over for your family at night? Will you feel comfortable counseling students about their personal problems, or would you rather leave such things up to their own parents or guardians?

There is no right or wrong answer to these questions, but if you know the answers before you begin teaching, you will be a happier, more successful instructor. Not everybody can or should be a super teacher. It is perfectly acceptable to be an excellent or good teacher. (Poor teaching, however, is never acceptable.)

Super teaching requires the highest amounts of physical, emotional, and mental energy. Super teachers usually arrive at school early and stay late. They also attend seminars and continuing education classes, volunteer for student activities, and make themselves available to students who need extra help, both in and out of the classroom. Because super teachers enjoy a solid rapport with their students, they don't have to focus so much time or energy on discipline in their classrooms. Instead, there is a give-and-take, an ebb and flow, the teaching equivalent of the runner's high that so many athletes find addictive. Unfortunately, unless they are extraordinary people with impressive reserves of natural energy or unless they make an effort to rejuvenate themselves regularly, super teachers may find themselves in danger of burning out.

Super teaching demands huge amounts of physical and mental effort, and depending on your budget it may absorb some money as well. If you are single, childless, and unattached, you may choose to devote the bulk of your energies to teaching for some period of time. However, if you are a single mother with three young children and have a close friend or intimate partner, you may not be willing or able to devote the amount of emotional energy that being a super teacher requires. Having children doesn't disqualify you from becoming a super teacher, it simply means that you will need to make sure that your family understands and supports your teaching. If your children are well-adjusted, self-motivated, and respectful of you and your partner; if your partner supports your career goals; and if you have a high level of energy, then you may be able to handle the stresses involved in super teaching. But don't beat yourself up if you can't be extraordinary. Being an excellent or good teacher is a true achievement.

Excellent teachers enjoy their work, but they limit the amount of time and energy they devote to teaching. They care about their students and do their best to help them—but not at the expense of their own families. Excellent teachers do work overtime, because teaching well requires a certain amount of unpaid overtime (grading papers, making lesson plans, and supervising field trips), but excellent teachers put a limit on the amount of overtime they are willing to work.

Excellent teaching requires less energy expenditure than super teaching, but excellent teaching may still wear you out if you aren't careful; you still need to make time to nurture yourself and your family. And you may have to explain more than once to your friends and family that your job is a high priority and that you need to spend some time in the evenings and on weekends developing your lessons and skills. Again, don't be too hard on yourself if you find that you can't juggle so many teaching balls as you thought you could, especially during your first few years. Mastering just the basics of sound teaching is a major accomplishment, and students still thrive in the classrooms of good old everyday teachers.

Good teachers do their jobs well, but know their own limits. They make a very clear distinction between professional and personal time. They treat their students with respect and do their best to make sure that all students learn the material required for the next level of education, but they don't feel obligated to save every single student. Good teachers arrive at school early enough to be prepared, but they don't hold open house before school or during lunch hour. And they don't spend hours in their classroom after school for informal chats or counseling sessions. They lock the doors to their classrooms at night and focus on their own lives, their own educations, their hobbies, their friends, and their families. By creating a distinct division between their personal and professional lives, good teachers conserve their emotional and mental energy. As a result, they often enjoy long and successful teaching careers; they are the ones who sadly wave good-bye to those excellent and super teachers who overestimated their personal resources and burst into flames after a few years of mach-speed teaching.

Sometimes teachers confess that they feel a bit guilty for not having the energy or natural ability to be a super teacher. I tell them—and I am absolutely sincere—that there is no shame in being an everyday good teacher. Not everybody can be a rock star, and not everybody needs to be. The world needs all kinds of people—those who are satisfied by doing good work, raising decent children, caring for their neighbors and contributing to their communities, as well as those who are compelled to create and invent or to seek fame and fortune. Not every teacher wants or needs to be a Jaime Escalante or an Esme Codell. And millions of students in this country are learning from—and loving—their everyday ordinary teachers. I may be biased, but I believe that an everyday ordinary good teacher is still a hero. (And I'm sure those millions of students in this country would agree.)

Regardless of whether you choose to be a super, excellent, or good teacher, you will still be contributing to society, performing honorable and necessary work, and helping to shape the future of our country. Aside from yourself, your students, and a few supervisors, nobody will know how much energy you devote to your job. But we don't become teachers out of a need for public recognition or reward. We don't teach out of a desire for prestige; we teach because we believe it's important. Teaching superbly is like running a marathon by yourself in the dark. Few people even notice what you're doing, and those who notice don't pay much attention—but their oblivion doesn't slow you down. You still enjoy the thrill and satisfaction of finishing the race, and you are definitely a winner.

## EARN SOME EXTRA CREDIT

Let us assume that you have a strong desire to help young people, a passion for your subject, a solid education, and a license from an accredited teacher-training institution. Are passion, motivation, education, and training enough? My answer is a very loud "No." Those attributes can create an excellent foundation, but teaching requires much more than knowledge and the desire to teach. Teaching requires a solid grasp of motivational techniques, leadership and conflict resolution skills, human psychology (child, adolescent, and adult), computer literacy, the ability to whittle an impossibly huge pile of paperwork into a succinct and teachable curriculum, and the ability to think on your feet (a pair of extremely comfortable shoes for those feet will help).

Some teacher-training programs include excellent components in some of those areas, but based on the e-mails and letters I have received and the conversations I have had with teachers throughout the country, far too many teacher-training programs are heavy on theory and light on practical skills and techniques that teachers must have in order to teach effectively. Designing worksheets, lessons plans, and exams requires important skills. Creating intriguing bulletin boards, art projects, and group activities can make the difference between a stuffy classroom filled with bored underachievers and an exciting classroom buzzing with the electricity that motivated little learners can generate. But even the most enthusiastic, creative, accomplished, and intelligent new teacher will struggle if he or she doesn't have a firm grasp on the basic concepts of human psychology and behavior: what motivates people to act the way they act, how to convince people to change their behavior voluntarily, how to challenge and inspire people to attempt difficult tasks, how to develop a solid rapport with people from diverse economic and cultural backgrounds, and how to quickly and effectively convince people to follow your lead.

Look for teacher-training programs that focus on successful leadership techniques instead of ineffective punitive disciplinary approaches. If possible, opt for a program in which teacher candidates do their student teaching during the first part of their education program instead of the last. Some people realize after just a few days in the classroom that they weren't meant to be teachers; it's a shame when those would-be teachers have to face the choice of continuing in a teacher program in which they don't belong or changing to a new major and spending thousands of dollars preparing for a different career. And heaven help both the students and the teachers when those teachers who know that they have chosen the wrong field decide to teach until they can afford to go back to school or find another job. Everybody loses in that situation.

If you have the choice, opt for a full year of student teaching (I would recommend two years), preferably at a number of different schools where you will have the opportunity to work with students at different age levels and from different backgrounds. (An Internet search for schools of education will allow you to review and compare different programs across the country.) You may find that although you thought you would enjoy teaching kindergarten, high school is where you belong. Or you may find that the squirrelly sophomores that everybody complains about are the ones you enjoy the most.

Make sure that your student teaching experience actually provides teaching experience. If you are assigned to a single master teacher for your entire student teaching time frame and that teacher does not allow you to interact with students beyond distributing papers (or, worse yet, expects you to sit in the back of the room and observe for weeks on end), then ask your college advisor to change your assignment. Don't complain about the master teacher, just say that you believe you need a more hands-on approach in order to make sure that teaching really suits you. Your advisor may try to discourage you from insisting on a change, but be firm. You are the customer. You are paying for your education, and you deserve to be taught how to teach. Your instructors may label you difficult, but I promise you that a little flak from your professors is nothing compared to the flak you will take from students if they sense that you are ill prepared to teach.

If your teacher education program allows you the opportunity to take elective courses, then psychology, leadership, conflict resolution, and time management are good choices. The more you can learn about what makes people tick (and how to wind and unwind them), the easier it will be for you to establish a controlled learning environment in your classroom. Community colleges often offer a variety of continuing education courses, as well as courses designed to improve the quality of life for local residents. If you don't have access to classroom instruction, countless courses are available online—although some are little more than advertising bait to sell books and other products. Some of the products may be worthwhile, but unless the Web sites offer you a generous sample of their materials and a money-back guarantee for instruction, you would be wise to check with librarians, teachers, or other people who might be able to point you in the direction of quality instruction.

Fortunately, thanks to the Internet, you can learn quite a bit about a number of subjects on your home or public library computer. The Web site www.teachers.net, for example, allows you to read the logs of conversations between teachers on topics ranging from classroom discipline to motivational lesson plans. If you enter "classroom discipline" or "motivational techniques" into a search engine, you will find a host of provocative articles, Web sites, and pointers for future reading.

## THOSE WHO CAN'T TEACH CAN STILL DO

Don't despair if you find that, in spite of your desire to nurture and guide young people, teaching children isn't your bag of books. Or perhaps you lack the resources to complete the increasingly complex licensure and teacher testing programs. Non-teaching jobs in education still enable you to provide instruction, guidance, and counseling: teacher aides, security officers, bus drivers, coaches, counselors, curriculum designers, independent consultants, test proctors, and career planners all make important contributions. You might consider working as an adjunct, adult education, or English as a Second Language instructor at a community college, library, or detention facility. Teaching adults requires many of the same skills as teaching youngsters, but adult students are much more likely to be motivated, well behaved, and receptive to instruction. In addition, there are opportunities to teach in day care centers, after-school programs, church-sponsored community service programs, mentor programs, literacy programs, tutoring programs, and school-to-work programs that match students with adults who help them prepare to enter the workplace.

If you have a burning desire to teach a subject you love, you may have to do some searching of your soul, your situation, and your options, but there are students who want to learn as passionately as you want to teach.

## WHAT IS TEACHING ALL ABOUT?

If you think carefully and analytically about your own favorite teachers, from elementary school through college, you will recognize some common traits and behaviors. Although they undoubtedly used different techniques and approaches to teaching, successful teachers communicate clearly their expectations for students, their attitudes about learning, and their basic belief about the teacher-student relationship. Many teachers say "Please come talk to me if you have any concerns," but we don't always accept that offer because we know that it isn't always sincere. How do we know? Because students learn very early on to pay more attention to what teachers do than to what they say. One young girl, a fifth grader who wrote to me about her own teacher, provided a perfect example.

"My teacher always says, 'Don't be afraid to ask questions,' but then if you ask a question she makes a face and says, 'Do you really need to ask me that?' so I stopped asking questions."

It's very important, especially at the beginning of a school year, and especially for new teachers, that your attitude and behavior are consistent with your words and instructions. One way to guarantee consistency is for you to be able to articulate your teaching philosophy simply and succinctly. If you can't state your philosophy or if you are unsure that your philosophy is "correct," then I'd suggest that you browse a few textbooks on teaching methods and ask other teachers to state their own philosophies. Often it's easier to start by articulating what we don't believe than articulating what we do believe. For example, I once met a teacher who told me, "I provide students with all the information they need. If they aren't interested in learning, f—k them." Naturally, I was shocked, but the teacher shrugged and said, "I'm burned out, but I can't afford to retire for a few more years, so I'm just hanging on by my fingernails." I tried to avoid spending time with that teacher because his negative attitude was so distressing to me, but his comments helped me define my own ideas about the teacher-student relationship.

Here are some common philosophies. Perhaps one of them represents your own approach, or represents an approach that you definitely don't want to take:

Teachers should never appear to know less than students. A teacher who makes mistakes, or admits making mistakes, loses the respect of students and is unprofessional.

Students should respect the teacher simply because he or she is the teacher. Teachers should never tolerate disrespect from students for any reason.

Mutual respect is the cornerstone of a successful teacher-student relationship and it is the teacher's responsibility to set the tone and model respectful behavior.

Students must be held accountable for their behavior. I want students to understand that their behavior has consequences, so they will learn to make better choices.

A teacher's job is to teach academic information and skills only. Parents are responsible for character education, values, and ethics.

Effective teachers set the stage for learning—then step aside and let students learn through discovery and experiment. A teacher is really a guide.

I will explain how I arrived at my own teaching philosophy in the next chapter, but basically my philosophy is based on one simple belief:

When students believe success is possible, they will try.
If they don't believe they can succeed, it doesn't matter
how easy the material or how smart the students, they will fail.
Therefore, my primary job is to convince my students that
success is possible and help them succeed.

Don't panic if you can't articulate your teaching philosophy this very minute. Let the idea percolate in your brain. Just as a computer can continue background printing or operations, your brain will tackle the topic and wrestle with it until, eventually, your philosophy will emerge. You may decide later on to do a little tweaking or a major overhaul. If you realize that you believe only certain students can learn, imagine yourself standing in front of your class, face-to-face, and explaining to your pupils why you don't believe some of them are capable of learning. Hopefully, that visualization will help you imagine what it feels like to be on the other side of the desk from a teacher who has low expectations for your success.

There's nothing wrong with changing your mind and adopting a different philosophy or approach based on experience, observation, or serious reflection—but if you enter your classroom with a clear idea of why you are there and what you expect from yourself and your students, you stand a much better chance of being a successful teacher.

## DISCUSSION POINTS

1. How do you feel about categorizing teachers as good, super, or excellent? Can you suggest an alternative method of categorizing teachers?

2. How important do you believe psychology and leadership skills are to new teachers? Is it possible to develop such skills on the job and still be an effective teacher?

3. Which of the teaching philosophies from the list in this chapter do you agree with? Which do you disagree with, and why?

4. Briefly state your own teaching philosophy. In small groups, take turns sharing your philosophy statements and discussing how you arrived at them.

# Do Your Homework

W hy do so many teacher candidates ace their education courses, read all the latest journals, carefully observe good teachers, shine like stars during their student teaching, and then crash and burn during their first year in the classroom?

Because education, desire, intelligence, passion, and talent do not automatically enable you to communicate complex ideas to other people.

Because in teacher training programs, the instructors are on your side, and they have a vested interest in your success, whereas your students (and, sadly, even some fellow teachers) couldn't care less if you fail. In fact, some of them find it entertaining to watch you flounder.

Because unlike your college classmates, who admired your pretty lesson plans and praised the cleverness of your lectures and worksheets, your students may not be at all interested in learning.

Because effective teaching is more a matter of psychology than pedagogy. As one young man wisely explained to me, "You can make me sit here and hold this stupid book all day, but you can't make me read."

Fortunately, psychology is interesting to read and think about, relatively simple to understand, and eminently applicable to teaching. Perhaps you have detailed instructions about what you are expected to teach, with curriculum guidelines that list specific reading selections and activities that your class must complete during a given time. Or perhaps you have the freedom and responsibility of creating your own curriculum. In either case, if you grab your students by their brains quickly, during the first days of class, they won't have the time or inclination to resist your instruction. In Chapter Five, "Start with a Smile," I will suggest specific activities for grabbing your students during the first days of school, but right now I would like to focus on developing and articulating your own philosophy of teaching.

When I first began teaching, I could not have stated my philosophy in one simple sentence. I was too busy trying to organize paperwork, plan lessons, referee arguments, convince students to cooperate, find a disciplinary approach that worked, and extinguish those thousand little fires that threaten to burn down every teacher's classroom every day. A struggling student helped me focus my thinking. When I was assigned to teach a class of sophomores whose regular teacher suddenly decided to retire, I entered the classroom with high hopes and boundless energy and found myself facing a group of students with zero hope and subzero motivation.

"It don't matter what we do," one girl explained. "Before she left, our teacher done flunked us all. Wrote a red F in the grade book beside everybody's name."

At the mention of the grade book filled with Fs, I saw those students' shoulders slump and their heads droop. As they issued a giant group sigh, I could feel their hopelessness. So I hurried to assure them that I didn't have their previous teacher's grade book and that I intended to start everybody in my new grade book with an A—in red ink. It may sound melodramatic, but I swear I could hear the hope fluttering in those students' hearts. Every single face turned toward me, even the faces of students who insisted that they didn't care one fig about school.

From the back of the room, I heard a boy whisper, "She's lyin'."

A second later another boy whispered, "Shut up! What if she ain't lyin'? I ain't never had an A before."

In that moment my philosophy of teaching was born, and it has served me well. As I mentioned earlier, my teaching philosophy is based on one simple belief:

*When students believe success is possible, they will try.*

I communicate that philosophy to my students frequently, to remind them that whenever I ask them to do something, my goal is to help them be successful—not simply to issue orders. Once I solidified my philosophy, teaching became much simpler and more enjoyable, and my students stopped fighting with me and started learning.

During the following years, using student behavior and achievement as my guides, I developed secondary philosophies about discipline, grades, and exams, which I will share with you in the coming chapters. Right now, however, I would like to ask you to consider the ideas and issues in this chapter before you step into the classroom, so that you will be better able to articulate your own teaching philosophy. I believe this consideration will help you become a much more dynamic and effective teacher.

## CHOOSE YOUR PERSONA

Your classroom is a miniature theater: it holds a small, captive audience and an even smaller cast—you. You are the star of the show, and when you first stand on that stage, your small audience can seem overwhelmingly large. The brighter your spotlight, the faster you'll capture your audience. Later on, you may choose to share the stage with your students, but until your students have learned their roles, you will need to take center stage. I don't mean that you should posture grandly and strut about your room. You do have a show to run, however, and specific goals to accomplish. Your responsibility is to lead your cast toward those goals; their role is to follow, although it is perfectly acceptable for them to politely suggest changes in the script.

Because your students will take their cues from you, it's very important that you decide before you step onstage how you will portray your character. What kind of image do you want to project to your students? How do you want them to see you? As the scientific expert, the hip dude who knows algebra inside out, the cool nerd, the toughest but best chemistry teacher on earth, the drill-sergeant grammarian, the stand-up comic who happens to know all about history, the serious student of literature or science, the hard-boiled journalist, the tough but tender coach?

You must be yourself. Pretending to be somebody you are not is a terrible idea and one that is bound to fail because students are very adept at quickly assessing their teachers' characters. They will decide during the first few moments they see you what kind of person you are. They will look at your clothes, your hair, your skin color (not to judge you, but to assess how you may judge them). They will note your most subtle body language, your gestures, your posture, the length of your stride, the tone of your voice, your expression as you observe other students, and most especially they will notice the look in your eyes when you make eye contact with them. They will decide whether you seem crabby or nice or tough or easy or scared or confident or boring. All of this will happen within the first few minutes of your first class meeting—long before you begin to teach. And once your students decide who you are, you'll have a hard time convincing them to change their perceptions. You can change their minds, but it demands so much time and energy that if you goof and get started on the wrong foot (as I have done more than once), you may be inclined to simply cope with the status quo and hope things will improve over time. Coping and hoping, however, are poor substitutes for self-confidence and leadership.

Whatever persona you choose, it should be one that is natural for you, one that you can maintain for the entire school year. I am not advising you to put on a mask or try to change your personality, but to consider how to make best use, as a teacher, of your unique characteristics, traits, and talents. You don't have to be an extrovert to be an effective teacher. Some extremely shy or introverted people blossom as teachers and enjoy a persona in the classroom that highlights their otherwise hidden talents and skills. But it is not a good idea to try to force a completely different personality in the classroom simply because you lack confidence in yourself. Instead of donning a false persona, it would serve you better to spend some time working on discovering your strengths, which will lead to increased confidence and self-esteem. And always remember—children tend to be more accepting of different personalities than adults may be. Students don't care so much about your good looks or your sparkling wit as they do about whether you treat them with dignity and respect.

It took me a while to perfect my drill-sergeant–stand-up comic–counselor persona, and I made many changes along the way. My first year I tried too hard to be "cool," and it caused discipline problems. I joked around a lot because I wanted the kids to like me, to think of me as an older friend. What I didn't realize at that time was that they didn't need more friends. They had plenty of friends—friends who offered them dope and cigarettes and plagiarized research papers; friends who thought heavy metal was great music and that Ripple was fine wine. What my students needed was for me to be a teacher, an adult who would accept my responsibility as their guide and a leader who sometimes had to be the bad guy in order to help them. During my second teaching year, I took the advice of a veteran teacher who said, "Don't smile until after Christmas." I decided to be the drill sergeant who could stare a student to death. I couldn't do it. I'm a smiling kind of woman, so my message was inconsistent and my students responded by misbehaving half the time.

Finally, I sat down and figured out what my biggest strengths and weaknesses were as a person. Then I combined my three strongest personal assets and came up with a combination that worked for me as a teacher. Once I could define my persona, I could communicate it to students effectively. Now I know who I am as a teacher. I am a strict but flexible professional educator who has high standards and expectations for my students, as well as a caring and compassionate human being. I am inclined to use humor instead of threats, intolerant of rude or disrespectful behavior, passionate about my subject, and willing to meet students halfway. I make a few important rules that cannot be broken under any circumstances; I take the time to know each student personally; and I use humor whenever possible to make my point without making students lose face.

## DRESS THE PART

In the search for my most effective persona, I discovered an interesting student response to my clothing: they perceive some outfits as more serious than others, and they behave accordingly. If the lesson for the day requires creativity, spontaneity, and lots of student input, I wear more informal clothing: corduroy pants and a sweater, perhaps. On days when I want to limit the amount of spontaneity, during an important exam or a lesson that will serve as an important building block for future lessons, I wear a suit.

Using clothes to project an image is basic psychology, and we see it all around us. The makers of TV commercials, especially commercials for pharmaceuticals or health products, often dress their announcers in white lab coats that give the impression of medical authority, so that viewers will be more inclined to believe them when they tell us that we'll have fewer gastrointestinal disturbances or sinus headaches. "Difficult" students often use clothing—leather jackets and ripped jeans, for instance, or turquoise hair—to advertise their contempt for authority and send a clear challenge to adults, a warning to keep our distance. Corporate executives are often very adept at power dressing. Young teachers or people who tend to be shy and introverted may take some tips from the fashion experts who advise young executives how to give the impression of authority: wear black pants and a white shirt, for example.

When you select your teaching wardrobe, keep in mind the persona you wish to convey. Make sure that your clothes don't send a conflicting message. If your goal is to create a very authoritative persona, for example, you may not be so successful if you dress very informally, especially if you wear the same clothes your students wear. They may tend to treat you as a peer instead of a teacher, in spite of your verbal instructions.

While we're on the subject of clothing, I'd like to suggest that you pay special attention to your feet. Many new teachers, myself included, are sorely surprised to find out how much their feet can hurt after just one day of teaching. Even if you are in good physical condition and are used to spending long periods of time on your feet, teaching will still take its toll on your soles. I most strongly recommend investing in a pair of well-made, comfortable shoes such as those made specifically for comfort by companies such as Born, Birkenstock, Clarks, Dansko, Mephisto, and Naot.

## TRAIN THOSE LITTLE PUPPIES

How do you want students to feel and act in your classroom? Do you want them to sit quietly and raise their hands before responding to your questions, or do you want them to speak freely, even if it means interrupting each other or you? Do you want them to feel free to come into your classroom early and chat with you or with other students, or do you want them to keep their socializing outside the classroom and focus solely on academic activities inside your room? Do you want students to engage in enthusiastic discussions in which they freely voice their personal opinions (which may lead to interesting arguments), or do you prefer to control any discussion to avoid conflict and keep the conversation on topic?

Consider your students' age, the difficulty of your subject matter, and the number of students in each group you teach. How do you envision them behaving during a given class period? Perhaps you picture them sitting at their desks, politely raising their hands for you to call on them. Or perhaps your vision involves a more energetic, less controlled environment, where students wave their hands wildly or feel inspired to shout out their ideas. After you have developed a good rapport with your students, you will be able to change the pace and procedures to fit different kinds of lessons, but you are likely to develop a better rapport and experience fewer discipline problems if you stick to one method for at least the first few weeks of classes.

Here's just one example. If you want students to raise their hands before speaking, you need to state your expectations and act accordingly. If you have stated a preference for hand raising and then acknowledge students who speak out of turn during your lessons, you will have just demonstrated that you don't mean what you say. If you persist in acknowledging your shout-out talkers, you may soon find that you have a lot of talkers and a lot of other students who have lost respect for your authority. On the other hand, if you don't mind the movement and noise that accompany student spontaneity, and you allow students to speak out during lessons, you may find it very difficult to get those students to sit quietly and raise their hands during a given activity if you decide later on that you need a more orderly classroom in order to teach a specific skill. Until you are sure that your students will follow your direction, it's best to stick to the one method that you would prefer them to use most of the time. I think of it as setting my students' default behavior. Unless I give specific instructions, how do I want them to behave?

If you aren't certain what kind of classroom environment you want to create, think about your own school days. Which classes did you enjoy most? Which did you dread attending? What kind of environment did those teachers create? How did they communicate their attitudes to you? Chances are good that you will teach the way your favorite teachers taught you—or the way your worst teachers taught you. Far too often, teachers whose own teachers humiliated them will turn around and use those same techniques on their students, without even realizing what they are doing. In my opinion, humiliating children is cowardly and emotionally abusive. You can be strict without being cruel, and students will accept a strict but fair teacher as well as they will accept a laid-back, tolerant teacher. But if you start the year using one approach and then try to change midterm, you may confuse some students; and they may not cooperate when you try to retrain them. Many people are resistant to change, especially children, who may feel insecure about many aspects of their personal lives.

Of course, you may choose to change your approach to one that you believe will improve your teaching, but be wary of changing your teaching style as a reaction to student behavior. If you begin the year as a soft-spoken, even-tempered teacher and then become a shouter or develop a short fuse that ignites at the smallest disruption, students will realize that they can control your behavior. Some students will then do their best to push your buttons because watching a teacher fume can be highly entertaining.

Training students is very similar to training puppies. If you let a puppy sleep on the bed every night for a week, she won't understand why you are punishing her by making her sleep on the floor the next week. She will wait until you are asleep and hop up onto the bed. And if you wake up and boot her off, her tender feelings will be hurt, and you will feel like a big bully. Likewise, if you train your little canine companion to sleep on the floor, and then one night you decide you'd like a foot warmer, she may be hesitant to jump up onto the bed. She may agree to warm your feet for a while before jumping back down to her proper place on the floor. Or she may enjoy the change of pace so much that she refuses to sleep on the floor the following night. Either way, you have one confused puppy on your hands.

## CONTROL YOUR CLASSROOM, NOT YOUR STUDENTS

Later, I will discuss discipline plans in detail, but right now I'd like to share with you one of the most important lessons I have ever learned. When I began teaching, after nine years on active military duty and seven in the corporate sector, I thought I had a good grasp of the basics of discipline. When my master teacher left me in charge of his sophomore honors English class, I was determined not to take any flak from my students. Unfortunately, my students didn't care one whit about my determination. The harder I tried to control them, the harder they resisted. They all threw their books on the floor at the same time when my back was turned, so I made a seating chart that separated friends from each other. They coughed loudly if anybody tried to answer a question that I had asked, so I gave them harder assignments. They crossed their arms and refused to look at me when I talked to them, so I sent the ringleaders to the office, where they sat for a while before returning to my classroom with a note asking me to be more specific about what infractions they had committed, because refusing to look at the teacher wasn't a punishable offense under the student code of conduct. So I sent them to lunch detention or after-school detention or in-school suspension. And when they returned, they acted exactly as they had before they left my room—except now they were determined to exact revenge.

One day I lost my temper and started screaming. I threw books and papers on the floor and pitched a proper childish tantrum. Those college-bound students looked at me, but they were more amused than impressed. The following day, I asked Al Black, a veteran teacher, to sit in on that class and observe the hostilities. After the students had left the room, Al sighed and shook his head.

"You don't like those students," he said.

"They didn't like me first," I protested.

"That doesn't matter," Al said. "You're the teacher. You create the classroom environment. And right now, you're creating conflict because you're acting like a bully."

After a sleepless night, I realized Al was right. It was up to me to fix the problem. I had been so focused on changing the students' behavior when I should have been looking at my own. I wasn't sure what to do, though, and Al refused to make it easy for me. "Figure it out," was the only advice he would offer. Since I couldn't figure it out on my own, I decided to ask the students for help. The worst that could happen is that they would refuse—which wouldn't change anything and I'd have to think of something else. The next afternoon, when the students arrived for class, I thanked them for arriving on time. They gave each other quick "what's up?" glances, but didn't respond. Then I said, "We started out all wrong and now nobody likes this class, including me. I don't dislike you. I just don't like what has been happening in this room. So, I'd like to start over. I'll be nice to you, if you'll be nice to me." After a few stunned seconds, one of the students—and one of the ringleaders—smiled, and gave me a thumb's up.

"Deal!" he said. Several others followed suit. And just like that, it was a different classroom. The human dynamic changed completely. Even the air felt different, lighter somehow.

Finally, I realized what those bright, capable underachieving students had been trying to teach me: I cannot control my students' behavior, but I *can* control myself and my classroom. As soon as I understood that simple concept, I stopped responding to their behavior and started making them respond to mine. After that day, when a student disrupted the lesson or refused to cooperate, instead of becoming upset or issuing warnings or threats, I immediately held a quick private conversation (sometimes five seconds was enough!) wherein I offered that student the opportunity to change his or her behavior without losing face. While they considered my offer, I returned to teaching the cooperative students and made sure to thank them for their cooperation. This may seem like a simple concept, but it makes a tremendous difference in the way teachers and students relate to each other. Once I stopped letting students dictate my behavior, I had far fewer discipline problems in every class, even when I taught at-risk and remedial students.

I don't mean to suggest that we ignore misbehavior, although it's not a bad idea to ignore small disruptions that may fizzle out on their own. I do mean that if we focus on giving our attention to those students who are cooperating with us, and verbally praising them for their excellent behavior, instead of letting students derail the teaching train, we are more likely to arrive at our destination and everybody is far more likely to enjoy the trip.

## PLAN FOR BATHROOM BREAKS

In a perfect world, teachers would be free to design reasonable and efficient procedures for student bathroom visits. But most of us have to contend with school-wise policies that are often inhumane because their focus is on preventing vandalism or truancy instead of addressing the very real biological needs of students. I have taught at schools where zero bathroom visits were permitted and at other schools where the standard practice was to allow students a limited number of visits per month or semester. And many teachers require students to "make up the time" they missed from class by coming in during lunch or staying after school. One teacher laughingly described the "pee dance" that he requires students to perform (grabbing their crotches and hopping from foot to foot) to show that they sincerely need to go to the restroom. (Oh, how I wish his boss would make him do the same dance!)

As always, I ask teachers to put themselves in the place of their students. What if your supervisor informed you on the first day of work that you would not be permitted to go to the restroom for any reason except during your lunch hour? Or that you had to work late or give up your lunch break to make up for using the restroom during work hours? That sounds ridiculous—because it is.

Using the bathroom is not a privilege. It is a biological need. It's inhumane and cruel, in my opinion, to deny people the right to use the bathroom because they are young or small. Some students have weak bladders. Others have medical conditions or take prescription medications that cause them to need more frequent bathroom breaks. These students, when faced with restrictive restroom policies, now face emotional pressures as well as physical ones. They are shamed by their need to go to the bathroom. And many students will stop drinking liquids in order to avoid having to go, which makes them dehydrated—not only unhealthy physically, but mentally. Our brain needs water and glucose in order to function well.

Another factor that many teachers overlook is safety. Sometimes students are reluctant to use the bathrooms during breaks or passing periods because of bullies, smoking, drugs, or sexual activities that take place in the restrooms.

So, what's the solution? As a group, teachers need to collaborate to design humane school-wise policies. Individually, teachers can do much to counter cruel school-wise policies that can't be changed. For example, when I taught at the high school where students were never permitted to use the restroom, I used to take my entire freshmen classes to the bathroom immediately after taking attendance. We were very quick and very quiet. Usually we took our books with us so that we could be on a "reading field trip" if questioned. We never were questioned because we didn't make noise or disrupt anybody else's learning. My students, grateful for being treated with dignity and respect, repaid me by working harder in my class.

Many elementary teachers have found, to their surprise, that young students can be extremely responsible about signing themselves out. Because they are treated like "big kids," they try hard to live up to the compliment.

If you are free to create your own policy, make it a small deal rather than a big one. Create a bathroom pass using an item that is clearly visible and not easily broken: a small stuffed animal, a wooden toy, a thick plastic ruler. Attach a keychain or string so that the pass can be hung near the doorway. Make a sign-out sheet for students to use. Then make it very clear that the bathroom pass is to be used *only* for visiting the restroom. Most students will not abuse the system. Serious consequences need to be assigned if students do go elsewhere (high school students like to coordinate their visits to meet friends or business associates in the hallways). I don't deny those students the opportunity to use the restroom in the future—but they have to have an escort until they prove themselves trustworthy. If the restroom is nearby, I escort them personally and wait in the hallway. If necessary, I assign a large and responsible student (or call a counselor) to act as my deputy escort. The offenders quickly shape up.

Your bathroom plan should suit your students. The point is to create a workable, flexible system that you can tweak as needed. But your primary goal should be to allow students to use the bathroom when they need to use the bathroom without punishing or shaming them. We have far better ways to teach students self-control than by making young people miserable or physically ill. By the way, teachers who do humiliate students often are the same teachers who have serious discipline problems in their classroom.

## YOUR OPTIONAL AGENDA

What are you really teaching in your classroom? During my first year in the classroom, I confessed to my master teacher, Al Black, that I was afraid I wasn't teaching my students enough. I explained that I believed students should reach a minimum standard to achieve a passing grade, but I wasn't sure where to set the minimum standard for my different English classes.

"Minimum standard of what?" Al asked me. "Commas, spelling, vocabulary? Should a kid know four ways to use a comma and the correct spelling of four hundred words? Should he know what *defenestrating* means? What if he doesn't know that particular word, but he knows a thousand other ones? What is the standard? I'm not talking about the district's objectives. I'm talking about your own standards. What is it you expect those kids to know when they leave your class?"

"I don't know," I admitted, "but I worry about whether I'm really teaching them anything."

"All teachers wonder whether they're really teaching anything," Al told me. "I used to wonder it myself, hundreds of years ago when I was your age. But then I learned something important. You aren't teaching English. 'What are you teaching?' you may ask. You're teaching kids how to analyze information, relate it to other information they know, put it together, take it apart, and give it back to you in the form that you request it. It doesn't matter what the class is; we all teach the same things. We just use different terms. You use commas and adjectives; biology teachers use chromosomes and chlorophyll; math teachers use imaginary numbers and triangles. And you're also teaching an optional agenda: you're teaching your kids to believe in themselves. So don't worry about whether you're teaching them grammar. You're teaching those kids. Trust me, you're teaching them."

After I had a chance to think about Al's comments, I realized that what he called the "optional agenda" is the most important factor in teaching, more important than school district objectives, because it is your optional agenda that answers the all-important question: What do you want your students to know when they leave your class?

What do *you* want your students to know? Naturally, as an English teacher, I want my students to have improved reading and writing skills, bigger vocabularies, increased comprehension of abstract ideas, better thinking skills, and an appreciation for literature. So I design specific lessons for vocabulary building and literary analysis and composing logical arguments—hundreds of different lessons over the years, tailored for different levels of ability. After my discussion with Al, when I spread out my various lesson plans and looked for common areas among them, my own optional agenda became very clear. Time and again I'd framed my lessons within larger lessons. One composition assignment, for example, urged students to write about a time they had faced and overcome a problem. A supplementary short story unit that I put together from a variety of sources included fictional accounts of people dealing with challenges such as divorce, the death of a loved one, peer pressure, and prejudice. The poetry I selected for special attention involved pursuing your dreams, standing up for your principles, admitting your errors.

My answer to Al's question is the same today as it was then: I want my students to have better academic skills, but I also want them to have a strong sense of their own ethical standards, an unquenchable thirst for knowledge, a desire to succeed according to their own definitions of success, good problem-solving skills, and the strength of character to treat all people with basic human dignity and respect.

What is your optional agenda?

Your values and ethics will shape your agenda. Even if you don't intentionally try to include your beliefs and attitudes in your lessons, they will be there, hidden within the context of the reading assignments you select, in the methods you use to determine who passes and who fails, in the tone of your voice when you address certain students, and in a thousand other subtle clues. Every day you will be teaching your students what you believe is important. You will be conveying your own ethics, attitudes, beliefs, and moral values to your students. If you can articulate your optional agenda, you can use that knowledge to enhance your teaching. Knowing your optional agenda will also help you avoid unintentionally teaching your students things you don't want to teach them—which brings us to the next area of consideration.


## FACE YOUR OWN PREJUDICES

Although most of us try very hard to rid ourselves of prejudices, I have yet to meet a person who is completely free of them. Our cultural and religious backgrounds, our families and friends, our experiences, even our biology, combine to make us prejudge people who are blond or brunette, tall or short, fat or thin, ugly or beautiful, extroverted or introverted, brilliant or dim, nerdy or popular, Catholic or Jewish or Protestant or Muslim, black or brown or white or yellow or red.

I believe it is important that we, as teachers, try harder than most people to eliminate our prejudices and minimize the effects of the ones we just can't seem to defeat, because so many of our students will remember the things we say and do for the rest of their lives. We spend more waking hours with most children, especially the youngest and most tender children, than their own parents do. Unless they have reason not to, most children love and respect their teachers. Many, many students learn to love and respect themselves—or despise and disrespect themselves—based on the way their teachers treat them. Think about your own childhood. If any teacher ever called you lazy, stupid, hopeless, ugly, clumsy, or worthless, I'm sure you remember the moment quite clearly. Just as I am sure you remember if a teacher ever called you intelligent, special, sharp, brilliant, charming, talented, or wonderful.

Skin color and ethnic origin are still primary sources of prejudice in our nation. Many people believe that because of our civil rights laws, affirmative action programs, and the many organizations devoted to promoting equality and justice, skin-color prejudice no longer exists in our country. We have made remarkable progress toward eradicating that prejudice, but we still have a long way to go. During the past decade, I have visited more than half of the states in our nation; in every state I met teachers who were dismayed and appalled at the racial and ethnic prejudices they witness on a recurring basis in their schools and communities. In fact, the only people I have met who truly believe racial prejudice is not a problem in our schools are white people. Those white people aren't stupid or lacking in compassion; they simply don't see what doesn't exist in their world. Brown people maintain that prejudice is still a big problem, and I believe they are in a position to assess the situation most accurately.

Here's why I continue to harp on the subject of racial prejudice: some years ago my sophomore class included a young man who happened to have extremely dark skin. He also had an extremely gentle and loving personality, an enthusiastic attitude toward school, and an extraordinary talent for football. The teachers on our team all liked Dante, and we agreed that his was the shiniest of stars in our class. One afternoon near the end of that school year, Dante stayed after school to talk to me.

"I just wanted to thank you," he said, "because you weren't afraid to make me do my homework. All the other teachers are afraid of me because I'm a big black man. They act like they think if they make me mad, I'll hurt them." As he spoke, Dante's eyes filled with tears. Watching him, I felt my own tears rising.

"So what do you do when those teachers act like that?" I asked.

"I act like I'm going to hurt them." Dante tried to laugh, but his chuckle turned into a cough that stopped just short of a sob.

For a split second, I nearly laughed myself, because it sounded funny. But I quickly realized that Dante's remark was not funny at all. Those teachers were prompting Dante to act as though he intended to hurt them. Whether intentionally or not, they were manipulating him into fulfilling their stereotype of black men as angry and violent. To fear a child simply because of his or her skin color is the same as saying, "I know that you are inherently violent simply because of who you are. It is only a matter of time before your true nature is revealed."

We all know how indignant we feel when someone accuses us of lying even though we are telling the truth and how outraged we feel when someone accuses us of doing something we haven't done. Adults are sometimes capable of rationalizing, justifying, or ignoring false accusations and insinuations. But children and adolescents are not experienced enough in human nature to justify or ignore adult behavior, and they don't know how to avoid being manipulated by adults. Most certainly, they are unequipped to cope with the overwhelming feelings of frustration, disbelief, indignation, and anger that arise when adults insinuate that they are violent (or stupid or worthless) because of their skin color or ethnic background. I believe that repeatedly exposing children to such subtle but serious prejudice is psychologically abusive and surely will have long-term effects on their self-esteem, their attitudes toward school, and their outlook on humanity. We all know that students tend to meet their teachers' expectations—high or low. So unless we have good reason to believe that a particular student is prone to violent behavior, we must expect the best from all of our students. And we must eradicate our irrational fears because we can't successfully teach children when we are afraid of them.

After my talk with Dante, I suggested that he read an essay by Brent Staples called "Night Walker," in which Staples describes how he has learned to control the rage he feels when people obviously fear him simply for his skin color alone. To defuse potential confrontations, Staples whistles well-known classical tunes to let people know he isn't a mugger—his "equivalent of the cowbell that hikers wear when they are in bear country." (This essay was originally published in *Ms.* magazine as "Just Walk on By," and was reprinted elsewhere under different titles. It can be found in a number of essay anthologies.) Although reading an essay doesn't solve the problem, it does provide an articulate, intelligent response that may help young minority males (and females) cope with a difficult world.

I said earlier that I have yet to meet a person who is free from prejudice, and I include myself in that sweeping statement. After talking to Dante, I sat down and forced myself to face my own prejudices. I had read the journal articles and the psychology textbooks. I knew that studies have proved that most white (and many black) Americans' anxiety levels rise when they see brown or black men approaching them in public. And I had to admit that my own anxiety level would rise higher if a black or brown man approached me than if a white man did. Yet I had never in my life been attacked by a brown or black male. I had, on more than one occasion, had an unpleasant social encounter with a white male. Therefore, it made no sense for me to fear black and brown men more than white. Because I had been raised in an all-white town in the North where I had no contact with anybody of any color other than white, I had no experiences to shape my attitudes. Other than Bill Cosby and Muhammad Ali, I don't remember another positive black male role model from my childhood through my thirties, at which point I stopped watching TV completely. During nine years of active military service before I became a teacher, I had had only one slightly antagonistic experience with a black man, but dozens of severely antagonistic episodes involving male Caucasian soldiers and sailors who didn't welcome women in their ranks. I could only conclude that I had formed my prejudice from hearing news reports of young black and Hispanic males waging wars on big-city streets and from watching movies and TV programs that consistently portrayed minority males as pimps, drug dealers, shiftless alcoholics, crack addicts, gangbangers, wife beaters, cop killers, and convicts.

My solution to purging my prejudice was to meet and talk to as many successful and educated black and brown men as I could. I sought them as mentors for my students. I befriended them in the school lunchroom and during community activities—not simply as research subjects but as human beings. After several weeks I knew I had made some significant progress in minimizing my racial prejudices when I met a black man I didn't like at all. Disliking that man was pivotal in my rehabilitation. Prior to that meeting, I would have felt compelled to like him or to act as though I did, in order not to appear to be prejudiced.

After nearly twenty years of ongoing self-treatment, I feel free to like or dislike anybody I meet, of any skin color or ethnic background, based on the way that person treats me—and especially the way that person treats children and dogs.

I don't pretend there is no violence in the world. I try to keep my distance from anybody of any color who appears to be drunk, stoned, sociopathic, or potentially dangerous. But I don't expect any particular person to be violent simply because of his or her ethnic origin. And I have learned to cope with students who have concerns or prejudices toward me because of my ethnic heritage, such as the young man who strutted into my sophomore English class one day and announced as he passed by, without making eye contact, that he didn't like white people.

"I can't help it if I glow in the dark," I told him. "I was born that way, and I can't do anything about it. If you're going to dislike me for something, please dislike me for something that I am directly responsible for, something I can control, such as my attitude, my politics, or my behavior. Why don't you cut me some slack until you get to know me? And I will do the same for you. I will decide whether or not I like you based on the way you act, not on your skin color."

My prejudiced pal just shrugged and pretended to ignore me, but he must have listened—although he rarely spoke to me and clearly did not feel any affection toward me. At the end of his second year as my student, he wrote in his journal that the most important thing he had learned in school that year was that "not all white people are bad." I considered that a high compliment from him. But even more important, I knew that he could no longer be 100 percent prejudiced because he had met at least one exception to his rule. He inspired me to try to introduce other students to their own exceptions.

As teachers, we can't eradicate students' prejudices, but we can—by our own example and by communicating our expectations clearly—lay the groundwork to make tolerance and compassion the rule in our classrooms.

## RESPECT YOURSELF

New teachers often ask, "How do I make students respect me, when they walk into the room determined to disrespect me before they even meet me?"

Clearly, you cannot *make* anybody respect you. You can demand respect all you want, but you can't force it. Children already understand this concept, so they aren't simply being stubborn when they resist teachers' demands for respect. They are insulted, just as you would be if a stranger marched up to you and demanded instant respect. Thus, the harder you try to force students to respect you, the more insulted they will be, and the more they will disrespect you.

Sometimes we find ourselves with an entire room full of disrespectful students. And some teachers draw the battle lines. They become more strict, establishing rigid rules and inflexible procedures. They allow students to draw them into the teacher-versus-student battle that so many young people enjoy because it is entertaining, easier than doing lessons, and, most important, because they already know how to act disrespectful. I know from experience how frustrating it is to try to continue modeling respectful behavior when students greet your efforts with disdain, defiance, disrespect, or complete disregard. And I know how tempting it is to let the children manipulate you into responding as they expect you to. But if you can resist, if you can continue to respect them as human beings, separating the child from the childish behavior, eventually most of them will realize that you are sincere, that you do respect them as people—and it is extremely difficult to go on hating somebody who truly respects and cares for you.

Here's how I approach the issue. I explain to my students on the first day in class that the one thing I value more than any other behavior is self-respect. I explain that I believe lack of respect for others stems from a lack of self-respect, so I will be working to help them develop self-respect, self-discipline, self-esteem, and self-confidence. Then I do my utmost to live up to my own high expectations. When a student disrespects me, I call the student out in the hallway to talk to me, but I still speak respectfully to that student. (On those infrequent occasions when the student has managed to push enough buttons to make me so angry that I can't speak respectfully, I either leave the student standing outside the room until I can gain control or ask a fellow teacher or counselor to take my class for a few minutes while I take a walk to calm down.)

Some students may not know how to respond to genuine respect because they have never encountered it before. You may have to continue being respectful for a very long time (an entire year or longer) until students realize that you aren't pretending. They may be suspicious. One boy told me that when he acted belligerent and I continued to address him respectfully, he assumed it was a trick.

"I figured something was up, you know," he told me later. "I'm like, she's slick, but what's she got up her sleeve? Ain't nobody gonna be that nice unless they want something. I finally figured out you was trying to show me how to act right. Do the right thing, man."

You don't have to like a student in order to treat him or her with respect. I'm sure you work with adults you don't particularly like, but you don't actively disrespect them, especially in front of your peers. Also, I think it's important to accept that not all students may like you. That is fine. Students don't have to like you, just as they don't have to like each other. They can still learn the information you teach. And they can learn to conduct themselves with self-respect so that they can survive school and go on to become successful people who enjoy positive relationships with other people in their personal and professional lives.

After observing both successful and struggling teachers, I have a theory about why some adults have trouble eliciting respect from students, even when those adults honestly believe they respect their students. When a teacher approaches students from a standpoint of wanting to reform, shape up, or save them, it comes across as condescending. Students sense that the teacher feels superior to them, and they resent the teacher's attitude, even though the teacher truly wants to help them. Imagine that another adult approached you and said, "You are such a mess. You make stupid choices; you waste your time and talents; and your values and ethics are inferior to mine. But I can show you how to be more like me so that you can be a better person. I promise I can help you, if you will only listen to me."

How would you feel if somebody said those things to you, even if the person were more accomplished and successful than you are? I don't think you would be receptive, because you would be thinking, What right does this person have to speak to me this way? Your emotions would block your intellect, and no real communication of information could occur. Instead, your attention would be focused on trying to assert your own strength, control your anger, express your anger, or return the insult.

If we want students to respect us, we must respect them as human beings deserving of basic human dignity. We must accept that they may have different values and lifestyles and that they may have made choices that we never would have made. But they are young, uneducated, and inexperienced (even if they are streetwise). We can't expect them to make logical, mature, and intelligent decisions unless adults have taught them how to think and provided them with role models who exhibit mature and intelligent behavior. Here's your chance to provide that role model. Instead of wasting their time criticizing and belittling students for joining gangs, taking drugs, having rampant unsafe sex, and cheating on assignments, you will be much more likely to earn their respect if you ask them why they have made the choices they have made—and listen to their answers. If they ask for your advice, feel free to give it. Otherwise, keep asking questions until they learn to question their own choices and behaviors. You can't save your students from themselves.

But you can teach them to think, to solve problems, to analyze choices, to be successful people, and they will save themselves.

"Are you asking me to say it's okay to be a gang member?" one teacher asked me. Of course, I am not asking teachers to advocate gang membership. I am asking that we refrain from judging students who happen to be gang members. If a student is a second- or third-generation gang member, as many of my own students have been, the moment I say something derogatory about gangs, I have insulted the family and lost any chance of ever gaining that student's trust. And it's very difficult to teach people who mistrust you. If we don't know all the circumstances of another person's life, we can't possibly know whether we would have made different choices if we were in the same situation, facing the same pressures. We can't possibly know the intimate details of our students' lives when we first meet them. So, I have learned to say, "I believe people have reasons for the things they do, even when they make different choices than I think I would. The important thing is that we think about the choices we make and if we decide they were not good choices, we make some changes." And I have to say that some of my smartest and best students have come from backgrounds where gang activity, violence, drug use, and frequent jail visits were the norm among the adults in the community as well as among students.

Another factor for teachers to consider is that street gangs are not like the Boy Scouts or Girl Scouts. Members can't just decide they don't want to attend meetings any more. One young man in my remedial reading class, an active gang member—I'll call him Ramon—was clearly intelligent and a quick learner, in spite of poor reading skills due to his past truancy. He attended class regularly for several months and then disappeared without a word. A few weeks later, I happened to encounter Ramon at a local department store. I expected him to avoid me, but he walked right over and said hello. I said that I missed seeing him in school.

"My girlfriend is having a baby," Ramon said, "and I was thinking about do I want my kids to grow up and do the same things I did. So I decided to get out of the gang. But they beat me down and told me if I come back to school, I'm dead. So I had to quit."

While I was still trying to think of something appropriate to say, Ramon turned so I could see his face more clearly. One side of his head was covered with bruises that still looked painful, although they were fading. Quickly, he pulled down his lower lip to reveal several missing teeth and wounds inside his mouth.

"I'm so sorry," I said.

"Hey, I'm cool," he said.

"That's wonderful. Good luck. I know you'll do well because you're an intelligent young man." I held out my hand and Ramon took it without hesitation. After a quick shake, he nodded and walked off down the aisle. I never saw him again. I never forgot him, though, and I hope he remembers me as somebody who looked past his appearance and his mistakes to see the fine young man inside.

As you consider how you are going to demonstrate your respect for your students as human beings, please take a moment to recall your own childhood teachers. I would bet my gigantic teacher's salary that you're not thinking of algebraic formulas or prepositional phrases. More likely, you remember a compliment that sent your spirits soaring or a humiliation that still makes your cheeks burn. I remember one of my own elementary teachers using masking tape to attach my glasses to my face because I kept taking them off when other kids teased me about wearing them. The teacher said she meant to teach me to keep my glasses on my face and stop acting silly, but what she taught me was how embarrassing and infuriating it is to be helpless under the control of an authority figure who misuses her power. After that day I left my glasses at home and refused to wear them to school ever again. I squinted in school every year until my high school graduation. I still remember the masking-tape-wielding teacher, but I also remember my fifth-grade teacher, Mrs. Hodak, who encouraged me to write and appointed me to the glorious position of class newspaper editor. When I acted silly, Mrs. Hodak would look at me over the top of her glasses and wait for me to come to my senses and settle down. Then she would hug me. Mrs. Hodak taught me to think about my behavior. She taught me to challenge myself and follow my dreams. She taught me the true meaning of respect, and I will love her until the day I die.

## GRADES: PERCENTAGE? CURVE? COIN TOSS?

How will you use grades in your classroom: to provide incentives, to record progress, to evaluate your teaching, to punish daydreamers and procrastinators—or all four? I opt to use only the first three, because when teachers use bad grades or deduct points as punishment, they contribute to the cycle of misbehavior and failure that undermines our school system. I believe grades should measure how well students have learned the material and skills, and their grades indicate how well I have presented the lessons and motivated my students. A grade book filled with Ds and Fs is a warning flag that I am not doing my job well.

Every teacher must create a grading policy that reflects his or her own standards and ethics, but the most effective teachers maintain high standards, a flexible attitude, and a constant focus on fairness. Effective teachers keep students informed of their progress at frequent intervals, to avoid surprises and complaints. Your school may use a pass/fail option, straight percentages, or a letter-grade system. Your department may add its own criteria, 95 percent required for an A, for example. But it will be up to you to assign the grades. Even a subject such as math, which is more objective than most, leaves room for subjectivity in grading. Will you give credit only for correct answers on homework, or will you allow credit for student papers that have incorrect answers but indicate considerable effort or basic understanding of important concepts? If a student has perfect attendance, completes her homework faithfully, cooperates during class but suffers from test anxiety that makes her fail every major exam, what grade will you assign her? Will you go strictly by percentage, even though it doesn't accurately represent her ability? Will you assign less weight to her exam scores? Perhaps you'll arrange an alternative testing program for her, allowing her to take her exams after school, perhaps orally, or with a trusted counselor in attendance.

What about your underachiever? If a student is clearly capable of earning an A without studying, but he decides to read comic books in the back of your classroom whenever he can and rarely bothers to complete a homework assignment, will you give him an A when he aces the midterm and final exams? Will your grade reflect his academic ability and natural intelligence, or will you consider his poor work ethic and laziness?

Will you grade every single assignment, or will you give full credit on some assignments for students who make a sincere effort to learn a new skill, even if they make a lot of mistakes? Will you allow students who work diligently on every task to earn extra credit that may raise their grade a notch to reflect their hard work, enthusiasm, and persistence? Will you start all students at ground zero and then make it as difficult as you can for them to work their way up to an A? Will you just start assigning work and figure out how to grade students after you see what they can do? Will you start all students with an A and work hard to help them keep it?

Because they believe we need to raise the bar, some teachers blast their classes with impossible workloads from the second the school year begins. And some teachers boast that "Nobody earns an A in my class because I'm too darned tough." My questions to such teachers is: What would motivate a student to try hard if he or she knows in advance that an A is impossible to achieve in your class? If the material in your class is learnable and appropriate for the students' ability level, then why shouldn't a motivated, hard-working student be able to learn what you have to teach?

The real question every teacher must answer is not so much "What grade does a student deserve?" as it is "What do you want your students to learn?" Of course, you must grade major exams according to your district policy. But although grading every assignment strictly by percentage teaches students that they must achieve whatever standards are set for them in a particular situation, it also may teach them that academic ability is more important than social skills, respect for other people, enthusiasm, a willingness to tackle challenges, and the ability to learn from mistakes.

At the end of the school year, you may wonder whether your grades accurately reflect and reward your students' efforts. You won't be the only teacher wondering. That's why so many teachers ask students to grade themselves or to write a paragraph or an essay arguing for their grades. I've used a variation of that assignment with great success. My students enjoy it, and I learn as much about my teaching as I do about their learning. I call my self-grading assignment "A Different Perspective."

I assign students the task of writing letters to themselves—from me. In their letters they must imagine that they are seeing themselves from my perspective as they describe their behavior and evaluate their performance in my classroom. They must assign themselves the grade that they believe I would assign, and they must justify that grade. Sometimes students find the assignment confusing and need help getting started. I write a few example beginnings on the board: "Dear Joey: It's been a distinct pleasure having you as a student" or "Dear Patrice: Wake up and smell your sneakers!" and so on.

One or two jokers usually write silly letters, but most students take the assignment to heart. They are honest and more critical than I would be. Sometimes a student who has an A in my book assigns himself a lower grade because he really didn't try his hardest. Other times I realize that a student spent an extraordinary amount of time and effort at home as well as in my classroom. I rarely lower a grade after reading the letters, but I sometimes raise one. In addition to letting me see whether my grades are on target, the letters give me insight into my own performance. They let me know that I spend too much time on one area and not enough on another or that I divided my attention unfairly between boys and girls. Those student letters remind me that I must work to earn my own A.

One final note about grading. If you teach subjects that involve abstract principles or concepts, such as ethics, economics, or algebra (especially algebra), be aware that some students may have problems because of their individual rates of development. There is a point in every child's development when the brain makes the switch from concrete to abstract thinking. This switch has nothing to do with intelligence. Conscientious, industrious students who are used to succeeding in school often become frustrated when they cannot grasp new concepts; and you may think they aren't trying, because they usually earn high grades. For example, when we study symbolism in literature, many bright students understand the definition of symbolism and the examples I give them to illustrate the technique, but they cannot create their own examples for an exam. Instead of deducting points from those students' papers, I give them credit if they can define the concept and remember some of my examples. My hope is that later on, when they are able to understand, they will recall those examples and use them as a model for creating their own.

## COVERING CURRICULUM IS NOT TEACHING

If you are a master organizer with a creative flair and the ability to teach advanced, regular, and remedial students, undeterred by myriad distractions and interruptions, then you probably have no trouble covering all of the curriculum required for your subject or course. If you don't spend a minute worrying about how you're going to fit everything you want to teach into one school year, then you're an uncommonly talented teacher who should skip this section. The rest of us worry, because it's common for teachers, especially new teachers, to fear that they can't teach everything they need to teach. There is too much material, too much paper shuffling, too many energy-consuming administrative tasks, and not enough time. Instead of sharing this fear and discussing ways to become more effective teachers, most of us worry privately and fear that our colleagues will think we're ineffective or unqualified if we admit that we sometimes feel inadequate to the task of teaching all the required skills and information for our courses.

The question every teacher must face is this: Given a conflict, where does my priority lie—in covering the curriculum material and preparing for tests or in meeting my students' needs? It's easy to err in either direction. Some teachers take the district guidelines to heart and race their way through the required textbooks and activities, leaving those students who can't learn fast enough trailing behind the pack. Unfortunately, sometimes an entire class ends up falling behind, and the teacher is the only one who really understands the material when it's time for final exams. Other teachers bend to the pressure from above and spend all their class time teaching a specific test. Their students may learn how to take that specific test, and the school district may look good on paper; but I believe those students could be better served if they learned how to think and read and write well, which would prepare them to succeed in college or at work, in addition to preparing them to pass exams. Still other teachers turn giddy from the pressure to perform or pay the price (not being offered a contract or granted tenure, for example), so they toss aside the textbooks and spend their entire class periods chatting with students about current events or designing fun projects that take weeks to complete, leaving their students unprepared for the following year's requirements.

It is possible, though not easy, to find a middle ground. My district supervisor gave me a big boost in the right direction when she explained her viewpoint at a meeting of our teaching team. Working together, we four teachers had the task of teaching fifty at-risk teens, students who had severe attendance problems, substandard reading ability, and apathetic attitudes toward education.

"Covering curriculum is not teaching," our supervisor explained. "Nobody expects you to address the problems these kids have, bring them up to grade level, and cover your entire textbooks in one year. I advise you to select the key elements in your texts and teach those elements well. Don't worry about covering every single thing; just teach the most important concepts and skills, and teach your students how to learn so they can pick up the slack." We took her advice and were amazed at how well it worked. Instead of dividing our textbooks into segments and arbitrarily deciding how long each new skill should take to master, we made a list of what we wanted to teach and started with the most important and basic skills. For example, our math teacher had to back up and reteach the number line and negative and positive numbers. We were a little nervous at first, but when our students realized that we would slow down as they needed in order to spend time on areas of special interest, they repaid us by working harder at the mundane tasks in between. Our students performed as well as the "regular" students in English, history, and computer courses; and our math students zoomed right past the regular geometry classes, earning higher grades and completing more of the same textbook!

Those students reminded us of a lesson we sometimes forget: children are capable of learning much more than we require during a given school year. If we slow down or back up to fill in the gaps in their knowledge base and if they are confident that we have their best interests at heart, they will accelerate their learning and accomplish goals far beyond any we set for them.

## THERE IS NO SUCH THING AS A CASUAL REMARK TO A CHILD

Sometimes I think we forget how impressionable children are (even adolescents). We forget how excruciating the smallest pain can be, how exhilarating the tiniest victory, and how lasting the effect of a comment from an adult they admire. One day before class started, a group of football players were boasting about their latest gridiron glories. I noticed another boy, Sean Campbell, blush and fidget as he watched the athletes trade playful insults in front of a group of admiring girls and boys. A skinny youngster, all elbows and knees, Sean often dropped things or tripped over his shoelaces. When one of the ball players complimented himself on a sixty-five-yard touchdown, Sean sighed and looked out the window. I walked around the room until I stood near Sean's desk.

"I'm very proud of you, Paul," I told the touchdown scorer. "But I hope you go on to achieve great things after school too. I'd hate for you to be one of those people who peak at age sixteen, whose lives are all downhill after high school."

"I'm cool," Paul responded with a grin. "You know the scouts are already looking at me."

I was looking at Sean, who was looking at Paul.

"You're going to be one of those men who peak much later in life," I said softly to Sean.

"Yeah, I was thinking that," Sean said. His cheeks flushed bright red, but he sat up straighter and stopped staring wistfully at Paul and his entourage. Pleased that I had boosted Sean's self-esteem, I took the scenic route as I strolled back to my desk.

In the far corner of the room, as I passed by the desk of an extremely shy girl named Marcy, I stopped and smiled at her. "You too," I said. "I think you're going to be a late bloomer, but you're going to be a big, beautiful flower."

Marcy folded into herself and hid her face as she did whenever anybody looked at her. Not wanting to embarrass her further, I quickly made some chitchat with other students and returned to the front of the room.

I forgot all about the incident until a few months later, at open house. Toward the end of the event, Sean's mother walked into my room and introduced herself.

As I reached out to shake hands with her, she took my right hand with both her hands. She squeezed my hand and held on.

"I wanted to thank you for what you said to Sean," she said. "He said you told him you knew he was going to peak late in life and he shouldn't worry about not being the best athlete or the most popular right now. You should have seen him smile when he told me. And he has been a different person ever since. You changed his life. I can't thank you enough."

I was so stunned at Mrs. Campbell's remarks that I just stood there, grinning stupidly at her until she left the room. I had completely forgotten about that day, but Sean had remembered. I floated through the rest of the evening on a little cloud of happiness. One incident like that can keep a teacher motivated for months. But just as I was ready to turn out the lights and lock the door, Marcy's mother peeked around the door frame.

"Am I too late to say hello?" she asked. Some children work hard to be different from their parents, but Marcy was definitely her mother's daughter. I welcomed Mrs. Bryant into my room and motioned for her to sit down in one of the student desks for a chat.

"Oh, I don't want to take up your time," Mrs. Bryant said. She held her purse tightly with both hands, and I had the impression that she was resisting the temptation to hold the purse up in front of her face to hide behind it.

"I just wanted to thank you," she said. "Marcy told me you said she was a late bloomer but that she is going to be a beautiful flower someday. She cried when she told me. We both did. She used to be worried about what would happen to her when she grew up, but she doesn't worry anymore."

I didn't say anything because I knew I would cry if I opened my mouth. I just nodded and smiled at Mrs. Bryant as she ducked her head and slipped out the door.

After Sean's mother had talked to me, I admit I was feeling a little proud of myself. But after Marcy's mother left, I felt a little frightened. Two students believed that a five-second forgotten conversation had changed their lives. If that was true, then what about all the other conversations I couldn't remember? Had I said anything that negatively affected children so strongly as those positive comments had? I tried to remember whether I had said anything harsh the last time I had run out of patience or had been frustrated by too much talking or pencil sharpening or giggling or note writing during class. I couldn't think of any negative comments I may have made, but then I had forgotten the late-bloomer comments too.

Before I turned off the lights and locked the door to my classroom that night, I wrote a note on an index card and taped it to the top of my desk as a reminder. My note read:

*Be careful. Everything you say, every single day, may be recorded in your students' hearts forever.*

## DISCUSSION POINTS

1. What is your teaching persona? How does it compare to your personal persona?

2. What is your optional agenda? What optional agendas did your own teachers have?

3. How can teachers effectively establish rapport with students who come from different cultural or ethnic backgrounds from the teacher's?

4. How can teachers design assessment tools that are accurate and fair indicators of individual student progress?

5. How do you prioritize when pressure to prepare for tests conflicts with the activities and lessons you believe are necessary to include in your curriculum?

6. Share some comments that you remember from your childhood teachers. Why do you still remember those comments?

# The Big Three: Preparation, Preparation, Preparation

Award-winning Realtors often list their top three criteria for success: "Location, location, location." And effective teachers often
list the top three criteria for their success as preparation, preparation,
preparation. If you don't get your ducks all in a row well ahead of
time, you may find yourself dealing with stray quackers all year long,
because once the school year begins, even experienced, effective teachers find themselves running at top speed on the teaching treadmill. In
addition to saving time and energy later on, you will find that spending a couple of weeks getting organized before school starts will allow
you to focus on the most challenging and interesting aspect of your
delightful job—your students.

You will need some equipment and supplies in order to get yourself organized. Because most schools operate on limited or shrinking budgets, supplies may be scarce. As soon as you sign your contract to teach, ask a friend or relative to host a teacher-to-be shower. Provide a suggestion list for gifts: file folders, storage crates and bins, portable bookshelves, colored markers and art supplies, poster board, construction paper, scissors, tape, staplers, pencils, pens, paper clips, three-ring binders, subscriptions to educational publications for young people, children's books, young adult books, dictionaries, notebook paper, pastel printer paper, and so on. If your friends and relatives are employed and generous, you might add bigger items such as a room-sized air purifier; a CD, iPod, or DVD player; or a video cam or digital camera. Don't be shy. You aren't asking for gifts for yourself; you are asking for donations to help you educate the future leaders of our country. People will be happy to contribute and even happier if you periodically provide them with an e-mail or printed newsletter highlighting your students' achievements. An especially nice touch and one that may bring tears to your donors' eyes is to have your grateful students send handwritten thank-you notes.

Another possible resource is Web sites where teachers can list their requests for funds to buy supplies, equipment, books, and other materials to aid their students. DonorsChoose.org is a national database where teachers can describe their classroom projects, and donors can search by area or need. To find state or local Web sites, teachers can do an Internet search for the term "teachers request funds" along with the local city or state. That search will bring up current Web sites.

Once you have supplies, where do you start? I'd suggest making three lists of things you need to prepare: your classroom, your paperwork, and yourself. You'll find my own checklists at the end of this chapter if you'd like to use them as a starting point.

## PREPARE YOUR ROOM

I often refer to attending school as children's "work," and I frequently draw analogies between the many common behaviors and conditions that lead to success in school and at work. In any profession, your environment affects your comfort and efficiency, and your interactions with other people affect the speed and accuracy of your work. As an adult, you have multiple options if you are uncomfortable or unhappy with your job. Students are stuck with whatever classroom environments their teachers create; your classroom environment can mean the difference between a room filled with cooperative, enthusiastic, motivated children or a group of apathetic nonparticipants and disgruntled whiners. Creating a dynamic classroom environment involves four basic elements: sensory details, seating arrangements, supplies and storage, and student information.

## Sensory Details

Children are much more attuned to—and distracted by—the world's sensory elements than most adults are. Students respond, often quite dramatically, to the way your room looks, feels, sounds and, yes, even the way it smells. You can do a great deal (even with limited equipment and funds) to address those four aspects of your classroom with an eye toward creating an environment that is functional, comfortable, welcoming, and inspiring.

Sound and smell are the easiest aspects to address. If your school is noisy because of traffic, loud air conditioning or heating systems, thin walls, or rampaging students, you can create an oasis of calm in your classroom by playing soft music before and between class periods. Scientists have repeatedly proven that music can either encourage (classical) or discourage (heavy metal) thinking and that classical music can improve IQ test scores. Light classical music, jazz, or music designed to enhance meditation can all be used to take advantage of children's natural affinity for melody and percussion.

If music is playing when students first enter your classroom, they will definitely notice; and many of them will make their opinions known. This is your chance to teach them how to be intelligent critics. If they criticize your music choice, ask them to listen long enough to be able to articulate an intelligent opinion about the music. Some students will resist listening to music that doesn't include screaming vocals or ear-numbing electronic drumbeats, but if you ask them to give it a try just for a few minutes each day, they will soon become accustomed to it. (If you have a large number of vocal complainers, don't argue. Just turn off your music, politely tell them you are sorry they weren't interested in your experiment, and drop the subject. Move quickly to the next academic activity. Chances are good that the students will change their minds and decide to give your horrible music a short listen.) One teacher I know spent weeks trying to convince her high school juniors to listen to light classical music before class started and during exams. Before long her students began complaining that the room was too quiet and that sounds were too distracting if she didn't play music during exams.

Music can also be a great tool for increasing student participation and motivation, but if you do play music, some student is bound to ask if he or she can change the radio station or listen to a popular CD. If your goal is to create a calm environment in your classroom, then I would suggest keeping the music choice as your domain, but include music in your student projects or allow students to have five minutes of music time at the end of any class period during which nobody has disrupted and everybody has completed the work assignments (you'll need to figure out a system for rotating choices, or a few students will dominate). I have had groups in which even confirmed nonreaders agreed to read difficult fiction in order to spend a few minutes at the end of the class period listening to their horrible, loud, screeching "really great music."

Next, let's talk about smell, an integral part of any school experience. If you close your eyes and let your nose drift, I would bet you can recall at least one distinctive smell from your own school days. My strongest olfactory memory is of new books. I have always loved their smell. But not all school smells are pleasant. In fact, when you take twenty or thirty warm bodies, plenty of well-worn sneakers, several quarts of perfumed personal hygiene products, dust from chalk or dry-erase markers, residue from the custodial staff's industrial-strength cleaners, and reams of old papers, you can end up with some nasty-smelling classrooms.

Fortunately, smell is a relatively easy aspect of your room to control, but buying a decent air cleaner is probably going to cost a few dollars (they are relatively inexpensive) out of your own pocket, unless you can find a local business to sponsor you or unless your department budget provides teachers with a petty-cash allowance. Even if you have to fork over the dough from your paltry paycheck, your investment will pay off. Not only will your classroom smell better, but also you'll find that you have fewer students sniffling during allergy season. And if you buy an air purifier with an ultraviolet light, it will kill many of the germs that congregate in classrooms during cold and flu season.

Do a little research before you buy an air purifier. There are a lot of urban myths surrounding negative ion generation and ultraviolet radiation. Negative ions are not harmful unless they are created in overabundance, and most new air cleaners have built-in controls. When an air cleaner generates the proper amount of negative ions, your room will have a fresh, outdoorsy smell. If you smell a distinctive tangy odor instead, you know that you need to make an adjustment to decrease the negative ions. Ultraviolet lights in air filters are not placed where they can injure people's eyes or subject them to radiation, and they very effectively zap airborne germs and pollutants.

Now we're ready to tackle the feel of your room. Take a walk around the block and then enter your classroom. Notice whether it's too warm or too cold, whether the lights are so bright that they create glare on the desks. Are the walls a nice warm color, or have they been painted an ugly industrial gray or tan to hide the dirt? (I know, I know, you aren't supposed to paint your room. But there are ways to get it done if you are creative.) If you do decide to paint, and you plan to paint without permission—I'm not advocating this, just suggesting that it is a possibility—be sure to consider buying a paint that does not give off gases. They are called low-VOC paints; read about them at the BioShield Paint Web site (www.bioshieldpaint.com) or ask your local reference librarian for help in locating information. If you go the law-abiding route and request permission, consult the OSHA guidelines to find out which paints can be used in U.S. schools. Your building custodians should have that information.

Does your classroom feel inviting? Is this a place you'd like to sit for a few hours every day? Wander around and visit some other classrooms. Compare the way they feel to the way your classroom feels. Then see if you can figure out what makes them more or less inviting. If your room is stuffy and overheated or too cold and drafty, find your school's maintenance supervisor and ask for his or her advice. Some school districts are inflexible about the dates that schools must use heating or air conditioning, regardless of the local weather conditions. And some buildings have a central ventilation system that doesn't allow for individual room settings. But if you explain that you are trying to make your room as comfortable as possible for your students, your maintenance professionals will probably find a way to help you; it has been my experience that they appreciate being recognized for their knowledge and training, and they are eager to help you if you approach them with a respectful and patient attitude. At one school, the custodians placed a transparent blue film over the fluorescent lights to reduce the glare and create a more natural color of light. At another school, when I asked about full-spectrum fluorescent lights, the head custodian said, "You tell me what you need, and I'll find it." When I painted my room one weekend—honestly, I didn't know I wasn't supposed to— the custodians shook their heads but agreed to pretend not to notice. (I didn't paint it a wild color, just a nice warm peach with light blue accents, and all the paint was provided by a professional painter who did the painting for free.)

How does your classroom look? Inviting and interesting? If you teach special needs students who are distracted by too much visual input, you may want to opt for a less busy decor, but if you do decide to decorate, in addition to the standard posters, maps, and magazine articles, try tacking up photos of students from your old high school yearbooks, copies of your childhood report cards and homework assignments, a collection of calendars, restaurant menus, theater playbills, jokes, flags, banners, colorful mobiles, plants (real or fake), or athletic memorabilia. Think of theme restaurants you like: the decor has nothing to do with the food, but we still like to sit in surroundings that are beautiful, interesting, or amusing. Put a fake palm tree and some floor pillows in a corner of your classroom, and kids will clamor to be able to sit there and read. (Don't ask permission to do this. Just do it, and if you get in trouble, apologize profusely. If you can prove that student behavior or grades have improved because of your decor, administrators are much more likely to give you permission to keep your unorthodox seating and decor.)

Does your room have some eye candy for those students who really need a daydream break now and then? Even when students aren't paying attention to your lessons, they will still absorb the information you have posted on the walls around them. Motivational quotations are especially effective. There are books devoted exclusively to memorable quotations, so you will be able to find some that will suit your students. If you have access to a computer, there are a number of tools that allow teachers to create their own posters with text and illustrations (BigHugeLabs.com and poster.4teachers.org are just two of many such resources). But if you make your own posters by hand, be sure to write them in very large letters so that students can read them from a distance.

Here are a few of my favorite quotes to get you started:

> *The hallmark of a second-rater is*
> *resentment of another's achievement.*
>
> —Ayn Rand

> *If you don't decide which way to play*
> *with life, it will play with you.*
>
> —Merle Shain

> *Nobody can make you feel inferior without your consent.*
>
> —Eleanor Roosevelt

> *If you can imagine it, you can achieve it;*
> *If you can dream it, you can become it.*
>
> —William Ward

*Great spirits have always encountered violent opposition from mediocre minds.*

—Albert Einstein

*The hardest thing about success is finding somebody who is truly happy for you.*

—Bette Midler

*There are two tragedies in life: one is to lose your heart's desire, the other to gain it.*

—George Bernard Shaw

*If your only tool is a hammer, you tend to see every problem as a nail.*

—Abraham Maslow

*One often learns more from ten days of agony than from ten years of contentment.*

—Merle Shain

*Light came to me when I realized I did not have to consider any racial group as a whole. God made them duck by duck, and that was the only way I could see them.*

—Zora Neale Hurston

*Rudeness is a weak person's attempt at strength.*

—J. M. Casey

*A life spent making mistakes is not only more honorable but more useful than a life spent doing nothing.*

—George Bernard Shaw

*Hold fast to dreams, for if dreams die, life is a broken-winged bird that cannot fly.*

—Langston Hughes

*Keep away from people who try to belittle your ambitions. Small people always do that, but the really great make you feel that you, too, are great.*

—Mark Twain

*We are each given the same twenty-four hours each day. How we choose to spend our time makes the difference between success and failure.*

—Kenneth Brodeur

*Just because you're right doesn't mean I'm wrong.*

—My mom, Alyce Shirley Johnson

## The Psychology of Seating

Student seating arrangements have a tremendous impact on students' motivation, behavior, and interactions with each other as well as with the teacher. For very young children who spend most of their time sitting on the floor or on pillows or mats, the important thing is that they can see and hear the teacher and teacher aides clearly. Once children are old enough that they spend most of their class time seated in chairs, seating becomes a more important issue. The shape and size of your classroom will limit your options, but two considerations should take priority, regardless of what arrangement you choose: vision and access. While seated, all students must be able to clearly see the board, any screens used for various projections, the TV or monitors, and the clock. And you must have quick and easy access to every student in your classroom. You will have far fewer discipline problems if you arrange your student seating so that you have a clear pathway to each student, with a maximum of two people between you and a given student at all times.

Creating access can be a challenge in a small room, especially in narrow mobile classrooms. In a smaller room, you may have to create three or more separate areas in order to have desks only three deep. Before you arrange your room, try sketching a few different ideas on paper. If you have a small room, you might consider eliminating your own desk if it's big and bulky and you have sufficient storage space. A small mobile computer desk and a small worktable might allow a more effective use of space.

Psychology plays an important role in seating: a round table indicates that all participants hold equal status, whereas a rectangular table usually has a chair at the head for the leader. Large tables with chairs that face across are conducive to communication and discussion. Chairs lined in long straight rows facing a stage (think of church pews or seats in a theater) create a clear distinction between the speaker(s) and the audience.

You can use seating psychology to send messages to your students. Long, straight rows indicate that yours will be a traditional classroom, governed by strict rules and regulations. A large circle or concentric semicircles send a different message, usually indicating that you expect group discussions or other student feedback. Small groups of desks or tables alert students to be prepared to participate in informal exercises, small-group activities, or teamwork exercises.

I take advantage of seating psychology by using different arrangements for different activities, but I have learned the hard way to avoid arrangements in which students face each other squarely from across the room. At one school where gang activity was a serious problem, both boys and girls would stare down students who sat directly opposite them when their desks faced each other head-on. Turning desks so that they face each other at even a slight angle can eliminate this problem; it's easy to judge whether you've got it right. Sit in one of the student desks in the front row. If your gaze is directed squarely at another student's desk, then shift your desk so that the direct line of your gaze includes several desks or a wall.

The only time I use straight rows of desks all facing the same direction is when we have an important test. Students understand that when they see test formation, they should sharpen their pencils, stow their possessions, and be prepared to work quietly. I don't like long, straight rows except during test periods, however. Students tend to misbehave or daydream when they are seated in rows of six or seven, because no matter where I stand, several students are far away from me. Worse yet, students cannot hear or see each other well. Students seated in the front and back of the room can't hear each other's comments, questions, or answers during class time. Everybody has trouble hearing when students read aloud during class because students are either reading into a void in the front of the room or into the backs of other students' heads— not conducive to creating a dynamic environment for participation or discussion.

In a classroom with a clearly defined front (a chalkboard or whiteboard and a projection screen permanently located along the same wall), my favorite arrangement is either a modified semicircle or U shape (Figure 4.1) that allows everybody to see clearly while giving me quick, easy access to all students, or a flexible plan (Figure 4.2) with worktables or grouped desks to the sides and a semicircle instructional area in the center.

The flexible arrangement can be tweaked to fit a number of different classroom shapes and sizes to facilitate small-group direct instruction and independent

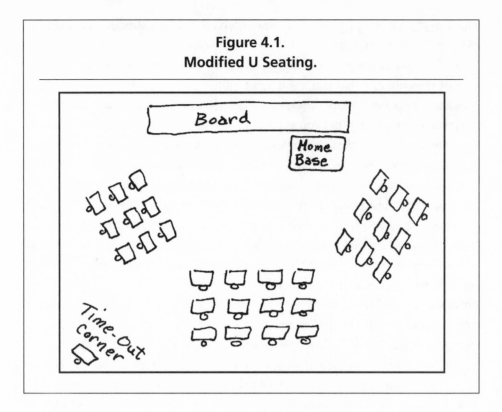

**Figure 4.1.**
**Modified U Seating.**

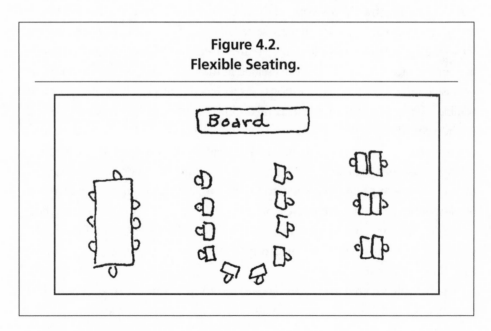

**Figure 4.2.**
**Flexible Seating.**

or group work at the same time. This is the most compatible arrangement for teachers who like to use differentiated instruction and independent assignments or projects. The teacher can provide direct instruction in the center of the room while students work independently in the side areas.

For small-group activities, I place the desks into clumps of three or four. I try to separate the groups enough to allow for private discussions and eliminate distractions from other groups. Some teachers ask their students to arrange the desks for group activities, which has the added benefit of giving students a bit of physical exercise; other teachers find that using student movers creates too much chatter and confusion and uses up valuable activity time. In either event, this is a perfect opportunity to teach students the procedure you would like them to use to prepare for group activity.

In a classroom with two possible fronts (with boards or screens on opposite walls or a board on one end and screen at the other), I use a double semicircle formation (Figure 4.3), so that the focus shifts from one side to the other without obstructing students' vision or necessitating rearrangement of student desks.

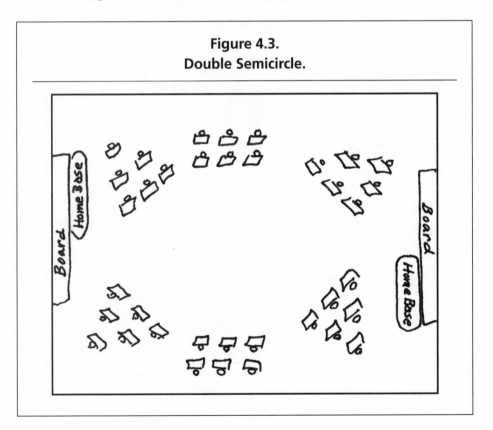

**Figure 4.3.
Double Semicircle.**

Although mobile classrooms will be illegal after I am crowned queen of education, at present many teachers have to work with them. Aside from aesthetic and comfort issues, one of the big problems in trailer-style rooms is vision. If your board and screen are at one end of the room, some students are going to be forced to sit where they can't see clearly. If your board and screen are attached at the side of the room, I recommend asking maintenance to provide portable versions, especially if you teach math or science. If you try to line up the student desks lengthwise, facing a board mounted on a side wall, you are going to end up with all your students crowded into a small space, and those on the ends won't be able to see well.

My approach to trailer teaching is to divide the students into two groups, one at either end of the trailer (Figure 4.4). While one group of students works independently at their seats, I instruct the other group using the overhead projector

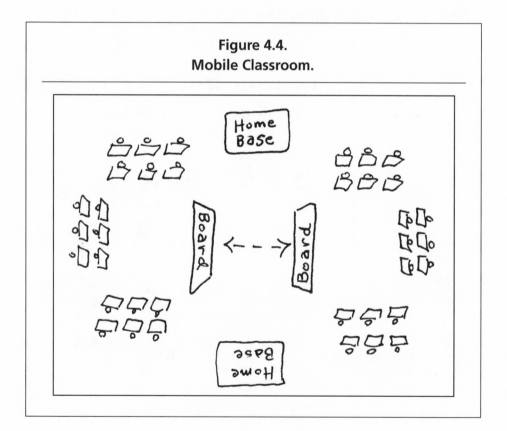

**Figure 4.4.**
**Mobile Classroom.**

and whiteboard (moving the screen and board for each group so that they are positioned where the whole group can see them). Although I have to present the same lesson twice, it doesn't deprive anybody, and it actually helps those students who process information more slowly, allowing them to tune in to both presentations as needed.

There are many other options for arranging desks, including getting rid of half of them and using conference tables, work centers, floor pillows, armchairs, futons, and the like. And even if you are stuck with a specific arrangement for some reason, you can still switch it up a bit. I read about one teacher who had trouble getting students to transition from one activity to the next. Her solution: she asked students to spin their desks 90 degrees or 180 degrees so they were facing a different wall. This simple shift in visual input helped her students shift their focus to the new activity.

## Open Seating or Seating Charts?

Some teachers swear by seating charts, and some students swear at them. Alphabetical seating is popular because it helps teachers learn names, take roll, and coordinate activities that require students to line up and move as a group. Alphabetical seating arrangements can be helpful to teachers, particularly if they work with very young children, but such arrangements can backfire with older students. Some students become irritated or apathetic after years of being assigned to the front or the back of every lineup, and some students will have been forced to sit year after year near students with whom they have serious personality conflicts. During junior high and high school years, personality conflicts can contribute to serious behavior problems. Unless your students are quite young or you already know them and their personalities, I recommend starting without a seating chart. Here's why: when you use a seating chart, you give up a great "power tool" and you miss out on an opportunity to learn more about your students.

When students enter a room for the first time and are permitted to select their own seats, you will find that some students make a beeline for the back of the room. Some prefer an aisle seat, just as some airline travelers do. And still others will choose to sit as close to the teacher's desk as possible. Not all students who sit in the back are troublemakers—some people simply can't concentrate when there are people sitting behind them—sort of like the poker player who likes to sit with his back against the wall, facing the door. Students who choose the perimeters of the room may have private lives where they often feel a desire or need to escape. They can't concentrate when they feel trapped. Front-row students may have hearing or vision problems—or they may be wary of sitting near somebody who has bullied or harassed them at some time in the past. All of this information can help you understand your students better, which will help you make the best choices when you design lessons and activities. And students may be more inclined to cooperate immediately if they are comfortable with the locations of their seats.

Another advantage of beginning a class with open seating is that it leaves you holding a good power tool. If misbehavior or disruptions become a serious problem, you can warn your students that if they don't improve their behavior, you will have to create a seating chart which might mean they won't have the option of sitting near their friends or in a favorite location. This puts the responsibility for their behavior squarely on their young shoulders, where it belongs. And if they haven't yet developed enough self-control to improve their behavior, then temporary assigned seats may help them along. When their behavior improves, you might allow them to try sitting in self-selected seats again as a test. This may take two or three tries, but if you use seating charts as learning tools instead of punishment, they can become an effective method for nurturing self-control and self-monitored behavior among your students.

One year, I had a very unruly class, so I threatened to create a seating chart and eventually did. Instead of resigning themselves to the inevitable, as my students had done in the past, this group whined nonstop for days, until out of frustration, I said, "Fine! You don't like my seating chart? You create one where we don't have so much talking and disruptions when people are trying to work." Those students welcomed the challenge. Working effectively as a group for the first time, they came up with an arrangement that sounded a bit complex at first, but it worked better than any of my plans. Here is the student-designed seating program, along with their justification for each step.

> Some students find it boring to sit in the same seats every day, whereas other students prefer the emotional security of sitting in the same seat. So the students who need to sit in the same seat get to claim seats, and nobody else can sit there even when those students are absent.

Some students who like to sit in the back also like to cause a lot of problems by throwing stuff or saying things that the teacher can't hear. So nobody gets to claim a seat that is far away from the teacher or in the back rows unless they have a B or an A in the class; anybody with a D or lower has to sit near the teacher's desk. If people bring their grades up, they can claim a new desk.

Finally, the students who get bored sitting in the same seats get to choose from the seats that are left every day.

Every quarter or semester, we redo the entire plan so that students who didn't get to claim their first choice of seats will have another chance.

Because the student-designed plan worked so well, I made it my default. I follow that plan at the start of the semester or school year—but I explain to students that if self-discipline becomes a problem, I will give them one warning. Then, if they aren't working effectively as a group, I will create a seating chart that stays in effect until the end of that quarter or semester. I rarely have to create a new chart.

If you do decide to use a seating chart at the start of the school year or semester, I recommend taping name cards to the desks the first time students are to sit in assigned seats, so that students won't sit down in one seat and then have to move to another. Better yet, stand in the doorway of your room to greet your students as they enter, and direct them to their assigned seats. Students, especially adolescents, are much more receptive to sitting in an assigned seat if they don't have to move after they have selected a seat. Changing seats after students are already seated can create confusion, animosity, and a poor rapport between you and your little scholars.

To head off most complaints, explain that you have created a seating chart in order to help your students be successful people, not simply because you enjoy being the boss. Tell them that you have put a lot of thought into the plan and you believe it will help them succeed. If students complain about their seats, ask them to come talk to you after school—not after class. If they care enough to stay after school, then you might strongly consider changing their seats. Often students will ask for a new seat because somebody is bullying them or they don't want to sit near a former friend. Some students don't want to sit by their own best friends because they know they won't be able to concentrate and they know they won't be able to resist the temptation to whisper or pass notes when they should be paying attention.

## Establish a Private Zone

Kindergarten and elementary classrooms usually have multiple cubbies and storage shelves. If you post pictures or photographs to show what goes where, children are usually delighted to retrieve their own books and supplies—and help you put things away. And many early-grade classrooms consist of workstations or activity centers instead of student desks or tables. How you arrange your classroom will depend upon whether you share the room with another teacher, what furniture is already in the classroom or available from storage, the standard practice at your school (ratio of individual seat work to group projects, for example), and your own teaching style. But you will still want to consider making your desk and personal property off-limits to students.

Choose a spot as your home base—the spot you will return to before and after class and during breaks between activities. You may choose to put your desk at home base, or you may opt for a lectern or podium on which to store daily lesson materials, leaving your desk elsewhere. If you use your desk as home base, be prepared. Unless you mark your territory and strictly enforce your no trespassing rule, students will buzz about your desk; because they are children (even teens can act like children), they are going to be curious about everything in, on, around, under, and behind your desk. They will sit in your chair and spin or rock. They will open the drawers just to see what's in them. They will jingle your key chain and look into your purse or briefcase. Student curiosity is the primary reason why so many teachers choose to make their desks off-limits. During school hours they sit at a work table or a small desk between activities, away from their desks and all those temptations.

Some teachers like to place their desks in the corner of the room farthest from the door. Others prefer to put their file cabinets and supply shelves in the far corner of the room but keep their desks near the door, where they can more easily monitor student activity. Regardless of the arrangement you choose, you will need to create one area where you can keep confidential files, student grades, exams, and lesson outlines and make that area strictly off-limits to students. Hang up a sign if you need to, warning them to keep their hands off. If a student ignores the warning, act quickly and forcefully. This is the one time you do want to reprimand a student in public. You don't have to punish the student, but you do have to make a big deal out of the incident; otherwise you give your students the message that you don't really care if they snoop and pry.

Even if your desk is off-limits, you should lock up (if your desk has actual working locks and keys) anything that can be thrown, spat, flung, or shot at or stuck to other students, such as paper clips, rubber bands, tape, and tacks. Be especially careful with black Sharpie markers; they are irresistible to children and will disappear faster than most other supplies. If your desk doesn't lock or you don't want to worry about keys, buy a plastic bin with a solid latch to store extra staples, paper clips, rubber bands, markers, and so on.

I have tried both arrangements—using my desk as my home base and keeping my desk private and using a lectern or podium during lessons. The second method works better for me. I don't stand at the podium and lecture. I move constantly. But having a podium limits my space, which forces me to stay organized, and I can move quickly from one activity to the next. Each morning I place the lesson plan and necessary materials at the podium. Between activities and class periods, I may make quick visits to my desk; but if students are present, I stay at the podium so that they can ask questions or request my help.

My own desk is off-limits to students at all times. I place my desk diagonally across one corner of the room, with a file cabinet behind my chair to store student records, exams, and other confidential materials. As shown in Figure 4.5, one corner of my desk meets the wall, blocking access from that side. I place a visitor chair against the other side of my desk and allow an opening just wide enough for me to walk past to my own chair. I place a computer workstation, another file cabinet, or a bookshelf next to my desk to create a narrow entrance to my personal area. This setup reinforces my no-trespassing rule by creating a physical barrier between my private territory and the rest of the room.

## Supplies and Storage

Once you have situated your desk and storage units, find a small shelf or table for student supplies. Keep this student supply table near your home base so that you can monitor student use and restock as needed. Your supplies will vary according to your students' age and the subjects you teach, but I recommend a few supplies for every classroom: a box of tissues, a bottle of hand cleaner, a small mirror (children get things in their eyes), and a box of Band-Aids. If you choose not to provide a bottle of hand cleaner year-round, I suggest that you consider supplying it during cold and flu season. Ask your students to use it after they have sneezed or used a tissue to blow their noses, especially those students who currently have a

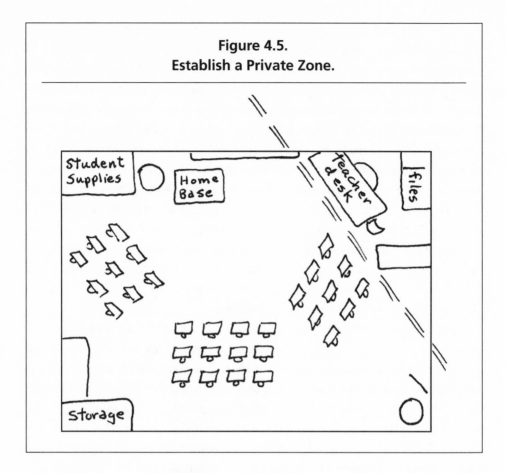

**Figure 4.5.**
**Establish a Private Zone.**

Student Supplies

Home Base

teacher desk

files

Storage

cold. Use it yourself between classes, especially after handling student papers. You will cut down on absences, including yours.

I also provide paper and pencils for my students. Although some teachers insist that parents or the school district should pay for all the paper and pencils, and the same teachers sometimes make a big deal when students forget to bring a pencil, I believe that we could save our energy for bigger battles and keep a package of lined notebook paper on hand, along with ten unique pencils (sparkly, polka-dotted, engraved, and so on). For classes with older students, I also provide ten unique and easily identifiable pens. I keep the pencils and pens in a jar labeled "Writing Utensils to Borrow" and assign a student to be the official pencil counter for each class or instructional period. The pencil counter's job is to make sure that ten pencils and ten pens are in the jar before students leave my classroom. This may seem trivial, but if you don't designate a pencil counter, your pencils and pens will disappear; it's easy for students to forget they borrowed a writing implement. But students do appreciate the option of borrowing a pen or pencil when they forget to bring theirs, and they waste far less time settling down to work.

If you feel very strongly that students need to bring their own supplies and you are certain that their families can afford to purchase them, then sell your students a sheet of paper or rent them a writing instrument and use the money to buy replacements when needed. But I'd think twice about wasting your time and energy arguing with children over pencils, pens, and paper. Many of them will "forget" their pencils every day just to procrastinate. We have many other opportunities during the school day to teach them responsibility.

Next fill your supply cupboard (or buy a big plastic bin) with trash bags, Band-Aids, Neosporin, disposable gloves, disinfectant cleaner, disposable antibacterial wipes, paper towels, a whisk broom, and a dust pan. When kids make a mess, unless they are very young, don't clean it up for them. Have them put on the gloves and get to work. (I know, I know, schools should supply these things; but if they don't, provide them yourself.)

Set one wastebasket near the tissue box on your student supply table and another near the door to your room (buy an extra one if you have to; your room will stay much cleaner). When wastebaskets are conveniently located, people are more apt to use them.

## Post Your Agenda

You can train your students to check certain locations for information each time they enter your classroom. For example, if you reserve the upper right-hand corner of your chalkboard or whiteboard for the daily agenda and make sure you post the agenda well before students enter the room each day, you won't have early birds hounding you with incessant "What are we gonna do today?" questions while you are trying to prepare for class. When students enter the room and ask you what they're going to do, point to the board and smile. Soon they will learn to look for themselves.

Make sure you post your agenda where everybody can see it. If you are very organized, you may choose to list details and specific times for specific activities. I prefer to make my agenda more flexible to allow for unforeseen circumstances. Sometimes students zip through an assignment that I thought would present a challenge; at other times they struggle with something I thought would be quite easy. So I make a simple list of general activities. Monday's agenda might read like this:

- Independent reading
- Spelling quiz
- Vocabulary review
- Journal writing or homework review
- Math worksheet
- Team assignments

Usually I post the following day's agenda before I leave the classroom at night so that it will be ready for even very early students. Some schools require custodians to clean all the boards, so if you post your agenda early, be sure to ask your custodian not to erase it.

Another option is to buy a portable erasable whiteboard, write your agenda with dry-erase markers, and post it above the student-supplies table. If your board is large enough, you might consider listing today's agenda, with a brief outline of the previous and next day's agendas for students who were absent or who like to plan ahead.

Having a daily agenda helps students focus, but some of them also need to see the bigger picture. Using poster board or giant construction paper, I create a classroom calendar big enough to be legible from across the room and hang it high enough so that it's clearly visible when students are seated. I mark all holidays, reviews, quizzes, exams, and special events. Quizzes are noted in blue marker, exams in red (for each quiz or exam, I count back three school days and post a reminder on that day for students to study and review). Special events such as graduation, picture day, and homecoming are marked in purple.

In addition to eliminating complaints from students that they didn't know about a test (no matter how many times you announce a test, somebody will forget), a classroom calendar provides a visual record of progress for students who feel overwhelmed by the length of the school year. Your calendar can also be a good motivational tool. One successful technique I have used is to place a star on the calendar for each day that I did not have to ask somebody to stop disrupting class; when a group earns fifteen stars, students earn a reward such as fifteen minutes of free time, a chance to play educational games, or a class visit to the library for thirty minutes of browsing. The only disadvantage of using stars to motivate classes is that you need a separate calendar for each class if you teach multiple classes. On the other hand, making separate calendars can inspire students in one class to work harder so that they don't fall behind another class. Although I don't like to focus on cutthroat competition, I do try to use positive peer pressure as long as students don't turn the process into a tool for humiliating each other. This is where your excellent teacher judgment comes into play.

Your daily agenda should always begin with your Do Now or Bell Work or whatever you call the activity that you want students to begin as soon as they come into your classroom. If you do nothing else to prepare for your school year, I recommend creating some interesting, fun, or challenging activities and assignments to get students started first thing in the morning or as soon as the bell rings to signal the start of a class. If you begin the first day with a Do Now activity and follow that same pattern for days two and three and four, you will find that by day five, students are already in the habit of getting to work without a lot of hoo-hah and nagging.

Please see Chapter Five, "Start with a Smile," for a full discussion and suggestions for Do Now activities and strategies.

## Rules of Order?

Perhaps you're thinking you should make a list of rules and post them on the wall where everybody can see them and be reminded how to act. My recommendation is to nix the rule list unless you are teaching kindergarten or first grade. Kids in second grade or higher know how they are expected to behave, because they have already gone to school where every teacher has at least one rule. Most have a list. Some have incredibly long lists. I think it's a good idea to create a behavior code or list of rules. But hang onto it. Don't hang it on the wall to remind students how to misbehave. Instead, give your students a chance to show you how well they can behave when you welcome them to your classroom and immediately engage them in an interesting or challenging activity. If everybody cooperates, then save your rules and regulations for later on, after you and your students have already created a good bond.

If you have one or two disrupters, quickly point out what you would like them to do—not what you don't want them to do. For example, instead of saying, "Don't talk when the teacher is talking," say, "It's my turn to talk now. Please be quiet until I finish." Then immediately thank the students who are being quiet. If you have a handful of students who seem determined to disrupt your wonderful first-day plans, then go ahead and whip out your rule poster or behavior code and make sure that everybody understands exactly what you expect of them.

Some administrations instruct teachers to spend the first minutes of every class going over the rules and regulations. I urge you to disobey that order (and I spent nine years on active military duty, so I know the importance of following orders). Let me restate my recommendation here. I urge you to delay obeying the order to make rules your number-one topic of conversation with a new class of students. I don't suggest holding back on rules out of pure orneriness or whimsy; I recommend holding back for a reason. My niece Lila explained it much better than I could. Excited about her first day of high school, Lila confided that she couldn't sleep for two days before classes started. She couldn't wait to be a freshman. I called her after the first day of school and asked how she liked being one of "the big kids." She responded with a long, melodramatic, teenage sigh.

"It was so-o-o-o-o-o boring," Lila said. "All we did was listen to a bunch of rules six times in a row in six different classes. It was just like kindergarten. I thought it was going to be different in high school. Now I don't even want to go back tomorrow."

Lila made a good point. Unless they are very young, students quickly become bored with needless repetition. Aside from boring and alienating students, a teacher who reads the rules on the first day can cause other logistical problems. When new students join your class, you have to repeat the rules for their benefit, which will once again bore the other kids who have already heard fifty million rules. Or you could hand students a printed copy of your rules, which they may glance at before throwing it in the trash or stuffing it into their backpacks. You could ask the new students to stay after class, which will irritate them because they have better things to do and because they heard the rules yesterday from the other teachers before their room assignments changed. Or you could cross your fingers and hope they behave.

If you prefer research to anecdote, here's another good reason for delaying your discussion of rules. The June–July 2007 issue of *Scientific American Mind* reported the results of a study conducted by social psychologists from Harvard and the University of California wherein subjects observed two-second video clips of professors teaching. The teaching ratings of those subjects accurately predicted the actual end-of-term evaluations of the professors' own students. The researchers reported that it takes six seconds or fewer to get a sense of somebody's energy or warmth. And another researcher spent twenty years conducting studies where he flashed images of faces and objects for just two-tenths of a second. People evaluated the faces and images within a quarter of a second, supposedly due to pathways that connect the human eye with the brain's rapid-response emotional-control centers, bypassing the cortex, where thinking occurs. Apparently, we humans feel before we analyze because our ancestors had to make immediate life-or-death choices when faced with strangers. Whatever the reason, it seems that we do often get a "gut feeling" when we meet somebody new. Opening the conversation by telling us what we can and cannot do in his or her presence might not be the best choice for that stranger to make, if mutual respect and trust are the goals, as they are in the classroom.

You have probably heard something to the effect that the first day of class sets the pace for the rest of the year. I have heard veteran teachers say (and I agree with them) that the amount of disorder you have on your first day of class is likely to be remarkably similar to the amount you will see on the last day. So on day one concentrate on grabbing your students by their overactive brains. Get a good grip. Focus on creating a classroom where good behavior is the norm. There will be plenty of time to talk about rules later on. In Chapter Six we'll take a long hard look at creating workable rules and discipline codes. But those things can wait. First, we need a plan for organizing the piles of paperwork that accompany every classroom, even as our society claims to go "paperless."

## PREPARE YOUR PAPERWORK

Your classroom is looking good and smells nice too. Your supplies are stowed safely away, and your student desks are arranged to give you easy access to each little darling who will soon be sitting there, looking to you for knowledge and inspiration. Now it's time to get your paperwork in order and put out the welcome mat.

Paperwork problems can overwhelm a teacher who isn't organized. You can do much to prevent those problems, improve your efficiency, and save hours of time if you design a workable file system. Your individual circumstances will guide you, but I would like to offer some suggestions for techniques that have served me well.

### Deep In-Basket

Place an in-basket on your desk that is deep enough to hold at least one hundred sheets of paper or thirty student reports or file folders. Instruct students to place all items for you in the basket—not on your desk, your chair, or on top of the file cabinet. (And if they have an item too large to fit into the basket, they should deliver it to you in person.) Also enforce a strict policy that makes it a classroom felony for a student to remove anything from the in-basket, including his or her own paper-work or folders. If students must retrieve something from the in-basket, they must ask you for assistance, in order to protect the privacy of other students and to avoid misplacing, disarranging, or losing important paperwork. At the end of each hour or class period, collect all student papers from your in-basket and stow them in the proper color-coded file folder until you have a chance to organize or grade them.

## Daily Lesson Folders

Keep one brightly colored folder for each hour or subject with daily lesson plans, assignments to grade, graded papers, and personal notes for students. If you need to take papers home to grade, tuck them into this file folder (if you teach multiple classes or subjects, keep your file folders in a binder that you use only for this purpose). After you have graded papers at home, return them to the file. Add your lesson plans or notes for the next day, and you have everything in one place for easy access.

## Your Own Emergency Plan

Accidents and illnesses happen, as do fires, earthquakes, and other disasters. Your school will have emergency procedures and instructions to follow during drills or evacuations. Place this information in a three-ring binder that has pockets to hold papers and a place to store a pen or pencil. Put a copy of your roll sheets in the binder, along with your own contact information (address, phone number, and name and phone number of a relative or friend). When an emergency occurs or a practice drill is announced, grab your binder and lead your students to safety. And in the event that you are called away without notice, your supervisor can easily find information to contact your family or friends or to give to your substitute teacher.

## Sub Folder

For use if you have an unplanned absence, create a folder that includes a copy of your roll sheets and three full days of lesson plans that focus on your subject and provide review of important skills and information, but that are not going to make or break your students' learning. If you know you will be absent, you may choose to provide lesson plans that continue your present unit of study, with associated activities. But be aware that not all substitutes are created equal. Some of them will follow your instructions to the letter; others will do nothing or—worse yet—create their own lesson plans.

Once, when I became ill with the flu, I came into school one evening to write out detailed lesson plans for my remedial freshman English class, which was reading *Romeo and Juliet.* Reluctant readers, the students had agreed to read it only because I promised they could watch the movie afterward. I provided the sub with page numbers, worksheets, journal-writing assignments, and a review worksheet. I specifically asked her not to show the movie until after the students had read the entire play. When I returned after three days, I found that the sub had ignored my lesson plans and shown the movie during her first day. During the subsequent two days, she held discussions and ignored the worksheets and journal assignments. When I complained about the sub, she countered by saying that I was "too controlling" and that she should be allowed to design the lesson when she was subbing, although she had no teaching license and her major field of study was science, not language arts. After that, I created a series of independent lessons that would enable students to practice important skills, but did not necessarily coincide with our current unit. When I have an unfamiliar sub or if I am called away suddenly, the students aren't thrown off track or bored by useless assignments.

While we're on the subject of subs, know that some schools permit teachers to request certain subs. If you find a good sub, ask if you might have her or his phone number so that you can call and check that sub's availability when you know you're going to be absent. Having one or two regular subs can be a real benefit. Students enjoy seeing a familiar face, and they often behave better for somebody they like and trust. And you can relax, knowing that your students won't be wasting their time while you're away.

Beware that if you work with students who are not emotionally secure, they may act out while you are gone, even if they have an excellent sub and even if they are normally well-behaved students. Instead of punishing those students severely on your return, you might consider holding a class discussion. Ask students to describe their feelings and think about why they misbehave when you are gone. Remind them that their behavior is a reflection on you; you are very proud when they can behave well for a sub. Suggest some alternative positive behaviors for students to use if they feel stressed or upset about your absence. They might ask to go visit with a familiar counselor, coach, secretary, teacher, or administrator for a few minutes (you might want to discuss this with the adult staff members involved, to prepare them). They could write you a note or make an entry in their journals. They could offer to help the sub by taking roll, erasing the boards, or passing out papers. Of course, if a particular student continues to behave disrespectfully after your discussions, the student will have to face some consequences. But try to make those consequences applicable to the behavior, such as a written apology to the sub, and not simply punishment.

### Fun Lessons Folder

Do a little research and find some quick, fun, entertaining, or challenging lessons. Trivia quizzes, brain busters, riddles, word games, and IQ tests are big hits with students of all ages. When your students zip through a lesson faster than you expected, when they behave especially well, or when they do something to make you proud, take a few minutes at the end of the hour or day to reward them with a fun lesson. Every bookstore has a section of books with educational games and puzzles, or you can create your own. You can also find suggestions on the Internet or in the Appendix of this book.

### Makeup Work Folder

Buy an accordion-style folder with alphabetical divisions and write "Makeup Work" in large bold letters on both sides. If you teach more than one group, buy a separate accordion-style folder for each class. Whenever you distribute any paperwork or assignment, pencil in the last name of absent students on the assignment and place it in the folder under the appropriate letter. If you cover material in the textbook on that day, make a brief note of what you covered and make copies of the note for each absent student. When students return to class, their missing assignments will be readily available, saving you time that would otherwise be spent searching for copies and explaining what they need to read to catch up.

Elementary-level students may need help remembering to pick up the papers and may require help doing the assignments, but you should expect older students to pick up their assignments and get them done. Make clear that students are responsible for making up the work, although you will be happy to answer any questions they may have or suggest sources for information or assistance.

### Prefilled Passes

Fill out the basic information (your room number, destination, and any specific instructions) on library, hall, and bathroom passes. Don't sign the passes, and be sure to number them so that students can't steal them. Then keep the passes tucked or locked away in a folder with a simple tally sheet showing which numbers you have issued. When you need to send somebody out of the room, you won't have to spend so much time filling out the passes. Usually I have students fill in their name and the date, then I sign the pass. With this system, you don't have to stop teaching, locate a pass, and make everybody else wait while you fill it out and sign it.

## Roll Sheet Copies

Make three or four spare copies of all your roll sheets as soon as you get them, and use them to create your own records for rewards, attendance, seating charts, teams for group projects, birthdays, field trips, fire drills, and other occasions for which you might need a list. I take a copy of my roll sheets home to use when I am creating lessons, such as vocabulary worksheets or quizzes, in order to use my students' names in sentences. They always perk up and smile when they read a sentence that contains their own or a classmate's name (be sure to check off names and use everybody's name at least once in order to avoid hurting feelings or giving the impression that you have favorites).

## Crates for Student Folders

This is my all-time favorite time saver and organizer. I buy a different color plastic file bin for each class I teach, and I label a file folder for each student in a particular class. For each class I use a separate color or folders cut on the same tab—all left one-third tabs, for example—so that I can easily identify folders and match them with the proper bin. If I can't find any colored file folders and I have to use all manila folders, I use a marker to draw a colored line across the tab, all red for one period, blue for another, and so on. (*Note:* At the start of the year, the folders will be slim, so you may elect to store two or three different groups in the same bin until the folders fatten up. Then you can transfer them to separate bins.)

Using my roll sheets, I lightly pencil in student names on the folder tabs and keep a few blanks for students who may transfer into my class later. During the first days of school every term, I distribute the folders as students are taking their seats and doing their first work activity of the day. I quickly see who is absent and keep those absent students' folders on my lectern, where I can insert copies of any handouts or reading assignments for that period. Personal folders help students learn to organize their work and make it easier for them to locate study materials prior to exams. Because the folders are personal, many students like to decorate them. I allow them to draw or write whatever they like on their folders, except vulgar, obscene, hateful, or gang-related words and symbols. Some teachers prefer to prohibit decorating to create a more businesslike appearance.

At the start of each class, I distribute the folders for use that day. I can immediately see who is absent, and as the class goes on I can place worksheets or assignments into my Makeup folder for those students who are absent. When students return, all of their graded assignments are waiting for them inside their folders.

When I return their homework or assignments, students have the option of taking the graded papers home to show their parents or placing them in their folders. I always suggest that students keep important assignments, quizzes, and tests in their folders for future reference and as a record in case of report card questions. Some students take their paperwork home and keep their own records, but many students (and parents) are so disorganized that they will lose anything you give them.

## Emergency Misbehavior Folder

Usually students wait until several days into the school year before they become truly disruptive. But sometimes you'll have an overachiever who will decide that the first few days of school would be prime time to act like a maniac. I'm referring to serious cases where a quick step out into the hallway for a private talk isn't an option because a student assaults or seriously threatens you or other students. You can remove the student who is out of control, lose the minimum amount of precious class time, and send a very clear message to the rest of your students that you will not tolerate outrageous behavior for even one minute in your classroom—*if* you have prepared an Emergency Misbehavior folder before the school term begins.

Fill out one or two disciplinary referral forms with as much information as you can, except for the date and the student's name. Where it asks you to describe the incident, write: "Student disrupted class, interrupted my teaching, and made it impossible for others to learn. I will provide full details as soon as possible. I request a student-principal-teacher conference before the student returns to my classroom."

Place these partially completed forms in a folder labeled "Misbehavior," where they will be readily available at the first sign of serious disruption. The first time you pull out that folder, whip out the form, and send your obnoxious student packing, other students will get the message that you are prepared and serious about teaching. Your principal will require specific details and you will have to follow up on the incident, but if you have a form prepared ahead of time, you will have provided enough information to remove the student from your classroom quickly, preventing more serious problems and establishing your control without wasting time or losing face by engaging in a prolonged argument.

## Assignments for Rude People

If you teach people who are old enough to walk to the school library without an escort, label a file folder "Assignments for Rude People." Fill this folder with five or six lessons that are challenging and pertinent to your subject matter. Meet with your librarian and let him or her know that you may send a student to work independently from time to time, but that you do not expect the librarian to tolerate any misbehavior. Fill out a library pass with everything except the date and student's name and write: "Rude Person Study Time" on the pass. Put your file away and hope you won't have to use it.

If the day arrives when a student repeatedly misbehaves just to trip your trigger or if you have a sneaky student who repeatedly instigates bad behavior in other students, a pupil whose parents have tried but failed to convince their child to act respectfully in your classroom, or a student who is perfectly capable of polite behavior but who intentionally ignores your requests—you have a rude person on your hands.

Don't argue or warn this rude student. Simply select the appropriate lesson from the folder, remove the other assignments, and hand him the Assignments for Rude People folder. Even if he pretends to think the folder label is funny, he will be pretending. Show the student the library pass and inform him that he must return the signed pass and the completed assignment to you approximately one minute before the end of that class period. Explain that if he doesn't return at the end of the class period, you will be obligated to report him as cutting class, and the school's disciplinary system will take over. Walk the student to the door of your room, wave good-bye, and shut the door firmly.

When the student returns with the completed assignment, say thank you and tell him you hope he will decide to control his behavior so that he can remain with the class in future. Most students will stop their disruptive behavior if they lose their audience, because they usually aren't capable of doing all their assignments independently. If you have a whiz kid who aces the assignments on his or her own and doesn't seem to mind being sent to work alone, you have identified the root of the misbehavior—boredom—and you can take steps to create lessons that will challenge the student.

*Note:* If the student refuses to go to the library or won't accept the Assignments for Rude People folder, simply return the folder to your file cabinet and take out your Misbehavior folder. Fill in the student's name on the referral form and call your security office or go to the nearest classroom to alert the teacher that you will be gone for a few minutes. Escort your student to the office and quickly return to your lesson without any further interruption or discussion with your remaining students. If they seem to be on the verge of an outbreak, look very slowly around the room and say, "Does anybody else need to leave?" My prediction is that nobody else will need to leave. If they do, repeat the procedure. (See Chapter Six for a more thorough discussion of disciplinary techniques—and for creating an environment where misbehavior is much less likely to occur.)

## The Grade Book

Create a system for your paper grade book (keep a paper book for backup even if you use a computerized grading system, because systems crash and some students are accomplished hackers). Don't write in your grade book during the first few days (or weeks if you work at a disorganized school). Instead, make a couple of copies of the first page of your grade book and use that to keep track of students' progress until after the administrative shuffling has ended and you have had the same students for a few weeks. Then enter the names in your grade book in alphabetical order. Enter the same names in the same order in your computerized grade book, so that student number one and student number fifteen are the same in each book. This will save you time later on.

With a little creativity, you can design a system so that your paper grade book functions as a record of attendance, participation, and extra effort, as well as a record of graded assignments. When students are absent, for example, you might outline the box for a specific graded assignment in red so that you can see at a glance which students were absent when you gave that assignment. (Some students will claim they were absent; if you don't mark it in your grade book, you will have to track down your attendance sheets and compare them to your grade book. You don't have time for such silliness.)

When absent students make up the missed assignment, you can enter the grade in the box, and you still have a record of the absence. If the student doesn't turn in the assignment by the makeup deadline, you can enter a red zero to remind you and the student that the assignment was not completed by the deadline.

If you include a column in your grade book for extra credit and one for negative credit, you can add or subtract points for students who do extra work and for those who cause extra problems and stress while you are trying to teach. This is one way to reward students who cooperate and work hard but may not be geniuses. They can earn points every day for putting forth real effort and acting like decent people. Likewise, smart-mouth, disruptive whiz kids can earn negative points so that they don't walk away from your class with an A just for being intelligent, in spite of the havoc they may have wreaked among their peers who were struggling to learn while they were entertaining themselves. (I usually enter negative points in pencil so that if a student decides to grow up a bit and stop causing trouble, he or she can still earn full credit for being brilliant.) I realize that some people object to such subjective grading, but I submit that all teachers are subjective to some extent, and at least this method is honest and transparent.

Some teachers assign each student a number in the grade book (if you teach multiple classes, it's a good idea to use a combination of letters and numbers, to avoid mixing up student papers from different classes). Instruct students to write their assigned numbers in the upper left- or right-hand corner of all papers they turn in. You can then place the student papers in order as you collect them and identify any missing numbers immediately. Read out the missing numbers to alert students that you do not have their papers, and place all the papers in a folder, making a note of the date and any missing numbers on the inside cover of the folder. When students turn in a late paper, make a check mark and write the date, creating a record of all missing or late papers. This method prevents lost papers, avoids arguments about whether students turned in assignments, and makes it easier for you to enter grades or notations for missing assignments into the grade book. If you have a particularly argumentative group, you might consider stapling papers together after they are collected as proof that those papers were collected on time.

Grading is one area in which computers truly are worth the headaches they sometimes cause. Even if you have to buy the software yourself and borrow a computer, find a way to use computerized grading. Your investment will save you time, energy, and frustration. Entering the student information to get started can take some time, but once you have the data in the program, you can manipulate it to change the weight of specific assignments and tests, provide periodic status reports, and be prepared to produce report cards quickly and accurately.

Electronic grading has another advantage. Because you can print out reports for an entire class or for an individual, you can quickly see how well your students are doing as a group. You can adjust your teaching, review specific problem areas, or add additional graded assignments as needed. You can also show a student his or her individual progress. Students who skip assignments are often shocked to see how much one grade can raise or lower their average. If a student has skipped two heavily weighted assignments, for example, you could show him what would happen to his grade if he had done the minimum amount of work and earned a C on one of those assignments. You can also print out interim progress reports to give fair warning to students who are in danger of earning poor grades, as well as an incentive to students who are working hard. Seeing their grades in print is a powerful motivator for most students.

## Master Lesson Plan Draft

Many schools require teachers to file lesson plans weekly or monthly. Even if lesson plans aren't required, effective teachers often create a rough draft of their plans for the entire quarter, semester, and year. If you teach high school and have multiple preparation periods, then mapping out your lesson plans for the year is even more important because you will have more planning to accomplish during your precious preparation period. Working from a master schedule enables teachers to adjust their daily lesson plans as needed, to allow for variations in student progress, changes in required curriculum, standardized tests, weather emergencies, and so on. And it's much easier to sleep at night when you don't have to worry about what you are going to do in the morning.

My preferred method is to make copies of a monthly calendar template so that I have one page per month. Then I consult the school calendar and mark every noninstructional day in red: holidays, teacher in-service days, midterm and final exam days, open house, and picture day. I also use red ink to block out days on which many students are likely to be absent or obsessed with some important social event such as homecoming, prom, baccalaureate, sports tournaments, college days, prearranged field trips, and so on. For those social event days, I plan a flexible lesson that will count toward grade credit for students who are present but will not include essential information that absent students will need in order to complete future assignments or exams. And I do not require that absent students make up the missed work, if their absences are excused. I simply place an X on the wall chart to indicate that the assignment was done. Students don't receive or lose credit for this assignment; they earn an X that has no value. (I don't announce my plan to the class, because I don't want students to skip class because they know they won't be penalized for missing the assignment.)

Next I highlight quarter, semester, and final exam days in green ink. One week before each major exam, I back up and schedule a day or two for review of material that will be on the exam. Then I plan two days without homework following the exam so that I will have time to grade and return exams quickly. Now I have a rough idea of how many instructional days are available for the various units in my curriculum.

At this point it's time to put away the pens and start using a pencil so that I can make changes later. On a separate sheet of paper, I make a list of all the elements I intend to teach during the year. Because I teach English, my list includes journal writing, informal essays, reports, research papers, poetry, short stories, plays, novels, literary analysis, grammar, parts of speech, spelling, vocabulary, analogies, and so on. I break my master list down further by assigning each element to a specific number of units to cover in each quarter.

Now that I have a rough outline of various units, I can figure out how much time to devote to a specific skill each day or week and how many weekly or monthly quizzes will be appropriate. Because some schools require a specific number of graded assignments during a given period, I can easily check to see that I will have enough. How you divide your time is purely your choice, but in my experience students of all ages and abilities do better when practice exercises and quizzes take place on a regular schedule—vocabulary exercises every Tuesday morning, for example, with a quiz on Friday. Regularly scheduled activities will also help you create lesson plans when you are ill, overwhelmed, under stress, or exhausted. My daily and weekly plans are very general and flexible, with optional activities and exercises that I can add or delete as time allows. With a very cooperative class, I can sometimes reduce my lesson plan to a few simple phrases.

Many education textbooks advise new teachers to make detailed lessons plans so that they use each minute of class time productively. That concept sounds good on paper. When I first began teaching, I planned each class to the second. I was so nervous that I didn't trust myself to remember what I wanted to cover during a specific time period. I imagined myself facing my students and not being able to think of a single intelligent thing to say. So I planned and outlined and made hourly, weekly, monthly, quarterly, and semester calendars, all filled in neatly and completely, down to the last spelling quiz. I also broke down each hour into five-, ten-, or twenty-minute blocks of time. I was prepared to walk into the classroom and be the superteacher I knew in my heart I could be.

Unfortunately, I hadn't planned time for the daily announcements, calls from the administrative offices, buses delayed by traffic, announcements over the squawking intercom, sick students, or an occasional spider dangling from an overhead light causing momentary chaos. I also hadn't planned—and nobody could—for the variances in student ability and behavior that drastically affect the speed with which a given class will grasp a new concept, master a new skill, or complete a given assignment. Often students would whiz through an exercise in ten minutes when I had expected them to take thirty minutes, leaving me twenty minutes to spare. Or they would labor for an entire class period over what I thought would be a simple ten-minute activity.

At first I spent hours revising those detailed lesson plans, but something always seemed to happen to throw my classes off schedule. I finally realized that I was far more likely to lose my mind than create lesson plans that I wouldn't have to change or frequently adjust. Now I make a very rough schedule of what I want to cover during a given time frame and I alter the plan to fit the needs of my students.

Some schools provide a template and require teachers to use it to prepare lesson plans. If that is the case at your school, don't despair. Fill in the template. But don't work yourself into a tizzy if you can't follow that template every second of every day. Unless you are in a very unusual situation, you won't find somebody standing in your doorway, checking to make sure that you are giving a spelling quiz at exactly 9:15 on Thursday morning. If somebody does visit your classroom and you are not right on target, explain that you realized your students needed a bit of extra time on whatever they are doing at that moment. Offer to do the activity on your prepared lesson plan the following day at a specific time if the observer would like to return. In most cases, they won't. If they do, teach that lesson and consider yourself warned. I think that's highly unlikely. What is much more likely is that somebody is tasked with collecting (and perhaps reviewing) lesson plans in order to fulfill a directive from higher up. As long as your students are well behaved, you rarely send students to the office, your students' grades on standardized tests are reasonable, and report card grades for your classes are reasonably good, nobody is going to be overly concerned about whether you are following your lesson plan to the letter.

Of course, I do include required curriculum in my plans, but I have found that I teach much more effectively and that my students learn far more (and do better the following year with their next teacher) if I concentrate on teaching them how to think and analyze information, instead of rushing them through materials just so I can say we covered the curriculum.

Sometimes we cover everything on the lesson plan. Sometimes we don't. I used to become very upset when we didn't cover all the things I wanted to cover. Then I made myself sit down and honestly consider what I wanted my students to learn and whether they were learning it. They didn't have my curriculum outline. I did post the agenda every day so they knew what I wanted to cover. But if we didn't cover every single thing, students didn't feel cheated. They thought the extra discussion or extended activities were very valuable. And as long as they are motivated and engaged and learning and produce good work and pass their exams, then it doesn't really matter that we didn't follow my beautiful lesson plans. Even now, I occasionally have to remind myself that my lesson plans are just that—plans. They are not directives or official orders.

My advice to new teachers is to make your lesson plans as simple and flexible as possible. If you need to structure each minute during your first few months (or years), do so. But as you develop more experience and confidence, shift your focus from planning to teaching, using your students' performance, instead of the calendar, as a guide.

## Welcome Handout

If you teach children who are too young to read, you might decide to write a short letter to send or give to parents and guardians, introducing yourself and providing your phone number and e-mail address, along with some basic information about your classroom. It doesn't take much time to draft a welcome letter, and it can be a great public relations tool. You won't seem like such a stranger, which can prove helpful as the year progresses and situations arise that require you to contact the families of your students.

If your students are old enough to read, consider designing a one-page Welcome to My Class handout that includes a short course outline, truly important information, a few tips for success in your classroom, and an abbreviated overview of your most important rules and procedures. If you don't like that title, try something more formal, such as "Course Outline and Objectives." (*Note:* Please don't title your handout "Classroom Rules and Procedures." If you do, you will create a dynamic of teacher versus student from the start, because so many students are resistant to rules of any kind.) Many students like to have something tangible that they can take home and read over (and maybe even share with their parents!).

Visual learners and students who are beginning middle school or who have multiple teachers for the first time really appreciate having handouts for their different classes because it helps them keep everything straight. One of the big fears of middle schoolers and high school freshmen is that they will forget where their classes are. Handouts from teachers can help allay those fears. Handouts also serve as reminders of different teacher personalities. Some teachers are sticklers for legible handwriting. Others have a zero-tolerance policy on missed homework. It's helpful for students to have that information in writing for reference until they learn their class schedules and teachers' expectations.

For two examples, see the handout I use to welcome my high school English classes in Exhibit 4.1 and a sample handout for third graders in Exhibit 4.2.

## PREPARE YOURSELF

With your room and your paperwork organized and ready and your philosophy of teaching fresh in your mind, you can now focus on physically and mentally preparing yourself to grab your students by their brains when they walk into your classroom. Don't worry if you feel nervous: almost all teachers get nervous before the start of a new semester or school year, even experienced teachers. (Sometimes the veteran teachers get more nervous than newbies because they know exactly what they are walking into!) Don't panic. Most of the time, students will cooperate if they know exactly what you expect them to do. Therefore, *you* must know exactly what you expect them to do.

### Plan Your Procedures

If you are underprepared and forced to create procedures as you go along, students will follow your example and create their own. So brainstorm every routine activity that will occur in your classroom and establish a procedure for performing it. (Sit in your classroom as you brainstorm, so that you will be reminded of physical obstacles or space limitations.) For example, how do you want students to request permission to do the following: use the bathroom, ask or answer a question during your lectures, or request help during classroom activities? How should they turn in late assignments, line up when the entire group needs to leave the room together, conduct themselves in the hallways, and so on? Make brief notes or use index cards to remind yourself of each procedure so that you can quickly teach it to your students. (You may have to repeat some procedures many

# Exhibit 4.1.  Miss J's Welcome Handout.

Welcome to Miss J's English Class!

*The Official Plan.* This class is designed to improve your communications skills through reading, writing, vocabulary, and grammar exercises; group assignments; and individual projects. We will read a wide variety of literature. Assignments will include timed responses, journals, essays, research reports, and literary critiques.

*The Rule.* Respect yourself and other people. No insults based on ethnic background, skin color, native language, gender, sexual preference, religion, body shape, or body size will be tolerated. It is unfair to erase somebody's face. We all have the right to be treated with respect.

*First Things First (FTF).* Every day you'll find an assignment posted on the Student Agenda Board. I expect you to be seated and working on the FTF of the day when the bell rings. Not five seconds or a minute after the bell. Please don't be a ding-dong.

*Be There or Be Square.* My job is to make this class enjoyable and informative. I will never intentionally embarrass you. Your job is to come to class. Be there or be square.

*Be on Time.* Don't you hate waiting for people? I do. Don't be rude. Be on time.

*Be Prepared.* Imagine how you would feel if you made an appointment to have your car fixed and when you took it to the shop, the mechanic said, "Oh, whoops, I forgot to bring my tools today. Sorry." Not cool. Bring your learning tools to school.

*Homework.* We won't have homework every night, but when we do, it's your job to do it—by yourself, using your own personal brain (it is perfectly acceptable to get help or share ideas with friends). If you have problems or questions, call me at 555-1212.

*Makeup Work.* When you return to class after any absence, it is your responsibility to check the makeup folder on my desk. You will have three days to complete the work. If you need more time, talk to me.

*Please Behave.* I prefer to deal directly with you instead of calling your parents. You are responsible for your own behavior. You behave yourself, and I'll behave myself.

*Fun.* We will have the maximum amount of fun allowable by law. Please bring your sense of humor to class. If you forget yours, I'll be happy to share mine.

## Exhibit 4.2. Third-Grade Welcome.

**Welcome to Mr. Bob's Super-Duper Third-Grade Class!**

Hello! Hello!

I'm Mr. Bob Witherspoon—welcome to my Super-Duper Third-Grade Class.

I believe every student (that means *you*) is super-duper in her or his own way.

Here is our class mascot, Digby the Dancing Dog.

What we are going to do this year? Dozens of things, including:

- Create exciting, fun projects to use our incredible brains.
- Spiff up our spelling skills. (We'll even spell supercalifragilisticexpealidocious!)
- Refine our writing skills by writing *our own books*!!!
- Make reading really, really, really, really interesting and fun. (I promise.)
- Watch some spectacular movies about things going on in the big wide world.
- Learn interesting facts about people, places, things, critters, caterpillars, and so on.
- Have *huge* amounts of *fun*!

My job as your teacher is to:

- Do my best teaching every single day.
- Be my best self every day.
- Make sure you are safe in my classroom.
- Make sure everybody in our super-duper class feels respected.
- Teach you what you need to know to rock in grade four.

Your job as a student is to:

- Be your best self every day.
- Do your best work on every assignment.
- Be respectful to yourself, to me, and to your classmates.
- Bring your learning brain to school with you every day.

Ready? Set? Let's rock and roll!!!!!!!!!!!

times before students catch on, so it's a good idea to have written instructions to help you remain consistent.)

Decide how and when you are going to teach your procedures. (For a more detailed discussion, see the section titled "Establish Routines and Rituals" in Chapter Five.) Some teachers like to teach all of their procedures, a few at a time, at the start of the year and add a short refresher course when it's time to implement a specific procedure. If you teach your students your procedure for walking to the library as a group, for example, but don't take them to the library until three weeks after school starts, many students will have forgotten what they are supposed to do. Some will forget the instant after you tell them, which is another good reason to write your procedures down. You can copy your procedure cards individually or as one list and distribute a copy to each student to keep in his or her folder as a reminder. Or you can practice them until students become familiar with them. Either way, be prepared to patiently repeat your instructions several times— especially for students who have multiple teachers. A middle or high school student may have five teachers, all of whom have different requirements for asking questions or requesting bathroom breaks.

## Design Your Discipline Code

Write down your discipline code. If it's too long or complicated to fit on an index card, you may find it difficult to communicate to students and even more difficult to enforce. When I first started teaching, I did the rule thing. Sometimes I created rules; sometimes I included students in the creation of rules. But every time I used a list of rules, I also had to make a list of consequences and then a list of increasingly punitive consequences for the students who broke the rules. I had to figure out a system for keeping track of offenses, consequences, follow-up conferences, and referrals to the office. Quite often I found myself bending a rule because of special circumstances; for example, a boy missed school to attend his grandfather's funeral, so I broke my zero-tolerance policy on late assignments and allowed him to turn in a project two days late. Other students then appealed for extensions based on their own "emergencies," which were very real to them. A sister went to the hospital. A toilet overflowed. A hamster died. Their requests put me in the position of deciding which emergencies were important and which weren't. Everybody was upset and nobody was happy, including me.

After that incident I read more books on classroom management, but I couldn't find the perfect discipline plan. So I branched out into psychology books, as well as books on salesmanship, leadership, and the art of persuasion. I tried different tactics with different groups and finally settled on one universal approach that has served me well with every group of students I've taught, from at-risk high school freshmen to university graduate students. After our welcome and get-to-know-you days, I lay out the ground rules for student conduct in my classroom. I make the following speech:

You are individual people with individual lives and needs. And life presents surprises and obstacles to us all. So I am not going to create a set of rigid rules and then argue with you about enforcing them. I reserve the right to make judgments as needed in my classroom. But I do have one rule that applies to every person in the room, including me, and it is absolutely unbreakable.

*The rule:* respect yourself and everybody in this room—no put-downs of other people based on their race, religion, ethnic background, skin color, native language, gender, sexual preference, intelligence, body shape, or body size. Those characteristics are not chosen by people; we are born with them. Yes, you can change your religion when you are an adult, but most children are required to accept their parents' religion; to criticize them for respecting their parents is wrong. Criticizing or insulting people for things that are beyond their control is not fair. It is not respectful, and I will not tolerate it in my classroom. You may comment on other people's behavior, as long as you voice your observations in a respectful manner. If you believe somebody is being cruel or insensitive, for example, you may say, "I think your behavior is cruel" or "You are being really rude." You may not, however, call the person a stupid jerk or blame their bad behavior on their gender or skin color. Which brings me to the subject of prejudice.

There are many, many forms of prejudice, and most of us have our own opinions and ideas about the world. You are entitled to believe and think whatever you choose. You are not entitled, however, to express your opinions in a manner that may insult, degrade, embarrass, hurt, or humiliate other people.

I always ask if anybody believes my rule is unreasonable. Nobody ever has. And since I have started using my one-rule policy without a list of specific offenses and consequences, I have had far fewer discipline problems. Again, the connection between expectation and reality proves true: I expect students to take responsibility for their behavior, and barring the occasional inevitable exception, they do.

We'll discuss discipline at length later on, in Chapter Six, but for now, if you can distill your discipline plan or behavior code down to one or two sentences that will enable you to communicate it clearly to your future students, you will be way ahead of the game.

## Rehearse Your Warning Speech

I hope this exercise will be a waste of time and you won't have to warn anybody to stop misbehaving. But just in case, it's a very good idea to know what you plan to say, should you decide you need to say it. If you can find a willing volunteer, it may be helpful to rehearse the warning speeches you will deliver to mildly disruptive or defiant students (those who are in fifth grade or higher) who may need a quick trip to the corner or to the hallway outside your classroom for a brief one-way discussion. You will do the talking, saying something along the lines of "Your present behavior is not acceptable in my classroom. You have the right to fail my class, if that is really what you want to do. But you do not have the right to interrupt my teaching or somebody else's learning. And you do not have the right to waste my time trying to get me to argue with you about your behavior. You are an intelligent person, and I know you know how to behave. So why don't you take a minute out here to consider your options? When you are ready, please come back and take your seat. Thank you." (Some teachers prefer to have students return when they are ready, while others insist that students remain outside or in the private conference spot until the teacher decides it's time for them to return.)

Younger students—up to about fourth grade (you'll have to make this determination based on the intellectual and emotional maturity of your students)—may not have the self-control to monitor their behavior for more than a few minutes after a quick chat. So you will probably want to come up with some catchphrases that you can use to remind younger students of your expectations. If you explain right from the beginning that you want everybody in your classroom to make good choices, you can ask a student, "Are you making a good choice right now?" That question fits a wide variety of behaviors and gives a student the option of discussing his or her behavior and then getting back on track without suffering negative consequences.

## Create Some Call-and-Response

Call-and-response is a very popular activity with students of all ages. The first day of class, you teach students the responses to your calls. For example, with young children, you teach them that when you say, "one, two," they are to respond, "eyes on you." You say, "three, four," and they respond, "talk no more." And so on. If you teach older students, try using the call, "W-W-W dot," and students respond, "zip-those-lips dot-com." You can also use a nonverbal rhythmic call-and-response, such as clapping your hands two times. Students respond by clapping three times. You initiate the clapping and stop when students are paying attention. I have seen this work quickly for an entire cafeteria filled with noisy students.

When you notice a student on the verge of straying off-track in your class, you can initiate a call-and-response to interrupt the behavior cycle—and then praise all your students for their quick response and good behavior. Keep an eye out for the student who had started to become disruptive. When he is behaving himself, stop by his desk and quietly praise him for his good behavior. This positive reinforcement is much more effective than repeatedly issuing individual or whole-group warnings.

### Check Your Wardrobe

Make sure that you have at least a few changes of clothing that are comfortable, easy to launder, and somewhat attractive, because students have to look at you all day long every weekday. At various times during discussions of what makes an effective teacher, students have suggested that teachers pay more attention to their clothing. You don't have to be a fashion plate, but as one student put it when he was describing a teacher he did not like, "It's a drag to have to look at somebody who looks like they just keep all their clothes in a pile on the floor." When I mentioned that I often speak to new teachers, he said, "Tell them not to wear the same outfit every Monday. It's like having those stupid underpants with the days of the week on them. School is boring enough without having to look at the same shirt every single Monday of your life." That's one young man's opinion, for what it's worth.

I've already suggested comfortable shoes, but your feet are important enough that I'm going to repeat the suggestion. If you are twenty-one and still indestructible, your feet may not notice the stress, but most teachers welcome as much comfort as they can find when it comes to shoes. Sore heels and achy arches can really ruin your day.

### Find a Friend

Make a reciprocal Chill-Out Pact with a teacher whose room is near yours. (If you can't find a friendly teacher, find an administrator, counselor, or secretary, but find somebody.) Occasionally you will have a student whose behavior doesn't warrant a referral to the office or an official warning, but who nevertheless jangles your nerves beyond your breaking point. And unfortunately, once in a while you may find yourself having a bad teaching day. Make an agreement with your ally that either of you may send a student to sit in the back of the other teacher's class for a short time (ten to fifteen minutes) to allow you and the student a break from each other. And if you realize that you are about to slip over the edge, you might ask your chill-out buddy to supervise your classroom for a moment while you supervise hers, if she is a teacher, or take a brisk walk, if the person is not a teacher and can spare a few minutes. You may never have to make use of your chill-out option, but if you need to, those few minutes can save the day with a minimum of fuss and paperwork.

## Meet the Admin and Support Staff

If you haven't had a chat with your principal and vice principal, request one. Find out how they handle discipline problems. Ask for information about the local community and how local politics affect the school. Let the principals know that you plan to send students to the office only if you are at your wits' end. Ask if you can call on them for support if you need it during the first days of class. I once had a very large principal who offered to come and scare my belligerent freshmen boys. It was very effective. The same boys acted out every morning, so the principal and I preplanned his visit. On the appointed day, when one of the boys began to disrupt, I called the office. The principal burst into the room and said, "Who needs to come with me?" I indicated the boy who had been acting out. The principal glared at the boy and then looked around the room. "Anybody else want to go?" he hollered. Nobody did. And after that, the boys toned down their behavior because they knew the principal and I were on the same team.

Don't forget the support staff. Seek out and introduce yourself to the maintenance crew, the audiovisual and computer gurus, the attendance monitors, the detention coordinator, and the custodian who is responsible for your classroom. Also, take time for a quick chat with your school librarian, classroom aides, and all the many secretaries who keep your school running. Recognize that these are valuable people without whom your job would be much harder. Ask if they require specific things from you or if you can do things to make it easier for them to respond to your requests. Knowing your classroom custodian and treating him or her with respect is not only the right thing to do, but you will find that a good custodian can provide advice, assistance, and an occasional miracle during the school year. And incidentally, it makes an incredible difference when stress levels rise to walk into the school building and find yourself greeted with smiles and encouragement from the adults on staff.

## Exhibit 4.3.
## Three Checklists.

**Your Classroom**

- ☐ Sensory details
- ☐ Seating arrangements
- ☐ Supplies and storage
  - Home base
  - Private files
  - Teacher desk
  - Student supplies
- ☐ Student information
  - In-basket
  - Agenda
  - Calendar
  - Student-supplies table

**Your Paperwork**

- ☐ Place in-basket on your desk.
- ☐ Create daily lesson folders.
- ☐ Create a personal emergency plan.
- ☐ Prepare a sub folder.
- ☐ Fill a folder with fun lessons.
- ☐ Create a makeup work folder.
- ☐ Fill out library, hall, and bathroom passes.
- ☐ Copy roll sheets.
- ☐ Buy plastic crates for student folders.
- ☐ Prepare a misbehavior folder.
- ☐ Create assignments for rude people.
- ☐ Copy a blank page from the grade book.
- ☐ Draft a master lesson plan.
- ☐ Design a welcome handout and make copies.

**Yourself**

- ☐ Plan your procedures.
- ☐ Design your discipline code.
- ☐ Rehearse your warning speeches.
- ☐ Check your wardrobe.
- ☐ Find a chill-out friend.
- ☐ Meet your admin and support staff.
- ☐ Inspect your classroom.
- ☐ Take a break.

## Check Your Classroom

Sit at your desk in your classroom and take a good look. Close your eyes and sniff. Make sure that everything is in place for the first day of school. Review your checklists and the index cards containing your procedures and discipline code; give your supplies and student folders a final inspection. Then turn off your teacher brain. Go home and try to be a regular human being.

## Take a Break

Give yourself a break, even if it's only for a few hours the night before school starts. Go out to dinner, rent a video, take a long hot bath—do something that is not connected with teaching. You may be tempted to stay at school as long as your security office will allow, but if you spend the weeks before school planning and preparing and the few days before school arranging your room, shuffling roll sheets, grade books, curriculum outlines, textbooks, and file folders, you will need at least a short break if you expect to greet your students with a genuine smile on the first day of school. You deserve the break, and they deserve the smile.

**Exhibit 4.3 provides a short version of the three checklists to help you get ready.**

## DISCUSSION POINTS

1. Which seating arrangements did you prefer as a child? Which do you prefer as a teacher?

2. For nonreaders, what might teachers do instead of distributing a welcome handout?

3. Which classroom procedures are most important to teach on the first days of class?

4. What can new teachers do if they have mild personalities and want to develop an air of authority?

5. What can teachers do to counteract the emotional and physical stress that accompanies teaching?

# Start with a Smile

We all know what's supposed to happen on the first day of school. You take roll, cover the ground rules, and get on with the task of teaching. Perhaps your school district is extremely well organized, the weather and rush hour traffic cooperate, and everything goes according to your careful plan.

But for far too many teachers, what actually happens on day one is closer to this: the bell rings and students continue to trickle in, late because their parents had car trouble or got stuck in traffic or because the elementary school pupils decided they weren't going to school after all and Mom or Dad had to carry them to your classroom and spend five minutes peeling them off their bodies. A few high school students got lost in the labyrinth of hallways or spent ten minutes searching through their backpacks for their class schedules. Somebody in junior high is really, really sorry, but she has to use the restroom right this minute because she had a soda for breakfast, and in elementary school a very small person throws up in the corner and cries because he is embarrassed and because school is very scary indeed.

Teachers are trained to carry on in the face of challenge, so you finally get everybody seated and listening. But the intercom interrupts your introductory remarks several times to announce changes in the bus schedule and remind students that free lunch tickets are available. Your students stop being scared and start to fidget. You hurry to begin explaining the rules and procedures for your classroom. Halfway through rule number one, somebody knocks on the door to explain that two students are in the wrong classroom. They should be in B103, not C103. You send them on their way and start again. You're on rule number two when a knock on the door interrupts, and you open the door to find a scared-looking girl who blushes and stammers that she thinks maybe perhaps somebody, um, told her she is supposed to be in your room. You hurry to your desk to retrieve your roll sheet and find that she is indeed listed. You direct her to an empty seat and call the class to attention. They respond reluctantly, and you resume your recitation. Another knock. This time it's a boy and a girl; neither child is blushing. They glare at you and thrust their schedule cards in your direction, as though it were your fault that the computer goofed and they won't be in the same first-period class with their best friends. Again you check your roll sheets, hoping the names of the two newcomers won't be there. But they are. And so it goes.

## DAY ONE: START WITH A SMILE

How you choose to greet your group is up to you, but keep in mind that human beings are naturally inclined to respond to a genuine smile with a smile in return. I say, ignore those old farts who warned you not to smile until Christmas. There is a huge difference between being kind and being weak, and students know the difference. It's possible to project a positive, friendly demeanor without sacrificing your authority or your students' respect.

Keep in mind that distance plays an important role in human interactions. If you stand behind your desk or podium, you will be placing a physical and psychological barrier between you and your students from the start—good for creating a separation between teacher and learner, but bad for developing a quick rapport or creating an environment of mutual trust and respect.

My recommendation is to stand near the doorway to your classroom as students enter. Standing just outside the door is more of a power position, if you are looking to establish your authority. Just inside is a bit more welcoming, but still projects authority. Smile, welcome each student to your classroom, and ask him or her to sit down (be specific—should they choose a seat or find the seat that has their file folder or name on it?).

Standing near the doorway has several advantages. First, it establishes that students are entering your territory as they cross the threshold to your classroom. Second, it sends a clear message that you are in charge of your territory and that you are allowing them to enter. This helps students understand that entering your classroom is a privilege and not a right. Third, your physical presence forces students to slow down and enter the room individually, which greatly reduces chattering and focuses their attention. One teacher, rather small and slim, said that he not only stands in the doorway but shakes the hand of each student who enters his room. He introduces himself by name and welcomes the students to his room. "They know right away that I am the boss and it is my classroom," he said, "but they don't feel threatened."

If shaking hands feels comfortable for you, then consider shaking each student's hand as he or she enters the room. That definitely helps create a connection, and you can learn a great deal from the way a student shakes your hand. Sweaty palms could mean the student is nervous about school—or she ran to get to class on time. Calloused hands might indicate that you've got a gardener, an artist, or a manual laborer in your classroom. A limp handshake may mean the student is shy or unused to being offered a handshake or uncomfortable touching a teacher. A very strong grip may indicate an athlete, a confident student, a leader, or somebody who may decide to test your authority. And so on.

Whether or not students make eye contact as they enter your classroom also gives you information. Those who don't look at you may have been taught not to look directly at an adult as a sign of respect. Or they may be shy, nervous, or uninterested in school. Pay attention to those who do make eye contact and how long that contact lasts. You'll soon learn to recognize signs of interest, intelligence, energy, humor, curiosity, fear, distrust, aggression, and all the emotions that students bring to school along with their books.

## Choose an Engaging Opening Activity

You can do much to ensure that your first day goes well, regardless of accidents, delays, and interruptions, by putting the focus on your students and not yourself.

Instead of starting with a teacher-centered activity that requires all your students to sit and listen to you, make a student-centered activity the first item on your agenda. Choose an opening activity that is simple but engaging. For example, provide large index cards and markers and ask students to create a tent-style name card for their desks. This activity is good for difficult or very talkative groups, and you can learn a lot about students from the way they write their names on their cards. Big bold letters usually indicate an attention seeker who either has confidence or would like to. Tiny letters may indicate shyness or lack of self-esteem.

You have literally hundreds of options for your opening activity, including:

☐ Place name cards or file folders labeled with students' names on desks before they arrive, along with colored markers or crayons placed randomly on desks. Ask students to find their names, take their seats, and decorate the cards or folders. Sharing markers or crayons will help them bond in a nonthreatening way. (This will also give you a good opportunity to remind them to say "please" and "thank you" if they need such reminders.)

☐ Distribute a questionnaire for students to fill out. Provide pencils.

☐ Design a bingo-style game where students must find other students in the class to match the squares on the bingo cards (Who has a puppy? Who can tap dance? Who likes green Jell-o?).

☐ Provide art materials and ask students to create "me" dolls that reflect their personalities (then tack the dolls to a wall in your classroom and admire them).

☐ Create a "treasure hunt" game for students to complete inside your classroom.

☐ Supply a sample "I am a person who . . ." poem (on the board or on a handout) and ask students to create their own versions. Give them the option of reading their poems, tacking them to the wall, or leaving them on their desks and then walking around the room to read each other's poems.

☐ Group students into threes or fours and give them a short, fun project to complete, such as creating a model, completing a jigsaw puzzle, matching pictures with words, or putting together silly sentences from phrases you have cut out in advance.

☐ Place different objects on tables spaced around your classroom (sports equipment, games, books, comics, electronics, and so on). Ask students to enter the room, look at the objects and go to stand near the table that holds the items that interest them the most. This will help them look at ways they are similar instead of viewing each other as strange and different. (One teacher said she used adjectives such as "friendly" or "energetic" instead of objects to show similarities in personality.)

- [ ] Ask students to draw a picture of their favorite animal, then ask them to share and tell why they chose that particular animal.

- [ ] Form a big circle. Ask each student to say his or her name and then make a movement (such as clapping hands, rubbing their tummy, wiggling their fingers, or tapping one foot). The class repeats the name and movement, adding each new name and movement as they go around the circle.

- [ ] Create a "crazy quiz" that consists of unusual questions: How many times does a hummingbird flap its wings in one minute? How much does a butterfly weigh? How long do baby kangaroos live in their mothers' pouches? How fast can an ostrich run? Have students work in pairs or teams to answer the quiz, and give the winners inexpensive "crazy prizes" such as bug-shaped clickers or gummy erasers.

- [ ] Distribute air-filled balloons and see who can keep his or her balloon in the air the longest using just noses or elbows to bump them up when they start to fall.

- [ ] Have students form a circle. Say your own name, then toss a bean bag across the circle to a student. She says her name and tosses it to another student. That student says his name and tosses it to somebody else. Continue until everybody has participated.

- [ ] Teach a call-and-response that you have preposted on the board or on a handout. Practice it several times, then complete the entire chant. A good format is the military-style chant where the teacher says "One, two" and students respond "three, four," followed by something such as "We are here to/learn some more. Five, six/seven, eight. We are awesome/we are great."

Remember that older students may have six or seven classes during one day and that several teachers may ask them to write, so if your opening activity involves writing, keep it short and easy. Your goal is to get to know your students' personalities and general abilities, not to intimidate, threaten, or bore them.

The primary purpose of the opening activity is to quickly engage students, so that if you are interrupted, they can continue their task until you can return your full attention to them. If you want to play a game or do some activity that involves your supervision, save it for your second activity. Your opening activity needs to be something that students can continue on their own if you must attend to some administrative detail.

A good opening activity reduces the chances of misbehavior, because students won't be bored and won't feel put on the spot, as they often do when they file into a quiet classroom and sit facing an unfamiliar teacher. A student-focused activity also gives you a chance to check out your students while they are otherwise engaged. You will immediately get a sense of which students are shy or unsure of themselves, which are gregarious and inclined to socialize, and which are reluctant to cooperate.

### Provide Clear Instructions

How you deliver your first set of instructions is very important. Your students are going to form their opinions of you and your teaching style within the first few minutes of your first meeting (remember the two-tenths-of-a-second judgment research I mentioned in the Introduction). You will project a very different persona depending on whether you are seated at your desk, perched on a stool, roving about the room, or standing in the doorway. Students will respond to the pitch, volume, and tone of your voice; your choice of words; and especially your facial expressions and body language. Arms crossed over your chest are a sign of defensiveness, for example.

Since this is the first day of class, some students will be eager, and some will be anxious or nervous. Make sure you provide clear, simple instructions for your opening activity. Don't forget the visual learners: it's a good idea to write the instructions on the board as you give them. And many students, especially kinesthetic learners, will respond faster and better if you model the activity for them.

While your students complete their first activity, you can take roll and handle any unforeseen tasks that may arise. Then it's time for you to greet your class. But don't distribute your Welcome to My Class handout yet or jump right into your second activity or game. Talk to your students first. Walk around a little. Let them have an opportunity to look at you without appearing to be rude. Tell them how much you look forward to working with them. Tell them how much you like your subject (or grade level) and why you chose to teach it. Tell them what they are going to learn during this school term, but don't go into great detail about what you will cover during the year. Keep your introduction short and simple.

## GRAB YOUR STUDENTS BY THEIR BRAINS

Once students have completed the opening activity and the first-day frenzy has had time to fizzle a bit, it's time to grab your students by their brains. Literally. Scientifically. According to Kevin Dutton, a research fellow at the University of Cambridge and author of *Flipnosis: The Art of Split-Second Persuasion* (Heineman, 2010), certain behaviors will disable the brain's cognitive security system—the brain does a "double take" that leaves it open to suggestion. When something unusual happens, brain activity increases in the amygdala (the brain's emotion center) and the temporoparietal junction (the novelty detector). For a split-second after something unexpected occurs, cognitive function is disabled, which provides a perfect opportunity for a persuasive person, such as a teacher, to introduce a suggestion. Surprised brains are far more likely, biologically, to follow the suggestion.

Students may expect you to go over your rules and discuss the consequences for a variety of misbehaviors. Your school administration may instruct you to discuss the school's disciplinary code during the first day. As I mentioned earlier, this is one time when I would risk ignoring those instructions, because most students already know how to behave. Even in the unlikely case that they haven't been to school before, their parents or other adults have repeatedly told them to sit down, be quiet, stop hitting or teasing each other, mind their language, and behave politely in public. If school attorneys are worried about legal liability, they may require parents and guardians to sign a statement when they enroll their students in school. Teachers are responsible for the safety of their students and for teaching them, but I don't believe it's fair or right to make the teacher the "traffic cop" when what they need to do is bond with students. So I hold off on talking about rules until the second, third, or fourth day of school. (If you simply can't bring yourself to ignore instructions from your administration, then find an entertaining way to present the rules. According to Dutton, humor is one of the most effective tools for disarming people and persuading them to cooperate with you.)

I usually begin by saying something like "We are supposed to go over the rules and regulations today, but I would like to save that for later this week because right now I'd like us to get to know each other." Then I do something to grab the students' attention. I entertain them with a slide show or a film excerpt, shock them with statistics about things that affect their lives, tempt them with a brain teaser puzzle, engage them with a goofy game, ask them to draw a picture of a dog that likes to eat poems, challenge them to beat me at a game of Scrabble—the entire class against me and they can use the dictionary. If they win, they all get an A for their first assignment (so far, that hasn't happened, but if it did it would be a good thing. They'd all be A students, temporarily at least). I do anything except what students expect me to do, which is talk about rules, regulations, course requirements, objectives, standard procedures, the importance of education, upcoming standardized tests, and ZZZZZZZZZZ.

What you choose to grab your students' brains with will depend on your subject, your personality, and your students. Whatever you choose, tweak the assignment to add an unexpected element. I am not suggesting that you use novelty for novelty's sake or that your job is to entertain students. But the first days of class are important—just as the first dates in a romantic relationship are important—because they set the tone for the long-term relationship. We use science to our advantage in creating that relationship.

For a scientific but accessible explanation of how brain chemistry affects students' attention and how stress affects learning, I highly suggest reading Eric Jensen's book *Teaching With the Brain in Mind* (Association for Supervision and Curriculum Development, 1998; see the Appendix for more information).

## STOP THE TEACHER-VERSUS-STUDENT ATTITUDE IN ITS TRACKS

There is an old Navy saying: "Kick butt first, take names later." Boot camp instructors use that approach to keep new recruits on their toes and to quickly establish who is in control. I use a modified, gentler version of that boot camp strategy, but my purpose is the same: I want my students to understand immediately that they are welcome in my classroom, but that it is *my* classroom and I am in charge. Also, I want to establish an environment in which students are working *with* me and not *against* me. I do not allow students to manipulate me into a teacher-versus-student stance (I did let that happen during my first year of teaching, but after I figured out how important it was for them to respond to me instead of me responding to them, I stopped letting them manipulate me). Instead, I try to show them that we are both on the same side and that we will work together to tackle the curriculum and have as much fun as possible while doing so.

This is another tactic that concurs with Kevin Dutton's research on persuasion. Empathy is a powerful persuader. If you can show that you share the same feelings as your students, they will mentally put themselves on the same side of the desk as you, so to speak. They stop viewing you as the enemy or the adult or the rule enforcer and start seeing you as a fellow human being (not a pal, but a human all the same).

You may choose to do something entirely different from what I do. What you do isn't so important as whether it works. But until you have students on your side, you can't teach them anything; you will be too busy trying to establish discipline and enforce your rules.

Getting students on your side isn't that hard. I have yet to meet a child who wanted to be a failure or who wanted to be disliked. But many children, especially teenagers, act obnoxious and unlovable when they are afraid, and children are afraid of a great many things. In school they have two particular fears: that people won't like them and that they won't be able to pass your class. Even smart kids worry about those two things, so I address their fears in my welcome. My speech goes something like this:

Welcome to my classroom. My name is Miss Johnson, and I'm very happy to have you in my class, because I like teaching school. I want to help you become more effective students, which will help you be successful people. I'm not here to pick on you or try to flunk or boss you around. I was in the military for nine years when I was young, and I got very tired of people telling me what to do all the time. So I try not to be bossy, even though my job is to be the teacher. Somebody has to drive this bus, at least until we get out on the road.

I promise not to embarrass you or humiliate you in my class because I know how that feels—it doesn't feel good to be embarrassed, does it? But I will expect you to think. If anyone dies from overthinking, I will take full responsibility for your death.

Now, how many people would rather go to the dentist than read out loud? Raise your hands please.

There are always hands. So I say:

Relax. I was very shy when I was young, and I was afraid to read out loud. You never have to read out loud in my class if you don't want to, so quit worrying about that right now. I don't want you to hate coming to my classroom. I want you to enjoy reading and writing and discussing the books and stories and essays we're going to read this year. I hope you'll feel comfortable enough to volunteer to read out loud later on, but I won't force you to.

Here's what I really want you to learn: I want you to be able to analyze other people's ideas, compare different ideas, and express your own ideas in an intelligent and articulate way. The more command you have of your language skills, the more successful you will be in school, in your work, and in your personal life—especially your love life.

They giggle. They think I'm joking, but I'm not. I explain:

I'm serious. Think about it. We use words to get many of the things we want in life. Of course, you use words to answer questions in school. But you also use words to ask somebody for a date. Or to explain to somebody why you don't want to take drugs or take off your clothes. Or to convince your parents to let you shave your head or borrow their car. And later on you'll use words to make your future mother-in-law like you—and if you don't think that's important, you're in for a big surprise.

And speaking of surprises, it may surprise you to learn that everybody starts my class with an A. Whether you keep the A or not is up to you, but I will do my best to help you keep it. And I promise you that if you come to class regularly, cooperate with me, and work hard, you will pass this class.

For years, I used the everybody-starts-with-an-A technique without understanding why it was so effective. The first time I used it, it was an accident, but it worked so well that I made it standard practice. Recently, as I delved into some research reports about effective leadership, marketing, and persuasion, I realized why that tactic is so effective. It has to do with people thinking they are getting something for free. Once they have something, they don't want to lose it. Marketing professionals use this technique all the time. Two-for-one sales, for example, may convince you to buy something you wouldn't have purchased in the first place, but since you are going to get a free second item, you buy the first one, which you already see as "yours." Coupons and memberships give grocery store shoppers the feeling that they are getting something free, even if prices on coupon items are higher than normal. Car salespeople will often place the keys to a car you haven't decided to purchase on the desk in front of you. Then they slide the keys toward you and say something about "your keys." They aren't your keys, but they feel like your keys and you are more likely to buy the car.

Starting students with an A isn't really giving them anything. They don't have any grades. But that A is there in the grade book, in ink, so it's real. And most students will make an effort to keep the A. Conversely, if they feel they are beginning with a zero and must work their way to an A, they feel as though they are starting with a debit. The debit doesn't exist any more than the A does, but sometimes reality takes a back seat to persuasion.

What you choose to do and say to create empathy between you and your students will depend on your personality, your students, and your curriculum. But I do urge you to tell them a bit about yourself and present a nongraded activity that allows you to get to know your students as people, and for them to get a sense of your personality. You don't want to be their pal, and you may want them to know you have strict standards for behavior, but you also want them to know that you are a compassionate, caring adult who is there to help them.

Sometimes I like to follow up on our opening activity by distributing index cards and asking students to provide some information. (I use a different color card for each class so that I can easily identify where a card belongs, and I can take that group's cards home with me for phone calls or parent communication activities.) Because so many kids are visual learners, I write the information prompts on the board:

Name:

Full mailing address:

Phone number:

Birthday:

Name of parent/guardian:

Student ID #:

*Note:* be sure to keep extra blank cards on hand for students who transfer into your class later, so you can add them to your files.

As my students fill out their index cards, I write the names of any absent students on blank cards for them to fill out if and when they show up. Then I walk around the room between the aisles, with my roll sheet in hand. I mentally test myself to see whether I can remember the students' names. If I get stuck, I sneak a peek over students' shoulders to check the names on their cards. When they finish filling out the information I requested, I ask them to turn the card over and write a little bit more on the back of the card.

I explain:

I want you to tell me anything I need to know to be a good teacher for you. If you have dyslexia or a speech problem or epilepsy or you just hate reading, let me know. If you have a job, I'd like to know where you work. If you have favorite hobbies or sports, please tell me so I can try to include those things in our lessons. If there is something special you'd like to do in this class, let me know.

I give students a few minutes to make the notes on the back of their cards (and for me to memorize more names). Instead of letting them pass the cards to me, I walk down the aisles and take each card individually. This serves three purposes: it brings me closer to them, which makes them nervous and more likely to behave; it gives everybody a bit of personal attention, which may prevent the attention-seekers from demanding extra attention; and it gives me another chance to match each name with the student's face. As I accept each card, I say, "Thank you," and repeat the student's name aloud. Once I have collected them all, I go to the front of the room and flip through them quickly, mentally testing myself. If I can't identify a particular name, I ask the student to raise his or her hand.

After a quick review of all their index cards, I tell the class it's time for our first test. Invariably, they gasp and groan and mumble.

"Relax," I say, "this test is for me. I am going to go down the roll sheet and see if I have learned everybody's names. If I get them all right, I win. If I miss one name, you all get an automatic A on your first test, and you don't even have to lift a writing utensil."

Of course, I have no test prepared for them, but they don't know that. And I have grabbed them. Even the kids who are too cool for school are intrigued. They are certain that I will make a mistake and they will receive that freebie A. Sometimes a sharp student asks what I will win if I remember all the names correctly. My response, "I win everything," delights them. They can hardly stand the excitement as I work my way down the roll sheet, identifying them one at a time. (If you decide to try this and your first activity was making name cards, be sure to have kids turn their cards facedown so that no one can accuse you of cheating.)

So far I have managed to pass the name test every time. Sometimes I forget half the names as soon as one group of students leaves my room, but they don't know that and it doesn't matter. I have another chance to relearn their names the next day. When I do make a mistake and forget a name, as I know I will someday, it won't be a disaster. The students will be delighted at earning a freebie A and even more delighted at having caught a teacher making a mistake. It will be a good lesson for them to see that adults make mistakes too, and yet the world goes on.

You may be thinking, "What a waste of time! My job is to teach, not to show off my memorization skills." I would argue that you will be able to teach much more effectively (and much faster) if you take the time to know your students before you begin your lessons. Names are much more than words; they represent us. In many cases children come to school empty-handed. All they have to bring with them are their names.

Or perhaps you're thinking, "But I could never learn a hundred names in one day!" If that's the case, and you haven't already done so, give your students sheets of 8-by-10-inch construction paper and pass around a few felt-tip markers. Ask them to print their first names in letters large enough for you to see from across the room and then fold the papers in half to make tent-style name cards that will stand up on their desks. Tell them that you have a terrible memory, but that it's important to you to learn their names.

Taking time to learn student names is worth the effort, because it eventually pays off. First, it demonstrates that you care about your students enough to be willing to take the time to get to know them. Second, people are much more apt to misbehave if they are anonymous members of a crowd.

At the end of our first meeting, I stand in the doorway and smile as my students file out. I wave and drawl, "Y'all come back now." Some of them laugh and wave; others roll their eyes and shake their heads at my silliness. But they leave my room smiling, and a group of laughing children is a lovely sight.

## TEACH YOUR PROCEDURE FOR ORAL RESPONSES

Even if you plan to teach a lesson on procedures later, now is the time to teach your procedures for answering questions in your class. There are endless variations on the theme of student responses, but students have three basic options:

- Students must always raise their hands before speaking and cannot interrupt people.

- Students may spontaneously respond to your questions or to each other's comments.

- Everybody must wait for a specific period of time (ten to sixty seconds) before responding.

Some of us believe we want students to raise their hands before speaking—until we actually start teaching. Then we realize that sometimes we want students to speak out quickly, such as during brainstorming sessions or when we are trying to generate enthusiasm or excitement about an idea or activity. During other activities, especially exercises that involve complex or abstract concepts, we might want students to take two full minutes to consider any question before making a response. Even if you opt not to use this method, I recommend trying it as an experiment. If you allow time for students who process information more slowly and for your quick responders to consider their comments before speaking, you will find that the complexity and intellectual level of student responses rises and that you will hear from students who normally don't volunteer an answer.

If you begin with just one hand-raising option and teach that as your standard procedure, students will soon learn to respond as you have taught them. If you then decide you want them to respond in a different manner, they may not be able to make the switch. Therefore, I recommend teaching all three methods, using a variety of exercises, and then announcing which method you expect students to use as you begin any new activity. One easy way to alert students (and remind them) is to make three posters like the images shown in Figure 5.1.

If you are creative, you can draw illustrations yourself, or you can ask an artistic student to make the posters. Then, when you begin an activity, prop the appropriate poster against the board or tack it to a wall where everybody can see it. For younger children, you might turn this into a fun project: students can make the three posters and store them in their desks so that they can put the appropriate poster on their desktops during a given activity.

## BE PREPARED FOR "TEST THE TEACHER"

So many factors affect student behavior that it's impossible to predict how students will respond to you. If you can get them started on the first or second activity and engaged in doing something challenging or fun, most students will forget to

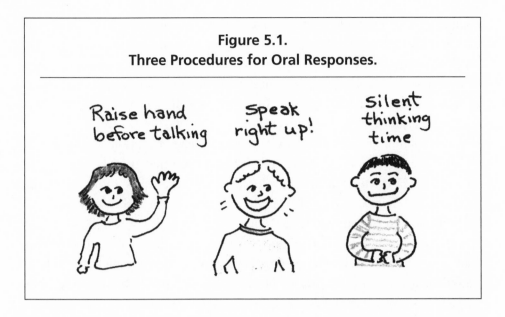

**Figure 5.1.**
**Three Procedures for Oral Responses.**

Raise hand before talking

Speak right up!

Silent thinking time

misbehave, which is your goal. But sometimes students may begin to test your tolerance during the first few minutes of the first day of class. A couple of kids seated farthest away from you may begin to pass notes or talk loudly while you're addressing the class. Some student may sit directly in front of you and start writing his name on his desktop. Somebody else may get up and boldly stroll across the room to talk to a friend.

What will you do if those things happen? Your reaction will set the tone for the rest of the school year. Remember: you are still establishing your teacher persona. Don't let students draw you into a confrontation over trivial misbehavior, or they will all realize that they can distract you any time they choose. Of course, you have to respond to their challenges, but you don't have to let them dictate your behavior. They expect you to yell at them, send them to the office, threaten to call their parents, or ignore them. So do something different from what they expect. For example, draw in your breath loudly so that everybody hears you, then freeze in place and stare at the student, wide-eyed. Hold that pose for as long as you can (or for as long as the other students stay quiet, awaiting the outcome). If the student stops the misbehavior, exhale and say, "Thank you so much," as though you just averted a major disaster.

If the same student disrupts the class again, walk right up to the student. Stand very, very close. Look very serious. And wait. If the student quiets down, you are good to go. Depending on your personality, you may wipe your brow, cross your eyes and give the misbehaving student a goofy look that nobody else can see, hurry to the window (if there is one in your classroom) and look outside, march to your desk, and pretend you are looking for something important. The idea is to break the tension and disrupt the behavior cycle. If you can distract students even for a second, you can often derail the disruptors. For example, you might choose to share a knock-knock joke or a riddle—when people laugh together, it actually creates positive chemicals in their brains, thus making them more likely to cooperate. You might smack your forehead and say, "Yikes! I forgot to bring my Taser." You might move away from the disruptive student, then turn to somebody else and say something such as "Oh, I love the first day of school, don't you? It gives me goose bumps!" You might announce, "I forgot to tell you. If you don't want to do the activities I have planned, we can always jump right into our text-books and get to work studying for our first test." Or you might say, "Everybody gets a little nervous on the first day of school. Who's nervous?" If anybody raises a hand, engage them in a conversation. If nobody does, just go on with your instruction or activity. Don't worry if students snicker at you or exchange glances that say, "What a weirdo!" You are a teacher. It's a given that you come from a different planet.

If you have a persistent troublemaker (or several of them), you have to do something. If the disruptions are minor, ignore them. Focus on the students who are cooperating and thank them for their excellent behavior. But if the disruptors are determined to stop you in your tracks, you need to act. Don't react. Try to make your behavior your choice and not a response to theirs. If students can continue to make you react to their behavior, they win. And because they aren't worried about covering the curriculum, they have an endless list of misbehaviors to share with you. You need to choose a behavior from your own preplanned repertoire of student motivators. Your goal is to get students to respond to you, not the other way around. If you have serious problems, see Chapter Six for specific discipline techniques and suggestions.

Don't let one or two rotten apples ruin your appetite for teaching. Remember your basic psychology: in a given group, the odds are good that at least one strong personality will challenge the leader just to see how the leader responds. If the leader demonstrates self-control, confidence, and courage, the challenger will usually back down—if given the opportunity to back down without losing face.

## Don't Take Student Misbehavior Personally

Don't take student misbehavior personally, especially at the start of a new school year or term. Children act in unacceptable ways for a lot of reasons, but you are very probably not the reason. Often, when students express anger, even if they express it in your direction, you aren't the real target. I can usually learn the reasons for student misbehavior by not reacting abruptly or automatically sending them to the office; instead I make them sit down and talk to me or write an explanation for their behavior in their journals. Following are just a few examples of student misbehavior in my own classes, along with the reasons why the students misbehaved:

- A boy leaped out of his seat, overturned his desk, and started shouting and shaking his fists, then ran out of the room. He refused to explain his behavior, but one of his friends told me in confidence that a girl had been sitting across from the boy, crossing and uncrossing her legs seductively while staring directly at the boy, and he wanted out of the room because he was embarrassed and physically uncomfortable.

- A girl jumped up and hit the boy seated next to her, then refused to explain her behavior. He told me to forget about it. Thinking that perhaps the boy had taunted her, I told her to sit down and behave herself. Her response was to hit a different boy in the head. I saw no choice but to call the office and ask somebody to come escort the girl out of my room. Later the girl confided that she had wanted to be sent home from school that day because she had to make a bowel movement and was afraid she would be assaulted in the school bathroom (older girls had twice assaulted her in the restroom).

- A boy threw a dictionary at my head. (If you read my book *My Posse Don't Do Homework,* you'll recognize Emilio.) He wanted out of my classroom because he couldn't read; he was afraid I would find out his secret and embarrass him in front of the class.

I could go on, but I'm sure you get the picture. Don't take your students' behavior personally, especially when they don't know you well enough to hate you. Don't assume that every challenge to your authority is an intentional sign of disrespect. Unless a student insults you specifically and personally, assume that it is your status as teacher, adult, or authority figure that is the target of the disrespect. Continue to demonstrate the kind of respect you want your students to show to you—and themselves.

## CREATE A DAILY "DO-NOW" ACTIVITY

Your "Do-Now" activity (or Bell Work or Warm-Up or whatever you choose to call it) is one of the most important and effective strategies you can use to eliminate time wasted trying to get students settled and focused. It is also one of the best deterrents to misbehavior. Instead of letting students enter your classroom and mill about, waiting for you to get ready or for the bell to ring, a Do-Now activity requires students to begin working on something as soon as they enter your room. When the bell rings to start class, they should already be busy (or immediately upon entering the room if you have a bell-less schedule). If you start your school year or semester with a good Do-Now every day, you'll find that in less than a week your students will be in the habit of making the transition from outside to classroom.

Students must know exactly what you expect, so it's very important that you provide clear instructions for the first few times they perform Do-Nows. You can print your instructions on the board in your room, project them onto a screen using an overhead projector or computer, print them on individual handouts, or present them verbally as you demonstrate the task. Simply presenting verbal instructions is not a very effective way to teach Do-Nows because so many students are visual or kinesthetic learners and will forget or misunderstand verbal instructions. The key is consistency. If you post your instructions on the board one day, post them there everyday. Likewise, if you project them on a screen, project them every day. Many teachers have found that it's easier and more effective to use a special location such as a portable whiteboard, a bulletin board, or one section of the stationary green- or whiteboard that is clearly visible to everybody.

Obviously, the content of your Do-Now activity will depend on the age, ability, and personalities of your students and will be influenced by the subjects you teach, but all good warm-up activities share some of these common traits:

- ☐ They can be completed by all students within five to fifteen minutes.
- ☐ They can be accomplished independently, without teacher assistance.
- ☐ They are interesting, fun, or challenging.
- ☐ They are educational, not just time-fillers.
- ☐ They are not graded as assignments, but do contribute to student grades.
- ☐ They are collected and filed—or discussed as a class or in small groups.
- ☐ They change periodically to add interest and avoid boredom.

Since one of the goals for Do-Now is to form a habit, it's a good idea to do the same kind of activity for at least a week to avoid having to provide different instructions every day. Once your students are in the habit, you may choose to change the activity once a week or at the start of every month, to maintain student interest and engagement. As students become experienced at different tasks, you can mix them up for more variety. If you teach science, for example, you could start with a week's worth of unusual animal photos. Each day students will find a photo posted in the room. Their task is to name the animal, spell its name correctly, and list three or four characteristics of the animal. The following week you might post photos of plants or try a completely different activity.

It's important to follow up with the students' Do-Now work after it is finished. Discuss it as a class or in small groups as a springboard to the first lesson of the day. Ask volunteers to share their finished product with the class. Collect papers, if applicable, and keep them in a file that you can refer to later. Let students compare answers and self-correct them, if they involve something like math problems or answers to questions. For example, if you teach math and you ask students to do a few math problems as their Do-Now, go over the answers with them or have them self-correct before they turn them in. If you teach science and your Do-Now requires reading a short selection about a specific animal or plant, then hold a short discussion about the reading before you move on. If you assign a Do-Now and don't do anything with it later, students will quickly learn that it isn't important and they may stop cooperating.

The possibilities are endless, but just to spark your imagination following are some popular activities from different grade levels that I have used or observed. Most can be adapted for older or younger students. You can find many more suggestions online at the dozens of Web sites devoted to classroom management and lesson plans (see the Appendix for suggested resources).

- Place an everyday object on a stand in the front of the room. Students must come up with a list of ten unusual ways to use that object.

- Three math problems are projected on a screen. Students must solve the problems and compare their answers—the class as a whole must submit the same answers.

- A yes-or-no question about something the class has studied is posted or projected. On one wall of the room, a large sign reads "YES." On an opposite wall, a sign reads "NO." Students must read the question, then stand on one side of the room or the other. The teacher moderates a brief discussion without revealing the correct answer, and students have the opportunity to change sides before the teacher shares the answer.

- Project a photo of a person on a screen. Ask students to draw a picture of something that person might have in his or her living room.

- Place a stack of handouts near the door. Students take a handout as they enter the room and must be prepared to write about or discuss the topic after a specified number of minutes (you must tell them exactly how long they have to finish). Each day, the handout contains a short article about something weird such as a three-legged pig, accounts of criminals who were arrested after doing something unbelievably stupid, or descriptions of unusual record-setters such as people who kiss for hours on end.

- A challenge is projected onto a screen: find out whose pulse in the room is the highest and whose is the lowest. Students must figure out how to take their pulses and how to time them.

- Post a single word on the board. Students must write down as many smaller words as they can, using only the letters in the posted word.

- As students enter, repeatedly play a short film clip that shows somebody performing a physical action. Students have three minutes to try to learn to perform the same action.

- Place stacks of three small bean bags on each desk—or on each pair of desks. Students have five to ten minutes to learn to juggle the bags (or at least try to learn). When class begins, they must explain what factors are involved in learning to juggle (balance and timing, for example).

- Project a list of words on a screen or board. Students have two minutes to memorize the words before they disappear. They will be asked to say or write the words correctly.

- Write an unusual word such as *flatulence* on the board. Students must figure out the meaning of the word and write a sentence using that word properly.

- Project a photo of several brightly colored objects on a screen. Give students three minutes to study the photo. Then ask them to list (or if yours is an art class, they can draw) all the objects and their associated colors.

- Post the name of a city on the board. Students must find out the country where that city is located and tell approximately how far away the city is from their own location.

- Project a close-up of a section of an object on a screen. Students must figure out what the object is.

- Project silhouettes of several everyday objects, then ask students to identify each one.

- Post or project a question for students to discuss: Do people ride zebras? How much does a camel weigh? Can puppies hear when they are first born? After two to five minutes, ask students to share their answers with the class.

- When students enter the gym, they find a circuit course like the ones used in military boot camps, with a sit-up station, a jumping jack station, a squat-thrust location, and so on. Each station has a picture and written instructions for the exercise to be completed and the number of repetitions. After they complete the circuit, students may jump rope or shoot baskets until everybody completes the course and is ready to begin class.

As you read this list, you probably thought of other ideas for good activities for your students. If you run out of ideas, ask your students for suggestions. They often come up with more difficult and challenging tasks than teachers do, and when students' input is incorporated by teachers, they often become more interested in doing the activities.

## INTRODUCE STUDENTS TO EACH OTHER

Choose your method of introduction carefully. Students are much more likely to treat each other well if they know each other's names, but many of the popular games designed to help people get acquainted are more effective with small children and adults than they are with older elementary, middle, and secondary school students. Why? Little kids are usually too innocent to be intentionally cruel, and adults are usually too polite or too concerned with earning a passing grade to insult each other. But preteens and adolescents are experts at humiliating and tormenting each other. Another consideration, which breaks my heart, is that many children are targets of gangs, cliques, or bullies. What may seem to you to be a simple game designed to give students a chance to become acquainted may create an uncomfortable or even dangerous situation for some of them.

I do not recommend pairing students or forming small groups until you know the students in a given class well enough to be sure that your grouping won't cause problems.

Another consideration is shyness. Some people are naturally introverted, and that is not a bad thing. We can't all be extroverts. Just as actors need an audience, leaders need followers, athletic competitors need spectators, and classrooms need listeners as well as talkers. Some teachers believe it is their duty to help shy people overcome their shyness and become comfortable speaking in front of groups. Others believe it is our duty to create a safe haven where students feel comfortable and then provide opportunities for them to naturally come out of their shells. The feedback I have received from shy people indicates that most prefer the second approach. I can't say which is correct, but I believe it's best to err on the side of comfort. I was a very shy child and although I have learned to overcome my anxiety enough to allow me to speak in front of groups, it still makes me very nervous (teaching is very different from public speaking, as you undoubtedly know). So I try to create activities that do not put shy students in the spotlight for more than a few seconds at most.

One of the most popular introductory games in school (and college) is student interviews. You've probably played this game more than once. The instructor asks students to pair off and interview each other, then introduce their partners to the class. This exercise appeals to teachers because it's quick and simple. But for many students this activity is an exercise in embarrassment and agony. Here are just a few reasons why so many students dread these peer interviews:

- Unless the teacher assigns pairs, a few students are always left out—nobody wants to be their partner. They feel rejected and unlikable. If the teacher forces people to join them, they feel even worse. And they never forget that nobody wanted to be their partner.

- Some students are so shy that having to speak in front of the class is a major trauma, especially on the first day.

- Children are quick to pick up on weaknesses such as lisps, accents, stutters, and blushing, and some will torment others.

- Preadolescence and puberty cause all kinds of physical situations that embarrass children: budding breasts, acne, sudden voice changes, random facial hair, uncontrollable physical responses to stimuli. Sometimes the worst thing teachers can do to students is make them the center of attention.

- Poverty, religious rules, or strict parents may force a child to dress differently from the norm. Their clothing may embarrass them or lead classmates to ask questions that they would prefer not to answer in public.

Please don't overlook the idea of using a game to allow your students to get acquainted. A number of games and activities don't require students to address the class or stand in front of the entire group. One of my college professors used a game that worked very well for adults, and I have had great success when I have adopted her game for use with my secondary students.

### The Adjective Game

1. Ask your students to think of an adjective to describe themselves at the moment. (You may have to remind them what an adjective is. I usually give a few alliterative examples, such as Rapping Robert or Talented Tiffany, and a few amusing examples, such as Hungry Sam.)

2. Beginning in one corner of the room, ask the first student to say his or her name and adjective. Ask the second student, and so on, until you reach five. Stop there.

3. Stand near the first student. Ask, "Who's this?" They will call out the name and adjective. Move to the second student and ask, "Who's this?" Continue until you have repeated the first five names.

4. Repeat the same procedure, stopping after each five names to begin at your original number one. When you reach the last student, start with the first student and repeat every name.

5. This step is optional, but it's a big hit with my classes. As the students give their names and adjectives, I jot them down on a numbered list. Now I instruct the students to get a pen and paper and number the sheet from one to thirty (or however many students are in the class). Reading from my list in random order, I give an adjective. The students try to write the correct name to match the adjective. When I have read all the adjectives and the students have listed all the names, I quickly go over the list, giving the correct names. Then I ask to see the hands of people who correctly remembered all the names, who missed one, who missed two, and so on. I award boxes of animal crackers or spiffy pencils to the students who correctly identify the most names.

Don't be put off by older students who shake their heads at your silliness. If they have enough sense of humor to laugh at you, they'll probably go along with the game. But if you have a truly tough class, as I have had, and you see that the ringleaders are going to ruin the game or refuse to play, you'll have to make some quick choices. You can ignore the party poopers and play with the kids who cooperate, which sends the message that students who cooperate are going to get more attention from you than the ones who don't—not a bad message. You can nickname all those who refuse to play as "Taking the Fifth Amendment" and show that it doesn't bother you if they can't play well with others. You can ask the nonparticipants to step outside until the rest of you are finished, which is risky because they may refuse to go; this spells success in their goal of getting you to abandon your plans and fight with them—not a good precedent to set. You can stop the game without explanation and move on to the next item on your agenda, preferably a challenging worksheet or reading assignment, which might be a good choice because you will have made it clear to everybody that if they don't want to play, you have plenty of work for them to do—another good message. Trust your instincts.

## ESTABLISH ROUTINES AND RITUALS

Standard procedures are probably the number-one way to eliminate wasted time in the classroom. You may have to spend a few minutes each day reviewing your procedures until students can follow them without your supervision, but once students learn them you're set for the semester or school year. Every teacher has his or her own teaching methods, curriculum requirements, and classroom logistics to consider, but many procedures are common to any classroom. For example, at times we all need to quickly get students' attention, collect papers, distribute materials, approve or disapprove requests for bathroom visits, check for understanding, clean up after projects, and so on. If we design and teach procedures for accomplishing those tasks that we must perform repeatedly during a school day or week, we can save time, prevent frustration, and make our classrooms more efficient, happy places to be.

If you are at a loss as to what procedures you should use and how to teach them, try to find a successful, happy teacher to observe. Even if your happy teacher colleague doesn't call them procedures, he or she will be using them. You'll notice that students in those classes know what to do when it's time to start an activity, collect papers, line up to go to the library, and so forth. If you can't find a teacher to observe, check the books, videos, and DVDs in your school district staff development library. If they don't have one, ask your administrators if they can recommend resources for you. Ask your fellow teachers. Do an Internet search for "classroom procedures" and visit Web sites hosted and designed specifically for teachers to share best practices and experiences.

In the meantime, to get you started, let's look at the situation where you want to transition quickly and smoothly from one activity or lesson to another. I watched a video clip where a class of elementary students got up from their seats and marched around their room in single file, singing their class song as they made their way to the storytelling area, where they quickly seated themselves and quietly waited for the teacher to begin reading. It took them less than a minute to make their way around the room, and during that minute every child was smiling and had the opportunity to expend some energy before sitting down to listen. That teacher faced a group of happy, receptive students. What a brilliant idea!

If you teach older students, you can use a variation of the singing march by playing the same musical passage to signal that it's time for everybody to finish up what they are working on and turn in their papers or get out their textbooks or find their art supplies or retrieve a calculator or a dictionary or a workbook from the storage center. If you use the same music to signal the same activity every time, students will quickly learn to follow the cue. And if you make the passage exactly twenty seconds (or thirty seconds) long, you can require everybody to be ready for the next activity when the music ends. Or you can play a few seconds of music and then count out loud slowly from ten to one, giving students just ten seconds to be ready to go. Using music or a countdown creates energy and enthusiasm without creating the resistance that often accompanies verbal instructions and requests.

I read about a teacher who used a similar strategy to signal cleanup time in her classroom following art projects that involved materials that needed to be gathered and stored for the next group. She played the first seconds of the *William Tell Overture* (DAH DAH DAH dum) as her signal. Her students responded with delight to such a dramatic cue.

### Attention, Please!

Another common requirement is the need to get your students' attention quickly. Successful kindergarten and elementary teachers are a great source for ideas. They often use call-and-response chants, nonverbal hand gestures, unusual sounds, or large colorful manipulatives posted on the walls at the front of their rooms. These methods also work very well for older students, although they may roll their eyes and pretend they are "too cool" to enjoy them. Some teachers shout. If that works for you, fine. But shouting tends to lose its effectiveness after a while, and it also gives the impression that the teacher is losing control. Calm people don't shout; calm, assertive authority is much more effective than panic or anger.

Chants or signals are usually much more effective—and less irritating—than shouting. Some teachers can silence a classroom by clapping their hands five times. Others may blow two toots on a whistle. The idea is to produce a sound that stands out from the voices of your students, and to let them know ahead of time that when they hear that sound they are to stop what they are doing, face you, and listen quietly. One teacher I observed in a video clip used a "rain stick" that produced a sound very similar to gentle rain. The first time he held up the stick and students heard the noise, they all became quiet and looked at him. He said, "Sometimes I need everybody to look at me and listen to me. That's what I want you to do as soon as you hear this sound." The students were intrigued and the rain stick worked very well to get their attention without creating a loud, startling noise. (I have since used a rain stick with my college students—they love it and it works.)

The same teacher had a Noise Meter that he made in the form of a vertical strip with self-stick material at three distinct points—Quiet Time at the bottom, Partner Work in the middle, and Group Talk at the top. He would place a large, easy-to-see laminated cutout of a soccer ball to indicate which level of noise he wanted for a given time period. Then he gave his students the opportunity to engage in three short activities, one at each noise level, so he could provide feedback to let them know when their voices were at acceptable levels.

Such feedback and practice are key steps to teaching any kind of procedure. We can't expect students to automatically understand what we mean when we say, "Talk quietly with your partner." What seems quiet to them may sound like shouting to us. It's so important to remember that students' failure to comply with our requests may not be due to lack of respect or unwillingness to cooperate, but rather to lack of clarity about exactly what is expected.

### Silent Signals and Nonverbal Cues

Sometimes a silent signal or nonverbal cue is more appropriate than a voice or sound signal. Students who need to make a quick bathroom visit, for example, can give you a prearranged signal such as three fingers raised, hand up, palm facing forward. They can give the signal even while you are speaking, without interrupting you. This allows you to nod or mirror the signal to give them permission. (Some teachers hesitate to allow students to sign themselves out for bathroom visits, but many teachers report that even young or "difficult" students respond very favorably to being given the trust and responsibility of signing themselves out for bathroom visits. They usually work very hard to maintain the trust and freedom that you give them—because they don't want to lose them. Students who abuse the privilege can be removed from the self sign-out list and will have to work to regain the trust and freedom that they have lost.)

At any time during your instruction, you can check for understanding by holding up one of your hands, making a "thumbs-up" gesture, and looking at your student questioningly. Those who "get it" also raise their thumbs. Anybody who is confused gives a thumbs down. This gives you the option, depending on the number of thumbs down, to back up and rephrase what you were saying, try a different approach, or put students to work individually or in pairs or groups while you circulate and assist.

Students can also silently initiate checks for understanding if you teach them to tap their index fingers against their heads any time they become confused while you are addressing the class. If only one student keeps tapping his head, then you know that you will need to spend some time with that student while others are working independently. If you have more than a couple of finger tappers, then you can slow down or vary your instructional method. This method prevents you from continuing to give instructions when nobody needs them or realizing later that you have lost students along the way.

Some teachers opt for a hand signal instead of verbal cues when they want students to stop talking and pay attention. The teacher may stop and cup his or her hand behind one ear while giving students a meaningful look. Students then stop talking and cup their own hands behind one ear. The teacher waits until every student complies, then says, "Thank you for listening," and proceeds with the next instruction or activity. Likewise, the teacher may simply raise one hand and wait for everybody to raise one hand in response before proceeding.

The excellent teacher I mentioned earlier used what he called "Give Me Five." He displayed a chart on the wall that showed five things he expected when he held up his hand: look at the teacher, stop talking, keep your hands to yourself, hold your feet still, and listen. Each expectation was numbered. Then, during his lesson, if a student strayed, the teacher quickly and quietly got the student back on track by saying, "Jenny, number two, please. Thank you." It worked brilliantly. The teacher didn't have to stop the lesson and the students responded without being put on the spot. This method can work with any age of student as long as you tweak the expectations to suit your class.

## All Aboard?

An important factor to consider when using verbal or nonverbal cues is the percent of student response you require. During regular lessons and activities, I think it's best to ignore minor misbehaviors and avoid being what students refer to as "a control freak." But if you use a verbal or nonverbal cue to check for understanding or to correct behavior, then ideally, you want 100 percent response. For example, if you ask for a student hand signal in response to your hand signal cue (you raise your hand and wait for everybody to stop talking, and they raise their hands in response) then you should probably insist upon a 100 percent response from students. If you proceed with only 95 percent, it may seem as though everybody is on board, but you may soon find that more and more students choose to opt out. Before long, you may find yourself back where you started—or even trying to regain lost ground. If you are teaching young children, they are usually delighted to respond to hand signals, so getting 100 percent is easy. Many older students will be very cooperative as well. But if you suspect that you may have some noncooperative souls in your classroom, you might choose to begin with verbal cues at first. That way, if you have a few nonresponders in the group, it won't be so obvious and you can ignore them, since they'll be swept along with the flow.

Don't make an issue of singling out one or two students who are not verbally responding to your cues. Most likely they are testing to see whether they can manipulate you into a showdown. You have far better things to do than engage in arguments with childish people. But if the same one or two students continue to flaunt their noncompliance, they may be begging for your attention. I suggest giving it to them—but not when you're in the midst of teaching. Find a time to give them your undivided attention when it's convenient for you and highly inconvenient for them. A good time might be when the other, more cooperative students are enjoying five minutes of free time to socialize as a reward for their good efforts at the end of an activity or class period.

## End-of-Class Procedure

Once you begin designing procedures, you'll find yourself creating new ones as needed. Be sure to create clear instructions for each new procedure and allow students the opportunity to practice until they get it right. Don't punish them if they require several practice sessions. If they aren't doing what you want, they may not understand exactly what you want. Don't worry about wasting time. The few minutes you spend teaching procedures will come back to you tenfold as you save time by not having to repeatedly request that students settle down and focus on their assignments or use their indoor voices or neatly stack their books on the bookshelf or clean up their messes or stand quietly beside their desks while they wait for the dismissal bell.

That reminds me of one of my favorite and most necessary procedures: the end-of-class, or EOC, procedure. I learned the hard way, during my first year of teaching, that if I didn't stop one or two students from edging (or thronging) towards the exit five or ten (or even fifteen) minutes prior to the dismissal bell, I'd soon have an unruly horde on my hands. And hordes are very unattractive.

During my second teaching year, I began teaching my EOC procedure to every class on the first day. It made a tremendous difference. You may choose to have students stand at their seats or line up along the wall (you can use the first places in line as a reward for good behavior—but be sure to rotate this privilege). Younger children are much less conscious of time and are more receptive to learning a song or chant and a routine for getting ready to leave. Older students often watch the clock. So my policy is: class ends when the bell rings. No early backpack zipping and paper shuffling. I give a three-minute warning, at which time they can prepare to leave. They can talk to each other, but they must stay within arm's reach of their seats. No edging and elbowing toward the door. If I see edging, elbowing, shuffling, and disorder, then they receive an additional homework and a quiz the following day. If students cooperate and follow the EOC procedure all week, their reward is five minutes of free time during class on Monday.

## TAKE TIME TO THINK

A psychologist who works with dyslexic students shared an experience with me that completely changed my attitude about time and my approach to class discussions. The psychologist told me about a teenage boy who came to her treatment center and asked her to give him an IQ test so he could prove to his father that he wasn't retarded, as the school claimed he was. The psychologist administered a standard IQ test under normal conditions, as requested. The boy earned a very low score—but he insisted that the score was incorrect and asked to be retested.

"Normally, a child who has been told for years that he is not intelligent will believe what he is told, especially if the parents believe it, too," the psychologist said, "but this boy wasn't having it."

So she administered a second test. The second time she allowed the boy to take as much time as he needed to answer the questions. He spent more than triple the amount of time normally allowed—but he scored in the genius category!

After hearing that story, I wondered how many little geniuses had been sitting in my classroom feeling stupid because I didn't give them sufficient time to process information. Those slower thinkers may have had better ideas, but they rarely got a chance to share them in my classroom. I realized I had inadvertently been teaching slower thinkers not to bother thinking because I was encouraging students who offered quick answers to my questions, regardless of the accuracy or depth of their answers. I liked a fast pace. It made misbehavior less likely, I thought, because students were engaged. But while I was busy racing along, encouraging the quick responders, I was teaching the slower thinkers not to bother, because by the time they arrived at an answer to the first question the rest of us had already moved on.

So I instituted a new policy that required a mandatory thinking period (ten seconds, then twenty and eventually a full sixty seconds) before anybody could offer an answer to a question, and the results were amazing. Students who normally didn't respond began raising their hands, and their thoughtful comments inspired deeper thinking from the quick thinkers. My own thought process improved as well. We didn't use the mandatory thinking time for every single class discussion, such as informal chats about school activities, but when we did take more time to consider important questions, it really changed the dynamic in that classroom.

If you have been rewarding faster thinkers in your class for raising their hands immediately, it might take you a few tries to teach your students to slow down and think. You may have to start with five or ten seconds and work your way up to a full minute of silence. Sometimes teachers find it hard to be quiet for ten or twenty seconds themselves. (Go ahead and try it now. Ask yourself a question and think about it for at least ten seconds. If ten seconds feels like a long time, you are probably a fast processor. If you didn't have time to really think, you are a slower processor. You may be smarter than you think you are!)

I strongly suggest trying this technique in your classroom. Students are usually very receptive to experimenting with longer thinking times, especially if you allow them to take turns being the official timer. That way they feel they are challenging themselves against the clock instead of being forced (by you) to be quiet.

## DO SOME DIAGNOSTICS

Give the counselors a day or two to straighten out student schedules before you distribute your one-page welcome handout. During those two days, give your students a diagnostic exam or create assignments that will let you judge their skills and abilities, their strengths and weaknesses. (Don't quench their enthusiasm by grading these assignments. Ask students to do their best, but don't assign grades. Another option is to give every student who sincerely tries to complete the assignment full credit, so that they are not punished for making mistakes.) Diagnostic exams and exercises enable you to adjust your lesson plans so that you don't bore students or frustrate them by giving them work that is too easy or too hard. On my diagnostic exam I include sample questions from chapter tests, semester reviews, and final exams to find out how much my students already know. If the results show that the majority of the class needs to back up and cover some old ground, we back up. On the other hand, if nobody misses more than one or two grammar questions, I eliminate the easiest lessons I had planned in that area.

For younger children, you might play games or do activities that will show you where students are on the learning spectrum for various subjects. Math games, science projects, and spelling or writing activities will give you a good idea of who knows what. For students in third grade and higher, responses to reading are an excellent way to find out what your students know about a given subject, in addition to giving you a good look at their logic and writing skills. Find an interesting or controversial essay, editorial, movie review, or feature article in a newspaper or magazine and make copies for your students. Have them read the article silently and write a response to the content (for younger students, I require a paragraph or half a page; for high school students, I require at least one full page). This not only gives you information about students' analytical thinking and composition skills, it also gives them good practice for the kind of writing they will be expected to do if they go on to attend college.

At one time I taught freshman composition at a four-year university. My freshmen, all high school honors students, had a terrible time coming up with their own theses; they wanted me to tell them what to say. When I returned to the high school classroom, I added many more open-ended writing assignments to my lessons, and my former students have reported that they were better prepared than many of their college classmates to produce the kind of writing that professors expected from them.

## WELCOME HANDOUTS AND FOLDERS

Once you are reasonably sure that the students in your classroom will be there for a while and you won't have ten new students the next day, it's time to distribute your one-page welcome handout and cover your ground rules. Read your handout to the class to ensure that everybody has seen and heard exactly what it says. After you read one section, stop and ask students if they have any questions or comments. Make sure they understand exactly what you expect in each area.

After you have read the entire handout together, ask again for questions or comments. Tell your students that this is their chance to argue with you, if any of your rules or procedures seem unreasonable to them. If anybody has a comment, consider it carefully and make a decision on the spot or tell them you will consider their ideas and let them know what you think at the next class. If you are an experienced or natural teacher or you have an unusually cooperative and well-behaved group of students, you may choose to open your rules to student input or votes. If you don't have much teaching experience or are feeling at all insecure about establishing your authority, you will probably want to keep the rule making in your court. Giving up control of the rules may sound positive and democratic on the surface, but you may find yourself giving up control of your classroom, which is not a good idea, even with intelligent or mature students. Somebody has to be the boss, and that's your job. Of course, it doesn't hurt to consider your students' comments and opinions. Listening to their ideas is a good way to avoid future misbehavior or mutiny.

If you have a well-behaved, cooperative group, you might reward students' good behavior by giving them a fun practice exam on your rules. I make handwritten overlays and use the overhead projector or create PowerPoint slides to ask questions such as these:

1. If you arrive to class tardy, you should

    a. Make lots of noise so everybody notices you

    b. Gasp and pretend that you just ran five miles to school

    c. Slap all your pals on the back as you pass by

    d. Take your seat quietly and get to work

2. What materials should you bring to class every day?

    a. Candy, gum, CD player, spiders, and assorted bugs

    b. A pen or pencil, paper, and your textbook (if applicable)

    c. Your dog, a pair of smelly socks, and two sodas

    d. A coloring book, a comic book, and a note to Santa

Students enjoy the "exam" and everybody laughs, which is very good because it dissipates tension and creates an immediate feeling of bonding among your students. I have said this before, but it bears repeating: groups that laugh together develop a quick rapport, and they tend to cooperate more quickly and efficiently.

Distribute your individual student folders on the same day that you distribute your welcome handout, so that students have a place to keep the handout and any other paperwork you may distribute. A blank page beckons to many students, so be prepared to answer the question, "Can we decorate our folders?" This is one of those small things that some students will try to enlarge into an argument in order to derail the teacher train.

If you find it difficult to tolerate immature or mildly defiant behavior, then it might be a good idea for you to insist that the students not write anything on the folders except their names. I allow students to decorate their folders with anything except gang insignias, racial slurs, or obscenities. I explain that the primary purpose of the folders is not for them to display their talents and political beliefs. Their primary purpose is to act as an organizational tool: the folders make it easier for me to communicate with students, they save time for everybody, and they help students store important paperwork. If students choose to use the folders to display political statements or provocative drawings, I allow them that privilege, as long as what they draw or write doesn't insult or intimidate others. For example, if they draw a marijuana plant, instead of creating a confrontation as they expect me to do, I say, "Oh, you like plants. Maybe you'll decide to study botany in college." Then I quickly pass on by so that they aren't sure whether I am stupid or just kidding. Either way, they get the message that I am the one who chooses the battles in my classroom and that I will not permit them to draw me into a petty argument that was designed to disrupt my teaching. (If a student persists in provoking me, we step outside or into a corner of the room for a quick chat; if necessary, I schedule a private after-school conference, at my convenience.)

## DELEGATE SOME AUTHORITY

Teachers tend to be nurturing souls. We like to help other people. But we also like to be in control, and many of us find it difficult to delegate any of our authority. Sharing your authority can reap huge dividends, however. By assigning jobs to students, you can conserve your precious time and energy for more important tasks. Student jobs also boost tender young egos, teach children how to handle responsibility, and encourage students to cooperate with you and each other. Some elementary teachers assign every student a specific task, with an important title to accompany the job: President of Pencil Sharpening, Official Attendance Taker, Certified Paper Collectors, Guest Greeter, and so on. High school teachers often take on student clerks or assistants who earn credits for providing administrative support during a particular class period each day. Even when a school doesn't have a formal clerking program, I often request that the office approve such arrangements; my requests have never been denied.

In my classes I always assign a student helper to take attendance, but since attendance records are legal documents, I always check to make sure the report is accurate (so students can't be pressured by others to record incorrect data). For each class period, I have an attendance monitor and a backup for days that the monitor is absent (here's your chance to recognize the memory skills of one of your students who remembered everybody's names). I also assign a door monitor for each class period to answer the door during class time. Instead of allowing people to walk in and interrupt our lessons, the door monitor greets anybody who knocks and accepts any notes, messages, or paperwork that doesn't require my immediate attention. I have taught at schools where two or three student messengers knocked on the door each hour to deliver notes from parents about after-school pickup times, birthday balloons, informal school surveys, notices of club meetings, and so on. Having a door monitor cuts down on disruptions and sends a message to your students that their work is too important to interrupt for trivial reasons.

The student cleanup crew is one of the most important student posts. I always request volunteers first. If I don't get at least four volunteers, I split the students into teams of four and rotate their assignment. The cleanup crew is responsible for making sure that no debris remains on the floor or desks when the dismissal bell rings. Students occasionally complain about being expected to do what they consider "the janitor's job," but when I explain that the custodial crew's primary responsibility is to create a safe and hygienic environment, not to clean up after slobs, they get the message. And when they are responsible for cleaning up their own or other students' messes, they encourage each other to be neater and more considerate of classroom furnishings and materials.

## DEMONSTRATE THE POWER OF CHOICE

When I was a college student, my psychology professor, Kenneth Brodeur, once gave our class the simple assignment of completing these two phrases with the first thoughts that popped into our heads: "I have to _____" and "I can't _____".

Next he instructed us to cross out the word "have" from the first sentence and replace it with "choose. "Then he instructed us to cross out "can't" and replace it with "don't want to." I objected to the new wording of my sentences, as did everybody else in class. But the professor insisted.

"Let's tell the truth," he said. He strolled to the front of the classroom and wrote on the board, "There are five things you have to do to stay alive: eat, breathe, drink water, sleep, and go to the bathroom. Everything else is optional."

"But there are lots of things we can't do," I argued.

"That's right," Professor Brodeur nodded. "You can't change your ethnic origin or your height, but there are really very few things you cannot accomplish if you are truly motivated and willing to work. When you go around saying, 'I have to' and 'I can't' all the time, you are telling the world you are a victim, and the world will treat you the way you tell it to. If you don't like your life, change it. You have that power. Whether or not you use your power is up to you."

That was the single most powerful lesson I have ever learned. It helped me realize that I could indeed change my life, my behavior, and my attitude. I have used Professor Brodeur's model to motivate my own students. We complete our power-of-choice exercise during the first week of classes. I complete the exercise each time too, because it's one of those lessons that teach you something new each time.

If you decide to use this exercise, make sure that your students understand your purpose. Reassure them that it isn't a test, that they don't have to read their answers out loud or share them with anybody else. You won't grade them on what they write; they won't even have to turn in their sentences. It's important for them to know that this exercise is for their benefit, to help them understand themselves better and to make them stronger people. (Of course, it will help you to teach them, but some of them may not be interested in helping you, so why mention it?)

Here are some typical starting sentences from students: "I have to do my homework, and I can't get an A in math." "I have to clean my room, and I can't wear my hat in school." "I have to go to school, and I can't cut classes." "I always have to babysit, and I can't lose weight."

Ask for volunteers to discuss their sentences with you, and allow the other students to consider theirs silently. Be prepared: some students will find this exercise very distressing, and for some it will take time and repetition. When you tell your students that they don't *want* to earn As and that they *choose* not to wear hats or cut classes, they will most certainly argue with you. And in some cases they may be right. If they give examples of goals that have legitimate limitations or physical impossibilities (a girl with severe astigmatism probably cannot become a commercial jet pilot, although some students may argue that it is possible; and a boy cannot have a baby, at least not yet). Accept and acknowledge any valid answers. But the majority of *have to* and *can't* sentences will not hold up to honest inspection.

I discourage the use of written instructions for this exercise because some people read an entire worksheet before they begin writing. If students know you are going to ask them to change words, the exercise won't be helpful.

Once your students understand and accept the truth of this lesson, they will have to admit that when they misbehave or fail in your class, it is because they choose to misbehave or fail. They don't *have* to let somebody copy their homework. They don't *have* to respond to another student's insult by launching an insult in return. They don't *have* to come to your class if they don't want to learn—they simply may choose to come because they don't like the alternative. And if they have a problem learning required material, they can ask you for help or arrange for a tutor or spend more time on homework. Unless they have a true learning disability, students have no valid reason for not passing your class, graduating from school, finding a decent occupation, learning to make friends, developing useful skills, and being successful people.

## REVIEW MASLOW'S HIERARCHY

Young people are more interested in themselves and in each other than in any other topic. They are also most confused about themselves, and that confusion often leads to problems in school. Perhaps you are thinking, "Oh, right. I need one more thing to add to my already overcrowded curriculum. Between school holidays, pep rallies, assemblies, and administrative busywork, I don't have time to cover my textbooks, much less try to teach psychology." If you are thinking along these lines, you are absolutely right. Teaching psychology isn't your job, so you may decide to skip this section. But if you have problem students who sometimes make you want to change professions, then you might consider discussing Abraham Maslow's theory with your classes. It will take only a few minutes, and it may save you many hours or months of aggravation.

At some time during your teaching training, you probably had a survey course, maybe two, in child or adolescent psychology. You've probably read at least one interpretation of Maslow's Hierarchy of Needs. I first discussed this idea with a class of students who had serious problems resisting the lure of gangs, drugs, shoplifting, and sex. One day we began talking about why people do what they do, and I told them that during my college studies in psychology, I learned that we often do things because we need to belong to something. No matter how many times we promise ourselves that we will be independent and stand our ground, we end up giving in and doing things we regret. Then we hate ourselves.

"That's me! That's me!" One of my students waved her hand in the air. "I'm always going shopping with my sister and her friends, and they always steal stuff from stores and I say I'm not going to do it. But then I go right ahead and do it again, and I always wish I didn't. I swear I won't go with them again, but the next time they ask me, there I go, doing what I said I wasn't going to do. And I feel so bad, especially when I go to church and sit next to my grandma and think about how ashamed she would be of me if she knew."

I assured Tyeisha that she wasn't horrible; she was simply human, because human beings need to belong and be accepted by a group of people. That's why we join clubs and social organizations, including gangs.

"How many of you have a family, people who love you, but you still feel like you don't really belong?" I asked my class. More than half the students raised their hands. "You aren't the Lone Ranger," I told them. "Lots of people feel left out, even in their own families. But we need to belong to something. So find something to belong to—a sports team, a hobby club, a karate studio, a church, a garage band, a choir, a group of sidewalk singers, a volunteer organization, an actors' group, even just a group of two or three kids that you eat lunch with or ride the bus with or walk to school with every day."

I explained that people who feel part of something are less inclined to join negative groups such as gangs, vandals, and shoplifters. My students were so attentive that I decided to introduce them to Maslow's theory. I outlined his theory briefly, and we discussed it. That night I made a chart for them to take home and keep where they could check it periodically to remind themselves to keep growing and moving up the ladder of happiness and self-fulfillment. Many students reported that knowing about human needs helped them make better choices.

Depending on students' age and maturity, I may use more or less sophisticated vocabulary and more complicated examples than those shown in Exhibit 5.1, but I've never had a group who didn't understand this theory. In fact, the "worst" classes were most interested in discussing these ideas.

---

### Exhibit 5.1.
### Maslow's Hierarchy of Needs.

*Level 1: Physical.* You need food, water, and sleep every day. If you're starving, you don't care whether you're wearing cool shoes—you care about finding something to eat. Until these level-one needs are met, you will spend your time and energy taking care of them. If you don't have these basic things, ask for help. Don't be embarrassed. Teachers can refer you to people who will help.

*Level 2: Safety.* Once your basic physical needs are met, you start to think about things such as keeping warm, avoiding harm, and staying healthy.

*Level 3: Social.* People—and lots of animals, like wolves—need to belong to a group and feel loved. You can have a family and still feel unloved. Sometimes this is why we hang around with people we don't really like or do things we know are wrong. Instead of doing these things, try finding something to belong to: a team, a club, maybe just a couple of kids you eat lunch with every day. Find somebody who likes you just the way you are. It doesn't have to be somebody your age—somebody older or younger will do just fine.

*Level 4: Ego.* Once we feel like we belong, we start to look for ways to increase our self-respect, because we all need to feel important and appreciated. We want other people to respect us, too.

*Level 5: Self-Fulfillment.* You have food, shelter, people who love you, and self-respect—now you're cooking! You know who you are and you want to become your best self. You are strong enough to walk away from a fight, but you stand up for your principles. You nurture your talents and learn just for the fun of learning something new. You follow your dreams!

---

## INTRODUCE METACOGNITION

One day a high school junior challenged a classroom assignment. He wanted to know the point of doing the work. I asked him what he thought the point might be. He said, "To waste our time and give you something to grade." I was tempted to hush him up, but decided to give him such a complete explanation that he'd never ask such a question again. As it turned out, the explanation blossomed into such a lively discussion of Bloom's taxonomy that everybody in class sat up and paid attention. The next day I presented the same lesson to my other classes, which all responded positively.

When I write "Bloom's Taxonomy of Cognitive Domains" on the board, I always hear whispers and a few groans. They don't know what a taxonomy is, but it sounds like taxes and nobody likes those.

I ask my students to try to figure out the meaning of the phrase. Usually they recognize the word *domain* as a kind of kingdom, but *taxonomy* stumps them. I grab a thick dictionary from the shelf and announce that I am going to "look it up in my handy-dandy pocket dictionary." Freshmen usually giggle; older students roll their eyes and make disgusted tsking sounds when I grab my dictionary. I ignore their ridicule.

Somebody usually says, "That's not a pocket dictionary."

I wink and say, "You gotta have big pockets."

I don't do those things just to be a clown but to model the behavior I want my students to practice. It works. Before long, students grab their handy-dandy pocket dictionaries to look up words they don't know during class.

After we define the terms, I tell the students that I'm going to share with them a lesson that teachers learn in college, but don't usually pass on to their students. I tell them I think they should know why we ask them to do the things we ask them to do. So we're going to try some *metacognition*—thinking about thinking. I explain the different levels of thinking, giving one or two examples. I ask them to think of additional examples from different academic subjects for each thinking level, and I distribute a handout on Bloom's taxonomy (see Exhibit 5.2).

Then we discuss the many ways we use critical thinking skills in daily life. My students are amazed to see that all the "boring, useless stuff" they are learning in school—even analyzing Shakespearean sonnets—actually will help them when they begin their "real" lives.

## Exhibit 5.2.
## Bloom's Taxonomy of Cognitive Domains.

**School Applications**

*Recall.* Remember information: recite your ABCs, identify different colors, list the fifty states, name all the planets.

*Comprehend.* Understand things: know that words are made up of letters, understand that subtraction means to take away, understand that the fifty states make up our country, know that skating requires balance, and know that mixing red and blue paints will give you purple.

*Apply.* Use things you understand: spell words correctly, add or subtract numbers, write a sentence, draw a picture of the solar system, pass a football, perform a skateboard stunt, or select the correct paints to mix a specific color.

*Analyze.* Compare and contrast information or ideas: compare two different characters in a story, identify the parts of an engine, find the misspelled words in a sentence, or state the differences and similarities between the human rights policies of three different countries.

*Evaluate.* Make judgments based on knowledge: conduct three science experiments and decide which one gave the best result, choose the most convincing of three different arguments on the same topic, state your opinion about why a certain book is worth reading or not, choose the best solution to a problem from three possible choices, or decide whether a country's nuclear arms policy is good or bad for the rest of the world.

*Synthesize.* Use knowledge and skills to create something of your own: write a story or poem, design and build a model, create a math problem, draw a picture to illustrate a scene from a play, form a theory about why something happens, or make up your own test for a class at school.

**Using Bloom's Taxonomy in Your Own Life**

*Recall.* Remember all the words to a song or all the items on your grocery list, recite the stats of a sports team, or name the parts of an engine or stereo system.

> *Comprehend.* Understand the difference between a receiver and an amplifier, know how a gasoline engine or computer works, or realize that some people are more sensitive than others.
>
> *Apply.* Hook up stereo speakers, copy a music CD, change your car's spark plugs, use a recipe to make guacamole, fill out a job application, fix a toaster or a bicycle, or ask a shy person for a date without scaring him or her.
>
> *Analyze.* Compare two different jobs; list the pros and cons of getting married, having sex, having a baby, sending your kids to private or public school, joining a gang, or quitting smoking.
>
> *Evaluate.* Decide whether your present job offers the kind of future you want, listen to all the candidates and choose the one who will get your vote, discuss with your partner various options for disciplining children, or determine whether you contribute your fair share to doing household chores.
>
> *Synthesize.* Make a plan for your life and put it into action, start your own business, write a song, build a doghouse, create your own secret barbecue sauce recipe, or design and implement a budget based on your income.

The day after we discuss levels of critical thinking, I bring in items from newspapers for my students to analyze. We read an editorial commentary, a movie review, letters to the editor, and a review of a music album. I ask the students to see how much they can tell about the writers from reading their work and whether they accept those writers' opinions. We look at all the ads in a particular magazine, and the students decide what kind of people are the target audience of that magazine, what political point of view the publisher is likely to hold, and what kind of people wrote the articles. This kind of analytical, critical thinking comes naturally to some students, but will be a new and exciting introduction to some students' own brain power.

Incidentally, after I teach my students to recognize higher-level thinking skills, they start looking out for assignments that push them to the highest levels.

Bloom's taxonomy has, of course, been updated, and some versions use different terms—*create* instead of *synthesize*, for example, and *understand* in place of *comprehend.* Some teachers, myself included, prefer the original words because we think they more accurately describe the actions. I don't think the specific terms are so important as comprehending and applying this information in our lesson planning.

One final note on this topic: Please don't assume that your students aren't smart or mature enough to grasp these concepts. I have discussed them with very low-performing students, disenchanted teenagers, and adults who don't speak English well, and they all understand at least the basic ideas. And they appreciate being treated as intelligent, capable people.

## SHOW YOUR GRATITUDE

Thank your students every single day for coming to class and cooperating with you. They won't get tired of hearing how wonderful they are. If we expect young people to behave well and to continue doing so, we need to acknowledge the good behavior. And we need to take every opportunity to shake their hands, pat them on the back, and encourage them to continue demonstrating their growing maturity and self-control. Like it or not, the children we teach are going to grow up to be just like us. They will treat other people the way adults have treated them. Since most children spend more time around teachers than they do with their parents and families, we teachers really do play a significant role in shaping their values and behavior. So we have an obligation to teach our students, by our own example, to be articulate, ethical, compassionate, and honorable people.

## THE HARD PART IS OVER—WE HOPE

Not bad—by the end of the first week of school, you know the names of all your students, they know your rules and expectations, you have a good idea of what you have to work with, students understand that you hold them personally responsible for their actions, and they know what they will have to do to pass your class. Students know some of your procedures, and you are prepared to remind them if they forget. You have kept them so engaged and occupied that they have forgotten to misbehave—or they have learned that cooperating is much more enjoyable than disrupting. With a little luck, they also understand themselves a little better and have at least a basic understanding of the different levels of thinking and how they will need to develop the highest-level thinking skills. So your second week should be easier than your first, and your third should be easier than your second. And so on. At least, that's the general idea.

Now you can create lesson plans that suit your classes, but don't get too specific just yet. If you plan your teaching days down to the minute, the administrative tasks and unavoidable interruptions (inoculations, club photos, field trips, career counseling, college days, armed forces information day, and so on) will drive you crazy, and driving you crazy is your students' job. You wouldn't want to spoil their fun.

## DISCUSSION POINTS

1. Should you smile before Christmas—or not? What is your opinion on this topic?

2. Share some good first-day activities you have observed or heard about.

3. Should teachers force shy students to stand up and speak in front of the class?

4. Design three nonthreatening introductory activities for students of various ages.

5. What are some specific things teachers can do to assess students' prior knowledge?

6. Create a one-page welcome handout for students in a specific grade level.

# Discipline Is Not
# a Dirty Word

If you mention the word *discipline* to most children, they immediately think of punishment, because they have been taught only one facet of that multidimensional word. In the military services, however, discipline has a more positive connotation, because military personnel understand that discipline allows them to function as an efficient team. They know that discipline will help them develop self-control and strength of character.

Classroom teachers can use the principles of military discipline to teach their students how to develop self-discipline and respect for others. Of course, I'm not suggesting that you conduct your classes like a military boot camp, ordering kids to hit the deck and give you fifty push-ups when they step out of line, but I do believe that children need and want strong adult guidance and leadership. The world can be a scary place for children, and they want adults to establish boundaries for behavior and set limits for them, so that they can relax and learn without having to be responsible for more than they can handle.

Adults don't want to live in a chaotic world either. We want reasonable laws that allow us the maximum amount of freedom and the minimum amount of danger. Children are no different from us. In spite of the books and newspaper articles and TV programs that tell us that today's children are apathetic, learning impaired, developmentally delayed, unwilling or unable to pay attention, impossible to discipline or teach, I don't believe those things for a minute because I have taught too many of those "unteachable" children. Children are naturally curious and eager to learn, but when they go to school unfortunately their natural curiosity and enthusiasm are replaced by fears: that they will fail their classes, they will be unpopular and lonely, they will be assaulted by bullies, they won't be able to get good jobs even if they go to college, their parents will get divorced like "everybody else's," or they will die from AIDS or a random drive-by shooting or a drug-crazed mugger on the streets outside their school.

We can't address all of children's fears, but if we can create an oasis of calm and order in our classrooms where students feel safe and protected, where they know what we expect of them and know that we will not permit other students to hurt or torment them, their curiosity and enthusiasm for learning will resurface and they will apply themselves to the lessons we offer. Positive discipline is the key to creating that classroom oasis.

## DEFINE YOUR PHILOSOPHY

Perhaps you have observed those "lucky" teachers who don't seem to have discipline problems. Luck does play a part, but preparation has a lot more to do with classroom management. You can prevent most discipline problems if you lay the groundwork. I like to think of classroom rules as scaffolding for children. Our rules provide support and keep children from falling and seriously injuring themselves. As children grow older, we can relax or remove the rules one at a time until the children stand alone, making their own decisions, taking as much risk as their confidence and abilities allow. If we make reasonable rules, enforce them fairly, and adjust them to meet children's changing needs, we teach children that, instead of restrictions designed to spoil all their fun, rules actually can create more freedom for them.

As you design your discipline policy, keep in mind your purpose. What is your goal when you discipline students in your classroom? (Be honest—nobody else will know what you're thinking.) Do you want to punish students for misbehaving? Do you want to scare them or teach them a lesson? Do you want students to accept responsibility for their behavior? Make better choices in the future? Do you just want to get even with them for disrupting your brilliant lesson?

In one of my teacher education courses, I ask teachers to do this brief journal assignment:

1. Quickly, in one or two sentences, articulate your goal when you discipline a student in your classroom. What are you hoping to achieve?

   _____

2. Now imagine that you have just been stopped by a traffic cop who says, "I have pulled you over because

   _____

   *[fill in the blank with your reply from step one].*

   How would you respond to the police officer? Would you be cooperative and grateful for the correction, the warning, or the ticket you just received? Would you be inclined to change your attitude and be more law abiding in the future? Or would you become defensive, argumentative, determined to be sneakier next time, or intent upon going to court to prove the officer wrong?

3. Let's go back to your reply in step one. If you honestly believe you would respond positively to what you originally wrote, you're fine. Otherwise please rephrase or revise your goal so that you would be more receptive if a person in authority said those very words to you.

The goal of this exercise is to come up with a statement in which your words match your intentions. Your goal should be the same in every situation where you discipline a student. You should be able to articulate your goal clearly and repeatedly, so students know what it is. You want your goal to be reasonable and, most important, you want it to be something that a student would agree with and accept in a positive way. For example, if you say, "I am asking you to stay after class because I want you to make better choices," some students would argue, "I think my choices are just fine." If you say, "I am giving you lunch detention because I want you to accept responsibility for your behavior," the student may argue, "But it wasn't my fault. Jimmy hit me and I told him to leave me alone and then you yelled at me for talking."

On the other hand, if you say, "I want you to know that you are responsible for the way you act, and you can change it any time you want to," a student can't very well say, "No I can't." Or if you say, "I am asking you to change your seat right now because I am trying to help you be a successful student," or "I would like you to stay after school and chat with me because I want you to pass my class," very few students will argue with you. Even if they say, "I don't want to be successful," it won't be true. Nobody wants to be a failure—unless failing will somehow achieve a goal, such as upsetting their parents. But for the most part, students want to succeed.

You don't have to be able to articulate your discipline goals perfectly right now. But it is important to spend some time thinking about the possibilities, because once you start teaching you may find yourself so busy implementing your discipline plan that you won't have time to think about refining or changing it. It can be very difficult to think quickly and effectively on your feet when trouble is brewing or boiling away in your classroom.

## WHAT GOES AROUND DOES COME AROUND

Punitive discipline techniques are designed to punish, embarrass, frighten, or pay back a student for some transgression. Punitive methods may temporarily change student behavior, but they do not encourage students to take responsibility for their actions or motivate them to cooperate with adults. Purely punitive disciplinary methods often result in a cycle of misbehavior and punishment that escalates, causing more classroom disruptions and declining grades. Look at the high number of high school students who are repeatedly sent to detention or suspended from school. Many of these students end up in dropout prevention programs because they miss too many critical classroom lessons. They blame their teachers or parents or schools for their problems, and become less and less motivated to achieve with each punishment.

Positive discipline techniques, on the other hand, are designed to make students think about their behavior, accept responsibility for their actions, make amends when possible, understand the effects of their behavior on others, solve problems, and learn how to make better choices. Instead of relying on humiliation or threats, positive discipline provides an opportunity for students to discuss the reasons for their behavior and helps them learn new ways to behave. Instead of blaming teachers or parents for their own misbehavior, students realize that they can control their behavior and affect the way they are treated in school and in the world.

We tend to teach the way we were taught, unless we make a conscious effort to do otherwise. If you can recall your own childhood, perhaps you will remember that standing in the corner or sitting in detention did not inspire you to turn over a new leaf but rather to be sneakier in the future—and perhaps you spent the time plotting revenge against the teacher who doled out the punishment. Perhaps you can also recall a teacher who insisted that you accept responsibility for your own behavior and who rewarded your sincere efforts with a handshake, a pat on the back, a hug, a complimentary note in the margin of a paper, or a phone call to your parents. Or perhaps you made a serious error and received serious punishment and stern lectures that actually caused you to change your attitude.

If you use humiliation as a tool for embarrassing students, don't be surprised if they follow your example and try to humiliate each other. In my opinion, humiliation is not only unprofessional, unethical, and unfair; I believe it is psychologically abusive to use humiliation as a method of controlling children. Perhaps you can't remember how you felt as a child when an adult intentionally embarrassed you. Or perhaps you are one of the fortunate few who were never subjected to humiliation. You may be better able to empathize with your students if you imagine yourself in the following scenario:

Your principal has forwarded an important fifty-page report to all teachers. You find a copy in your mailbox on Friday with a note from the secretary saying that the principal expects all teachers to read the report before the staff meeting on Monday. You put the report in your bag and take it home, but between chaperoning your son's birthday party, doing the laundry, driving your daughter to a soccer match, visiting your mother in the hospital, and trying to squeeze in a few minutes for your spouse, you don't get a chance to read the report. You do glance through it, though.

At the staff meeting on Monday morning, the principal asks how many people read the report. You raise your hand because, technically, you did read a bit of it. Imagine that the principal then looks directly at you and asks you to stand.

She says, "Please summarize the main points from the report." Clearly, she thinks you are lying. She senses that you haven't read the report, and she is going to make you do one of two things: try to fake your way through this experience or admit in public that you lied when you said that you had read the report. You now have the choice of discussing details of your home life in front of your peers or looking like a liar. The principal's only point in asking you to summarize the report is to embarrass and humiliate you. Perhaps she believes this tactic will make you want to read her next report in order to avoid being embarrassed, but it's far more likely that you will skip the next staff meeting or call in sick that day.

There are better ways to supervise and motivate people than using humiliation and punishment for the sake of punishment—and far better ways to teach.

## COWBOY PHILOSOPHY

One year, at the Southwestern New Mexico State Fair, I had the unforgettable experience of watching Craig Cameron, "the cowboy professor," in action. I was struck by the similarities between breaking wild horses and taming wild students. Cameron worked with two wild horses that afternoon—one that had never been ridden at all and one that had resisted being forcibly saddle broken. In both instances Cameron was able to mount and ride the horses within an hour, without raising his voice or using any force whatsoever. As I watched Cameron tame those horses and listened to him explain his actions, I realized that I was in the presence of a master teacher. I took copious notes.

"Many people set out to break the spirit of a horse," Cameron told the crowd that had gathered outside the round pen where he worked the horses. "The last thing I want to do is break down the spirit of any horse: I'm out to build it up so that I can utilize it. I want to relate to the horse on his own level and on his time schedule. If you want a horse to have a good attitude, you can't force things on him. You have to give him time to decipher what it is you want him to do."

As he spoke, Cameron picked up a saddle blanket and took a step toward the horse he was breaking. The horse took one look at the blanket and started running in the opposite direction (just as our students try to escape from difficult lessons). Instead of chasing the horse or trying to corner it so that he could place the blanket on its back, Cameron stood still and waited until the horse stopped running and, overcome by curiosity, approached the unfamiliar blanket to investigate. He allowed the horse to sniff and nibble the blanket, then he brushed it gently over the horse's legs and belly before placing it on the horse's back. Immediately the horse bucked the blanket off and ran away. Cameron picked up the blanket and waited until the horse returned to inspect it again. Satisfied that it posed no danger, the horse finally stood still and accepted the blanket. Cameron could have saved time by hobbling the horse and tying the blanket to its back, but he would have faced the same struggle every time he wanted to saddle the horse.

"People bring me all sorts of 'problem' horses," Cameron said, as he placed a saddle on top of the blanket and let the horse run until it realized that the saddle wasn't going to hurt it.

"Usually the problem is the way the horse was taught in the beginning," Cameron explained. "Somebody tried to force a lesson on him, or he was punished harshly for not doing right. If he doesn't do the right thing, he knows you're going to jerk harder or spur harder or get a bigger mouth bit. So now he's nervous, scared, and defensive. He is just flat-out turned off to learning."

Again, the horse circled the pen several times, then slowed down and walked to Cameron and allowed him to tighten the cinch on the saddle.

Students, like horses, resist having their spirits broken or being forced into performing uncomfortable or unfamiliar actions. If we give them time to get used to us and time to understand what we want from them, they are much more apt to cooperate. We can beat, scare, or bore children with endless repetitions when they don't cooperate. Children, like horses, may cooperate temporarily out of fear, pain, or exhaustion, but unless we gain their trust we're going to have to fight the same battles over and over again.

One comment that Cameron made during his training session struck me as particularly applicable to classroom teachers who must deal with students who resist accepting authority. "Horses naturally understand a pecking order," Cameron explained. "Your horse can accept the fact that you are the leader of the herd and he is the follower. That doesn't mean that a horse won't test you from time to time. He's going to test you. But you can establish that you are the leader, number one in the pecking order, without causing your horse pain or fear. The way you do that is to control your horse's mind instead of his body."

If you back a student against the wall and demand respect or obedience, you are not apt to receive either one. Children's natural instinct is to escape when they feel frightened or threatened, or to fight if escape is impossible. If you make clear from the start that you are the leader in your classroom and that your leadership is necessary in order for you to teach and for your students to learn, you allow students to accept your authority without feeling any loss of dignity. Instead of demanding cooperation, effective teachers make it a choice.

After seeing him work, I bought Cameron's videos, *Gentle Horse-Breaking and Training,* and *Dark into Light,* to watch at home. The longer I watched, the more I became convinced that teacher-training programs should assign his videos as required curriculum. If you'd like to read about Craig Cameron, you can find archived articles about him online or in equestrian magazines such as *Western Horseman* or the *Quarter Horse Journal.* For information about his videos and workshops, visit www.craigcameron.com or call toll-free 800-274-0077.

## RULES VERSUS PROCEDURES

Rules and procedures are two very different things. Rules are rigid and inflexible; procedures can be adapted as needed. Rules are not made to be broken. Like laws, rules make no allowance for individual differences or circumstances. If you establish a list of rigid rules for your classroom, you may regret it later. For example, you may make a rule that you will not accept late work or that one missing homework assignment will preclude a student from earning an A in your class. What if a student cannot complete an assignment because of a true emergency, such as a serious illness, accident, or death in the family? You have two choices: stick to your rule or bend it. Either option has disadvantages.

If you adamantly stick to your rule, innocent students will suffer and you may earn a reputation as a harsh and heartless person. If you bend your rules for one student, other students will quickly line up to ask for special consideration because they too have emergencies (some of which may seem trivial to you but very important to young people). No matter where you draw the line, some students will feel that you have wronged them, that you play favorites. That's why I suggest making rules only about things that you will *never* tolerate, things that cannot happen by accident—hitting, kicking, biting, racial insults, or sexual harassment.

Procedures, on the other hand, don't legislate behavior; they provide guidelines for completing specific activities, such as using the restroom, completing makeup work, requesting permission to miss class, requesting admittance to your class when tardy. Establishing procedures for your classroom provides clear guidelines for student behavior while also allowing you more options. If special circumstances arise, you will be able to make changes without causing a lot of complaints or confusion. You will be able to make decisions based on individual circumstances. If students complain that you treat them differently from each other, respond by pointing out that you treat them individually because they are individuals. "One size fits all" does not apply to education, because each student has unique talents, abilities, goals, challenges, and circumstances.

One teacher reported that the first time a student complains about being treated differently from another student, she says, "Sweetheart, you *are* different from each other, and I am not going to treat you all the same. Same doesn't necessarily equal fair. I will always be fair. And you can take that to the bank."

You can reduce the amount of disorder in your classroom if, early on, you establish a procedure for distributing and collecting papers, grading papers in class, turning in homework, collecting makeup work, dismissing class, issuing hall and library passes, allowing visits to other teachers, and so on. Instead of reviewing all your procedures during the first few days of class when students are often too excited or overwhelmed to remember them, cover each procedure as it arises. Remember that many students learn by seeing or doing, so don't just talk. Show them what you want them to do, then practice each procedure until your students know the routine, especially with young children. You may opt to give students a copy of your procedures in writing. You may feel like you are wasting time at first if you spend five minutes at the end of each class for two weeks discussing the procedure for leaving the room after the dismissal bell, but you will save yourself a lot of time and heartache later. Kids know that if they can get you to ignore their behavior once or twice, they can ignore your procedure.

Don't create procedures unless you think they are important, and if you make them make sure you demonstrate and follow them. Otherwise you weaken your authority and lose students' respect.


## RULES FOR CREATING RULES

You may have to experiment to find the best discipline methods to fit your unique personality and your students, but you are much more likely to succeed if you focus on these three key concepts as you create your classroom rules:

- Limit the number of rules.
- State rules positively.
- Consider the consequences.

The more rules you create, the more time you must spend enforcing them, the more complicated your list of consequences, and the more likely students are to misbehave out of defiance. Long lists of rules box in everyone, stifling creativity and hindering your efforts to develop a strong rapport and an environment of mutual respect. My preference, after testing many methods, is to create one over-arching rule for my classroom: Respect yourself and everybody in this room.

This one simple rule covers any situation that may occur. For example, it is not respectful to chomp loudly on gum, stick chewed gum or candy on desks or books, hit or insult people, carve obscene words into a desktop, arrive late to class, throw litter on the floor, interrupt other students who are trying to work, disrupt the teacher's efforts to teach, and so on.

State your rules positively whenever possible. Remember the old joke that instructs, "Don't think of an elephant"? The same idea applies to rules. Don't give kids more ideas than they already have. Negatively stated rules—such as no gum chewing, no shouting, or no running with scissors—provide a list of suggested misbehaviors for students who crave attention. Negative rules also provide a challenge for students who want to distract you from teaching a difficult lesson or simply want to push your buttons. And, finally, negative rules can inspire further negative behaviors. For example, if you make a rule that no gum chewing is permitted in your classroom, then some students are going to forget they have gum in their mouths or may risk breaking your rule because they really like gum. When those students believe they are in danger of getting caught breaking your no-gum rule, they may hide their sticky wads under their desks, on your bookshelves, or in their textbooks. If, on the other hand, you have a positive rule in your classroom, "Dispose of all gum properly," then you leave it up to the students to choose their own behavior and they are far more likely to cooperate.

Sometimes you won't be able to state a rule positively. Or you may have to add an addendum using negative words in order to avoid creating a mouthful of gobbledygook. My own one-rule policy, for example, includes a list of prohibitions for those students who require specific information. The addendum specifies no put-downs of other people based on their race, religion, ethnic background, skin color, native language, gender, sexual preference, intelligence, body shape, or body size. But because I state the main rule positively, the overall rule doesn't have a negative connotation and students don't feel compelled to break the rule just to show that they can.

Consider the consequences of your rules on everybody, including you. Doling out demerits, for example, requires that you keep records of student offenses and spend time assigning punishments and consequences. Assigning lunch or after-school detention may seem like a good idea, but it punishes you as well as the student, because you have to spend your time supervising your detainees unless you want their detention time to become a social hour. Making students write essays or reports is a popular punishment, but using writing as a punitive tool may backfire on everybody—you, the student, and the other teachers at your school—by teaching students to hate writing. Sending students to the principal, another popular tactic, may remove the student from your room, but sends a clear message to students that you feel incapable of handling the situation alone.

## IDENTIFY YOUR BULLIES AND OUTCASTS

Bullies are nothing new. But whereas bullies used to use their fists to blacken an eye, today they are apt to use any number of weapons to cause serious, sometimes even fatal, physical injuries. Many schools have successfully implemented antibullying and character-building programs. But it's still not unusual to encounter a bully or two in any modern classroom. The problem is that sometimes it's difficult to catch bullies in action or even to identify them. Even harder to identify are the instigators who don't do the bullying themselves, but who are experts at manipulating other students into insulting or assaulting each other. At one high school where I taught, students seemed to enjoy setting each other up. One student would confide to another, untruthfully, that a third student had been "talking trash" about her. The second student would then confront or attack the innocent third student who would end up being disciplined, sometimes suspended, along with the second student, despite her protestations of innocence. Nothing happened to the first student, of course, because she was not involved in the confrontation.

One day, by accident, I hit upon a way to identify the bullies and instigators in my classroom. In preparation for assigning students to small groups for discussions and projects, I asked students in every class period to take out a sheet of paper and write their own names at the top. Then I asked them to list the names of three or four students they would like to work with in small groups. As an afterthought, I added, "And if there are one or two people you never want to work with, please list their names. I don't want any details, just names."

When I reviewed the student lists later that night, at home, I realized that in every class, the same names appeared on the "Do not want to work with" lists. I realized that I was looking at the names of my bullies, my instigators, and my outcasts. Of course, I wasn't able to magically fix everything, but knowing who I was dealing with helped me monitor my classes better and significantly reduced friction among students. I tried to find adult mentors for the bullies. I kept an eye on the instigators and intervened when I suspected they were stirring things up. And I did my best to befriend the outcasts and help them develop social skills and self-confidence.

A quick Internet search for "antibullying" will bring up hundreds of Web sites with resources for teachers and parents. I wish there were as much help available for teachers who want to help the outcasts in their classrooms. Aside from the fact that some students suffer humiliation and cruelty every single day of their lives for years at school, ignoring students who are bullied can be dangerous. The bullies are not the ones who bring weapons into schools: it's the outcasts who can no longer tolerate being tormented by their peers.

Teachers are the first line of defense. We may not be able to eliminate bullying, but we certainly can reduce it by refusing to tolerate verbal abuse of any kind in our classrooms—and by making sure that we don't lapse into bullying ourselves.

## CHARACTERISTICS OF SUCCESSFUL DISCIPLINE POLICIES

You can find any number of training courses, books, workshops, and journal articles that offer keys to effective classroom management. Much of that advice may be contradictory and confusing. Experts disagree vehemently about whether rewards have positive or negative effects on long-term behavior and motivation, for example. Some experts insist that assigning consequences is the key to molding behavior; others believe that consequences equal punishment and that we should view misbehavior as a problem for which we must brainstorm solutions. Every classroom management program offers examples and testimonials to its effectiveness, and so many different approaches exist that you may be tempted to throw up your hands and wing it or just pick a policy and hope it works. I suggest that you select or create a program that incorporates the following common characteristics of effective, successful discipline techniques:

- Consider cultural differences.
- Model the behavior you expect from students.
- Separate the child from the behavior.
- Make the student accept responsibility.
- Allow the student to back down gracefully.

- Seek solutions instead of simply assigning consequences.
- Assign consequences that address specific behaviors.
- Clearly state your expectations for future behavior.
- Provide positive feedback when behavior improves.
- Wipe the student's slate clean.
- Identify the reason for repeated misbehavior.
- Focus on rewarding good behavior.
- Send students to the principal as a last resort.

## Consider Cultural Differences

In today's multi-ethnic society, it is essential that teachers consider cultural customs and differences before assuming a student's behavior is rude, defiant, or disruptive.

In my own experience, for example, I have had students from countries where children are taught to avoid making eye contact with adults as a show of respect. In other cultures, students were discouraged from asking questions because to do so might imply that the teacher had made a mistake. And one boy surprised me by explaining that in his country, touching a person on their head was the ultimate insult—something I never would have guessed.

Recently, one of my online students posted a thought-provoking comment on the class discussion board. He wrote: "I actually had an experience a few years ago with a Korean exchange student who would smile when disciplined in class. I was initially enraged until it was explained to me that that was his method of showing shame under chastisement. It was this newfound understanding that opened my eyes to individualization of discipline and the concept of respecting the individual student. I now make more of an effort to understand the context from which every single one of my students are emerging before I wade into classroom discipline."

## Model the Behavior You Expect from Students

No matter how brilliant your plan, it won't work if you don't set the example. You cannot mandate respect, for example. If you want students to treat each other with respect, you must show them how it's done (and in some cases, show them and show them and show them, because this will be a new experience for some of them). If you want students to use a logical approach to solving problems, you must demonstrate the techniques for them by modeling the behavior when you encounter problems during the school day and explaining how you work through each step.

Yes, modeling behaviors takes time, but spending that time at the start of the school year will save you hours of time later: your students will cooperate with you, and you won't have to waste so much time on discipline.

*Note:* Do not let other adult staff members disrespect your students. Often adults will insist that they are "just kidding" when they insult or intentionally embarrass students, but because teachers hold positions of power, students may be afraid to protest or admit that the teasing is offensive or insulting. Even when students do protest, some adults persist. Of course, you can't dictate adults' behavior, and it's hard to criticize them without stepping on their toes in front of students. You can't very well say, "Please stop abusing your authority," but you can call the adult aside and say, "Please help me out here. We have had a problem with teasing in my classroom, so we don't engage in that behavior at all. Sometimes students don't understand when teasing crosses the line, so we just don't do it. It's hard for me to enforce that rule when they see adults teasing students." Even if the adult isn't so receptive as you had hoped, pretend that he or she agrees with you. Smile and say, "Thanks for helping me out."

(I know, I know. You want to keep your job. You don't want to make enemies. But if you see adults bullying children and you say nothing, you are giving your tacit consent. Ignoring bullying is the same as ignoring sexist or racist jokes or ignoring physical child abuse. It's just not acceptable.)

## Separate the Child from the Behavior

Sometimes a child will intentionally misbehave just to irritate a teacher, but most misbehavior is a result of immaturity, impatience, frustration, or the desire to fulfill some imagined or real need. Children act like children because they are children (and many teens are still children); as imperfect human beings, students are prone to making mistakes. Don't take your students' behavior personally unless it is clearly a personal attack on you—and even then you may simply represent authority. When we take children's behavior personally, we limit our ability to assess a situation objectively and choose the best response, but if we can separate the child from the behavior, we can follow the excellent advice, "Hate the behavior, love the child." This attitude helps us focus on solving problems and helping students learn to make better choices, instead of simply punishing the student or assigning meaningless consequences.

## Make Students Accept Responsibility

When we assign consequences and dictate behavior, we take control of and responsibility for a given situation. If we place the responsibility squarely on the student's shoulders where it belongs, we create a completely different experience. For example, if a student disrupts your class and you immediately reprimand him and assign a consequence, you focus everybody's attention on you, and some students will automatically sympathize with the culprit just because he is in the less powerful position. If you ask the student to stop and think about his behavior and decide whether he wants to continue or make a change, the focus shifts to the student, and he now controls the outcome of the conflict. He cannot blame you for his behavior or for any resulting consequences. Many teachers find that asking students to step outside for a chat, fill out a form describing their unacceptable behavior, or sign a contract agreeing not to repeat specific behaviors are more effective approaches than assigning punishments.

## Allow the Student to Back Down Gracefully

When students have the opportunity to retreat gracefully, many of them will decide to cooperate with you. But when you back them up against the wall, most students will become stubborn and defiant, and many will lash out. This holds true even for very young children, who often have a stronger sense of dignity than many adults give them credit for having. When we allow a student to back down the first time he or she engages in a specific inappropriate behavior, we teach that student and any observers several lessons: we are all responsible for choosing our own behavior; everybody makes mistakes; most mistakes are not permanent; and a good leader exhibits compassion, forgiveness, and respect. Our students imitate our behavior whether or not they like us, so it behooves us to set a high standard and a good example.

When a student acts disrespectfully, you may ask, "Do you believe your present behavior shows self-respect and respect for others?" At this point, the student has the option of behaving differently without losing face. Because it is his or her choice, the student may be more inclined to choose a different behavior and will not feed a need to exact revenge upon you for meting out punishment if you must assign some consequence in order to restore calm to your classroom. When I give students the option of choosing to behave, I don't assign consequences if they do choose to cooperate. Instead, I thank them for making such a mature and responsible choice. Then we go on as if nothing happened.

The first time I tried that technique, the obnoxious student said, "That's it?" I said, "Yep." He said, "That was easy." I said, "Yep." He shrugged and sat down. And, by the way, his behavior improved. It's hard work to hate somebody who truly likes and respects you. And it's really not fun when they refuse to fight.

## Seek Solutions Instead of Merely Assigning Consequences

Sending a tardy student to detention does not address the problem of tardiness and will most likely result in a worse student-teacher relationship and possibly in academic problems. Requiring a student to spend ten minutes helping you clean your classroom would reduce the amount of effort and paperwork involved. Better yet, require the student to use a problem-solving model to brainstorm possible solutions to his problem. Then discuss his solutions and help him choose and implement the best course of action. In addition to addressing the current problem, you'll be teaching that student how to solve future problems.

## Assign Consequences That Address Specific Behaviors

If you do assign consequences, try to select ones that actually address the misbehavior you want to discourage. If a student draws a heart with black marker or scrawls obscenities on her desk, sending her to detention just leaves you with a dirty desk. Making the student clean her desk—or all the desks in your classroom—would be more appropriate. Likewise, sending a disrupter to detention doesn't teach him to be quiet and respectful. Asking him to stand outside your door or stand at the back of the room until he feels able to control his behavior will give him an opportunity to practice self-control; if he makes an effort but fails at first, he may succeed if you provide a few more chances to practice.

## Clearly State Your Expectations for Future Behavior

One year I had a student who repeatedly interrupted my lessons by standing up, loudly clearing his sinus cavities, and walking across the room to spit in the trash can. Because he was a well-behaved student otherwise, I opted to warn him to be more polite instead of assigning punishments. Finally, I called the student aside. He insisted, "But I am being polite!"

I asked, "Do you think walking across the room and spitting in the trash is polite when I am trying to talk to the class?"

"Yeah," he said, earnestly. "I'm not spitting on the floor."

That conversation taught me to be more specific in my instructions to students. My warnings no longer leave any room for misunderstanding: Now, I might say,

"Keep your hands on your own desk." or "Throw things only in appropriate places, such as the gym."

## Provide Positive Feedback When Behavior Improves

Everybody responds to positive feedback, and students are especially responsive. After any incident that results in a private conference, consequences, or punishment, watch for an opportunity to praise the student who misbehaved. When she behaves appropriately, let her know you noticed and that you appreciate the improvement. Youngsters often believe that the teacher no longer likes them after a confrontation, even a minor incident. I frequently remind students that I still like them as people, even if I don't always like their behavior. *Note:* Some students prefer not to have their good behavior recognized publicly in front of peers, but they will not object to a positive phone call to their parents, a quick note, a handshake, or a comment on the margin of a paper.

## Wipe the Student's Slate Clean

In addition to providing positive feedback, make sure your students understand that a mistake is not a permanent condition. Just as we release criminals who have served their time, we must allow students a second chance. Of course, the more serious the offense, the longer it will take for a student to regain your complete trust, but if you make clear that you don't hold any grudges, the student will be much more likely to cooperate in the future. After I invite an unruly student to step outside for a private chat, for example, we shake hands before we re-enter the room. Then I make a point of making eye contact and making a positive comment to that student a few minutes later. The following day, I greet that student when he or she enters the room. I want it to be clear to that student, and to the rest of the class, that we all make mistakes and when we do, we need to address them, learn from them and move forward.

## Identify the Reason for Repeated Misbehavior

If you keep assigning the same consequences for the same misbehavior, nobody is gaining anything from the experience and everybody is losing valuable time. When a problem recurs repeatedly in your classroom, the student is sending a clear signal that he or she needs help in some specific area. Identifying the reason for a behavior may take some time and effort, but the time will be well spent if a casual conversation, a brief nonpunitive conference, an exchange of comments in a journal, a phone call, a confidential chat with close friends, or some similar method can help you figure out why a student is behaving in a certain way. Often students misbehave repeatedly because they want the teacher to send them to talk to a counselor or psychologist or they want you to inquire about their home situation. If you can't communicate with the student, ask around. Most students have a favorite teacher, coach, secretary, bus driver, security guard, school police officer, custodian, or counselor.

## Focus on Rewarding Good Behavior

For some reason, looking for negative behavior seems to be our default setting. And unfortunately, if you look for bad behavior, you will find it. But we can train ourselves to look for good behavior instead. When you focus on rewarding good behavior instead of punishing bad behavior, you create a different dynamic in your classroom. Rewarding or praising students for being considerate people is not the same as bribing them. A bribe is intended to entice somebody to do something for the sole purpose of earning a reward. Of course, we don't want to teach children that they will receive a reward every time they cooperate or work— because they won't. That's not the way the world operates. But they certainly will be rewarded for behaving responsibly and considerately as citizens and workers. We all respond to positive feedback, which may come in the form of verbal praise, high marks on our assignments in school, good performance appraisals on the job, promotions, monetary raises, certificates, employee-of-the-month awards, or other acknowledgment. Sometimes adults say, "We shouldn't reward children." And I ask, "Would you go to work every day if you never got paid?"

## Send Students to the Principal as a Last Resort

A hundred years ago when I was young, being sent to the principal's office was a very big deal. The principal would paddle you, your parents would paddle you, and your siblings would shun you for embarrassing the family. If you send a student to the principal's office today, there is a good chance that the student will refuse to leave your room or that he will leave campus entirely. Even if he cooperates, he may spend an amusing hour trading jokes with other students in a waiting area or sit in a detention room reading comic books, doing word search puzzles, or staring at the walls.

When your wayward student arrives at the principal's office, the result may be very different from what you intended. Principals don't always support their teachers. Most do, but some simply don't. Students don't always care whether they pass your class or graduate. Parents don't always accept reality or the responsibility for raising their children. And in the worst cases, students or their families may raise legal issues—valid or not—to avoid the real issues of personal responsibility.

In addition to the obvious reasons, my primary reason for not sending students to the office is that I don't like the cycle of behavior that usually results. What we hope will happen rarely does: the student doesn't accept responsibility for his or her actions, learn from this mistake, and resolve to cooperate with you in the future. What usually happens is more like this: the student misbehaves; you send the student to the office; the student becomes angry or embarrassed and blames you for causing those feelings; the student also blames you for whatever punishment the principal metes out; the student misses hours or days of valuable lessons in your class and other subjects; the student returns to your class amused or still angry or ashamed or eager for revenge; and you're back to the beginning of the cycle, ready for another round.

With compassion and creativity, you can break this destructive cycle and offer alternative solutions. Again I'd suggest sitting for a moment in your students' seats to change your perspective. Imagine how you would feel if your supervisor at work objected to your behavior and, instead of explaining the objection, discussing the problem, and giving you a chance to change your behavior, the supervisor marched you past your coworkers to the company president's office for a reprimand. That may sound silly, but an office isn't so different from a classroom. You're the company president, and your students are your employees whose job is to learn their lessons and complete their assignments in exchange for credits toward an academic promotion or a diploma. When they make mistakes or become ineffective workers, your task is to correct them quickly and without damaging their dignity any more than is necessary. Of course, just as employers do, you must deal with serious offenses differently from everyday problems such as tardiness, inefficiency, forgetfulness, and general bad attitudes.

## TWELVE STEPS TO BETTER DISCIPLINE

"Theories are great, but I need practical advice," one young teacher told me during a workshop. "Could you tell me exactly what to do and say to my students?" The following sections list my twelve-step response to her question. I have experienced good success using these techniques with a wide array of students, from troublesome teens to overachieving college-bound scholars. These steps are listed in order of power—beginning with the most subtle and least forceful responses from you. After you gain some experience, you may want to add your own variations, but this list is a good starting point. It will give you a solid basis and will provide opportunities for you to practice and evaluate different techniques.

### 1. Ignore the Offender

Often students act out just to gauge the teacher's response. If you are easily upset, flustered, or angered, they will take advantage of your short fuse. On the other hand, if you ignore mild misbehavior, it will often go away. A student may whisper the F-word under her breath, for example, just to see if she can make you blush or yell. If you pointedly ignore the behavior, the student may get the message: *this is my classroom, and I will decide when and how I respond to student behavior.* If she doesn't get the message, you have plenty of other options. Read on.

### 2. Send Nonverbal Messages

We all respond to body language. In fact, most students of human behavior agree that 80 percent of our communications are nonverbal. Take advantage of this powerful tool by using eye contact, changes in your voice and posture, and gestures. Practice in front of a mirror, if necessary, but learn how to use your eyes to communicate a warning. It may be helpful to think of a threat while you practice your warning look. "Stop that right now or you will be very, very sorry," is a good one for starters.

Silence is much more effective than shouting. Trying to shout over rowdy students only makes them louder or more excited—and it makes you look weak. However, if you suddenly lower your voice and slow your speaking pace, students will immediately pick up on it. Imagine that you are biting each word in half. It will convey a silent warning. And if you stop talking in midsentence and look fierce, it's very likely that a student sitting near you will draw in her breath or otherwise communicate her concern through a change in posture. Within seconds, that concern will be communicated to everybody else in the room. You will actually be able to feel the change in the energy. Let that energy percolate for a few seconds. Then continue as though nothing had happened. Most students will get the message.

You can also use movement to alert students that their behavior is approaching a danger zone. Some behavior experts divide the classroom into three zones: red, yellow, and green. When you are across the room from a student, he is in the green zone and free to act out. As you move closer to the student, the zone becomes yellow; caution is advised. (Consider your own response when a police car pulls up along side you on the highway.) When you are near enough to touch a student, she enters the red zone and will usually control her behavior until you move away.

The lesson here is to keep moving. Teachers who rove around their rooms experience far fewer behavior problems because students automatically react to the distance between them and the teacher. If this distance changes at random, students are much more likely to monitor their own behavior.

### 3. Use Humor to Defuse Tension

There is a reason why so many effective public speakers begin with a joke. It changes the entire dynamic of a room. And you may be able to make use of that fact to defuse the tension between you and students. (Also recall the research on persuasion discussed in Chapter Five.)

I discovered by accident just how useful humor can be. I was trying to get my high school juniors to write haiku. One tough boy refused to even try. He didn't respond to coaxing. I knew that warning him was unlikely to inspire creativity, so I gave up. I dropped to my knees and clasped my hands. "I'm an old woman," I said. "Please don't make me beg. It's so unattractive and it hurts my old knees." The boy shook his head and rolled his eyes at his classmates, but he couldn't resist smiling. And after I gave up and walked away, he wrote a haiku.

Another time, two Hispanic gangster wannabes strolled into my classroom wearing sunglasses. I knew they expected me to order them to remove the glasses and that they were prepared to start a confrontation. Instead, I walked behind them and started singing "Lo mucho que te quiero (How Much I Love You)" softly in Spanish: "Nunca hablo a ti con la mentira/ Siempre hablo a ti con la verdad/ Quisiera que olvides el pasado, que vuelvas a mi lado, que tengas compacion." They started laughing, which totally destroyed their tough image. And later on, I looked up and saw that they had both removed their sunglasses.

### 4. Drop a Behavior Card

Because so many students are visual or kinesthetic learners, or because they are simply stubborn, they may not respond to verbal requests. Or they may forget a few seconds after you have reminded them to be quiet or sit down. So create some behavior cards. Use colorful index cards so that you can easily locate and retrieve them.

For young students, write this message:

> Stop and think: How am I acting right now?

For older students, write this message:

> Your present behavior is not acceptable.
> Please be more polite.
> Return this card to me—in person—after class.

The moment a student begins to disrupt your class, walk over and drop a card on his or her desk. Don't say anything. If you are in the midst of talking, keep right on talking. Stay near the student for a few seconds. In most cases the student will stop the current behavior. Leave the card on the desk—it serves as a visual reminder for students who tend to forget. Collect the cards after class if you teach multiple subjects or at the end of an activity with younger children. When you collect the card, thank the student for choosing to stop the inappropriate behavior. (If you drop a card and the student ignores it or throws it on the floor, see the next step.)

### 5. Have a Quick Chat

If nonverbal signals, humor, and behavior cards fail to motivate your student, ask him or her to step outside the room (or to the back of your room, if you have small children or a strict policy that would prohibit having a student stand in the hall temporarily). Don't worry about the other students. They will be interested in seeing what happens, and though they may make a little noise while you are in the hallway, usually they will be quiet when you return.

Ask your student if there is a reason for his or her disruptive, defiant, or disrespectful behavior. If there is and it's reasonable, figure out a way to address it. If the student can't offer a reason, ask the student if you have somehow offended or insulted him or her. If you have, apologize and offer to shake hands. If you haven't, tell the student that it is time to think. Here's the warning speech I make (you may choose to change the wording for younger students, but the gist of the message should be the same):

> You have the right to fail my class. If you truly want to fail, then I would like you to put that desire into writing and sign it so that I can keep it in my file to show you and your parents in the future if you question your grade. If you don't like the activity I have assigned, I'm sorry, but I am the teacher and I chose that assignment because I believe it will teach important information and skills. You don't have to do the assignment. You have the right to sit and quietly vegetate,

but you do not have the right to interrupt my teaching, stop anybody else from learning, or waste everybody's time with obnoxious disruptive behavior.

Ask the student if he or she feels ready to come back to class and cooperate. If so, ask the student to shake hands and give you his or her word of honor that they will not disrupt your teaching or anybody else's learning. (Don't skip this step. Most students take their word of honor very seriously. And if that same student starts to disrupt again, you can often stop that behavior dead in its tracks by quietly reminding the student, "I thought you gave me your word.") Then get back to business. Forget about the incident. And if the student behaves well for the rest of that class period or activity, offer a word of private praise. He may shrug and act as though he doesn't care, especially if he is a teenager, but teens do care. They just hate to admit it.

If your disruptive student opts *not* to rejoin the class, it's time for the next step.

## 6. Give a Time-Out

Just as adults sometimes need some time alone to clear their heads or regain their composure, sometimes students need a break from the pressures of school (or life). If your disruptive student chooses not to rejoin your class the first time you issue the invitation, don't push. Leave the student standing outside your door. Remind her that if she runs off, you will have to refer her to the office as being truant and then the matter is out of your hands. Be firm, but kind. Tell her you are trying to help her be a more successful student who has excellent self-control. Leaving your disruptive student alone gives her time to think about her behavior.

Go quietly back into your room and continue teaching. Thank the other students for waiting and tell them you appreciate their patience and cooperation. (You want them to realize they will receive more attention from you by cooperating than by disrupting.)

Occasionally, when it's convenient and other students are occupied, you can step outside to see whether your disrupter is ready to talk to you. If not, leave her there. If necessary, leave her there until the end of the class period or activity period or school day. Often students will pretend the entire incident never happened. You can then do the same. Once or twice, I have had students who stood outside the classroom for an entire period, disappeared the moment the bell rang, then returned the following day and behaved like little angels. Okay, maybe not angels, but definitely not devils.

## 7. Rewire Your Connection

Sometimes a teacher and student get off on the wrong foot for one reason or another and end up at odds with each other. Once a student confided to me several weeks into the semester that she almost cut my class the first day because, in her words, "You looked at me mean." I insisted that I certainly had not. I had never seen her before she walked into my classroom. "I know," she said, "but I walked by your room and you looked at me mean." I had no recollection of ever seeing her, but apparently she had walked by my room when I was thinking hard about something and frowning in concentration. Fortunately, after she got to know me, she realized that I wasn't mean, but it took weeks for her to warm up to me.

This example illustrates the fact that you may not even know why you and a particular student don't seem to click. But if you find yourself repeatedly having to correct the same student for this or that, before you blame the student step back and assess your relationship. You can't be expected to love every student you meet, and not every student will like you. But you do need to get along, for both your sakes. If you realize that you dislike a particular student or just don't have a good connection, then it's up to you to change it. You have the grade book and the authority. You can afford to be kind and generous. Assign the student to be your classroom aide or helper and get to know each other a bit. Use a private journal to make a written connection. Send a positive note to the student's parents, complimenting him or her on something valid, or ask a counselor to meet with you and the student for an unofficial meeting where you try to learn to communicate better. Tell the student you'd like her to visit your room during lunch hour and surprise her with a tasty treat and a chat. She won't expect the gift or the conversation, and it may break the ice. When you do meet with your student, don't rush. Take your time. Often students will try to wait you out if they know you only have fifteen minutes or a half-hour to spare, because it's uncomfortable to have an honest conversation. Talking makes you vulnerable. Don't expect immediate results, and don't be dismayed if the student shrugs off your attempts to talk and acts like he doesn't care. Trust me, they care. Even teenagers.

Another option, if you enjoy a good rapport with your students, is to discreetly ask students you trust to keep your conversation confidential if they know why your disruptive student misbehaves so frequently. Once a girl confided that a boy in our class had started acting out after his twin brother was killed in an accident. The girl said. "He didn't used to be like that." My awareness of the situation didn't change the boy's behavior, but it certainly changed my perception and my attitude toward him.

## 8. Call the Culprit

One evening after a particularly trying day, I called the father of a student who had tried to drive me crazy by whistling softly at a very high and annoying pitch for ninety minutes in my classroom. Father wasn't home, and junior answered the phone.

"You know who this is?" I asked.

"Yes," he whispered.

"I was very disappointed in your behavior today," I said. "I like you, but I don't like the way you acted. It was very annoying, and it disrupted my teaching. It's important to me to be a good teacher. I don't want you to do that again. All right?"

"All right," he said.

Junior never whistled again, and I realized that I had happened upon an effective deterrent. I began calling students directly to discuss their behavior. In most cases those phone calls were much more effective than calls to parents, because the students were entirely responsible for their behavior. Often when the student behavior improved, I did call the parents—to tell them how much I enjoyed having their child in my class. The students didn't know what to think, which kept them on their toes. A good place for them to be.

## 9. Create a Contract

Just as behavior cards serve as an effective visual reminder to students who forget verbal instructions, student contracts serve as effective written reminders to students who have promised to cooperate. Your contract doesn't have to be elaborate, and it doesn't have to be a form. Some teachers use a form on school letterhead to make the contract look official; all they have to do is fill in the blanks. Other teachers ask the student to write out an agreement about what behaviors will improve and what consequences the student will suffer if he or she breaks the contract.

Just as positive reinforcement produces quicker and more lasting results in behavior, positively stated contracts result in quicker cooperation and a better relationship between student and teacher. Instead of listing things the student won't do, list things the student will do. And, if possible, incorporate some reward—not a bribe—for example, if the student does not break this contract for thirty days, the student will earn ten points for good conduct and this contract becomes null and void. Think about how much more responsive you would be if a traffic officer gave you thirty days to prove you could drive safely instead of issuing you a ticket.

Just for the record, I prefer a verbal contract and a handshake. It works for me.

## 10. Send for Reinforcements

Sometimes even the best teacher runs up against an immovable student. If the first nine steps fail and the student still causes major disruptions, don't waste time blaming yourself. Clearly, the problem is bigger than a simple personality clash or routine misbehavior. Don't quibble. Send for reinforcements. Meet with your principal and ask for suggestions and support. Request a meeting between you, the principal, and the student to see if you can come to a resolution. Call the parents and request assistance or a conference. If parents or guardians are unhelpful or if you suspect after speaking to them that they may be contributing to the student's bad behavior, see if you can find an adult relative or older sibling. Check with the student's bus driver and your school security personnel; sometimes school staff members enjoy good relationships with students who don't respond well to teachers. Consult your school counselors and psychologists. Ask a coach to counsel the student. If your school or community has a mentor program, put in an emergency request. (If you can't locate a mentor program, find out what social programs and services may be available.)

## 11. Request a Student Transfer

Ask a counselor if he or she would be willing to have your troubled student complete assignments in the counselor's office. Once I had a principal who agreed to take my chief troublemaker under his wing and supervise the boy during my class period. If these aren't viable options and if your school is large enough to have another teacher at the same level, find out whether that teacher would be willing to accept your disruptive student as a transfer into his or her class. Of course, teachers can't make this transfer themselves, but if both teachers agree, your administrators will be much more likely to cooperate with your request. At small schools where a transfer is not an option, you may be able to find a fellow teacher who also has a problem student. You can agree to switch students for a specified period of time each day, even ten minutes, to give yourselves and your students a break from each other.

## 12. Remove the Perpetrator

You may be stuck with an incorrigible student for any number of reasons: a small school with limited options, lack of administrative support, uncooperative or irresponsible parents, or inflexible guidelines from your local school board. If you have exhausted every possible avenue, tried every intervention you can think of, and a student continues to disrupt your teaching and other students' learning, but your administration won't agree to remove the student from your classroom, then you need to remove the student from your classroom—unofficially. I have used this method successfully myself, and I have recommended it to other desperate teachers, who report that it worked for them as well. It's best to keep this procedure to yourself, however.

First create an assignment folder for your troublesome student. Include the next two or three assignments that you intend to complete during class and a brief but complete description of any special activities or projects. Next talk to your school librarian and ask whether you may send a student to do independent work as long as that student does not misbehave in the library. If the librarian agrees, explain that you will give the student a pass each day and that the student is to ask the librarian to sign the pass and indicate the time that the student enters and leaves the library. (In schools with no library or no cooperative librarian, find a counselor, coach, administrator, or teacher who can supervise the student and agree on a time period and location for this experiment. If no other location is available, place a desk outside your classroom door and have the student sit outside and do his work. If he leaves the desk and wanders off, he is now in violation of your school policy, and you must refer him to the appropriate office.)

Do not make any preface or provide any warning before you implement this plan. Simply call your student aside, hand him the folder, and explain that he will be completing his work independently. Provide an instruction sheet that states your expectations about conduct in the library (or other applicable location), the procedure for getting his passes signed, and his responsibility for returning the completed work to you at the end of the class period each day. Do not argue with the student. Hand him the folder, show him the door, shut the door, and teach the students who cooperate.

If your troublesome student decides to take a vacation, simply fill out the proper reports and let the discipline system handle him. If he complies with your instructions, continue this policy for as long as necessary. Once I had to remove a student for an entire quarter, and I'd like to add that the day I reached the end of my patience and removed him from the class, several students stopped by individually to thank me for removing the troublemaker and making it possible for them to learn. As it turned out, he had threatened some of the boys and sexually harassed some of the girls, but they were all afraid to file formal complaints against him because he was a member of the prize-winning varsity football team.

Of course, there is a chance that your administrators (or, sadly, your fellow teachers) may object to your emergency independent-assignment procedure. If that happens, explain (and follow up with a letter summarizing your conversation to cover your back in case somebody decides to file a report at your district office) that you had exhausted every legal option and the student still made it impossible for you to teach and other students to learn. Provide dates and times when you asked administrators for support or assistance, copies of disciplinary referrals, minutes from any conferences, and dates and times of phone calls or meetings with parents.

## IF YOU HAVE TO HAVE DETENTION, MAKE IT WORTHWHILE

Some schools insist on having a detention center, and many schools require that teachers take turns supervising detention. If that's the case in your school and you can't convince your administrators or fellow teachers to try a different approach, then do your best to make detention useful.

Instead of simply enforcing a no-talking rule or overseeing time-wasting activities such as word search puzzles (which seem to be popular detention room assignments for some strange reason), find some interesting articles—interesting to young people, not necessarily to adults. For example, my students have responded enthusiastically to critical reviews of popular movies; feature articles about sports stars or musicians; essays about controversial subjects such as UFOs, tattoos, and body piercing; pop psychology quizzes; self-help articles on handwriting analysis, dating success, anger management, ways to gain popularity, and so on.

Don't make your reading assignments mandatory if you have a room full of little rebels. Just pass out the papers and say, "Here's something interesting we could read." Then give them a few minutes to look it over. Read a little bit out loud. Some students will follow along, though they may pretend they are ignoring you. If anybody seems interested at all, ask for volunteers to read. If nobody volunteers, read the entire article aloud yourself. Encourage the students to discuss the article, but if they prefer to remain mute, don't take it personally. Detention rooms may have some nasty bullies among the crowd, and many students prefer to keep a low profile. That doesn't mean they aren't interested, however. Hold your own discussion—with yourself. State your opinions. Collect the papers. Let the students go back to vegetating. Vegetating is boring, so some of them will think about what you just read. Some of them may even be inspired to think for several minutes in a row. That's a good start.

*Beware:* Your efforts to stimulate thought may backfire. One teacher reported that when she began using short psychology lessons and discussions about developing social skills during her assigned detentions, students often complained when the bell rang to signal the end of the period. After a few weeks, some students began asking to be sent to her detention because they enjoyed her lessons so much!

## KEEP RECORDS

Regardless of what behavior policy you choose, create a folder for discipline problems. Keep track of your efforts to help students, with dates for each disciplinary action. You don't need to record quick chats and time-outs unless a student starts to show a pattern of serious misbehavior. If that does happen and you find yourself with a determined problem child, document everything—warnings, behavior cards, phone calls, notes to parents, referrals to the office (students can disappear en route to the office or forge signatures on their passes). Also document your conversations and requests for help from administrators and other teachers. This record will not only provide evidence in the unlikely event of a legal problem, it will also show you whether you have a pattern of becoming too stressed and short-tempered at the end of a grading period or the beginning of a new unit.

## CONSULT THE EXPERTS, BUT TRUST YOUR INSTINCTS

Investigate resources and explore your options before you settle on a discipline program. Find a method that makes sense to you and that fits your own teaching style. Don't adopt somebody else's rules just because you think you should have rules. Children instinctively understand when adults are sincere, and heaven help you if they sense that you aren't. If you try to impose a behavior code that you don't really support, then nobody in your classroom—including you—will honor it.

After asking for advice from your professors and colleagues and conducting your own research, if you still find yourself at a loss for how to approach classroom discipline you might start with a modern translation of the Golden Rule: treat people the way you would like them to treat you. Don't merely post the rule in your classroom. Follow the rule yourself. Treat your students the way you would like them to treat you. They may be a little slow at first, and some of them may need a short vacation (or two or three) from your class, but if you sincerely respect them and maintain your own high standards of behavior, eventually they will come around. And eventually you will find an approach that works for both you and your students.

There are a number of popular programs such as Love and Logic, Positive Discipline, and Discipline with Dignity that many teachers recommend. My education students like to read the articles on the various Web sites and pick and choose their favorites. Some of them complain about the commercial aspects of the Web sites; one online student wrote: "I resisted reading the articles on those Web sites because I was so put off by all the ads urging me to buy this or that, but after reading the positive comments posted by some of the other students, I took another look and found some really helpful advice. I guess teachers should be happy to take what they can get for free, considering."

Should you encounter a plethora of die-hard, incorrigible little stinkers in your classroom who steadfastly refuse to appreciate you, hang in there. And hang a calendar in your bathroom where each night as you brush your teeth, you will have a visual reminder that you have survived one more day. Don't give up hope. Don't take the students' actions personally; they would torment another teacher just as they torment you. Do give up feeling guilty or unworthy. Most of us have had "one of those years."

## EMERGENCY MELTDOWN DISASTER PLAN

Occasionally several factors combine to drive a teacher past the point of his or her tolerance. Even the best teachers can crack under certain conditions. When students sense that a teacher is near the breaking point, a handful of sympathetic souls may behave themselves, but most students will become relentless in their efforts to break the teacher. This can happen even with students who are not vicious or unfeeling. It is a result of specific ingredients and group dynamics that are beyond your control.

I remember a very professional young teacher with seven years of experience successfully teaching advanced-level classes at a California high school. Her students adored her, and graduates often came back to offer their thanks. One day a student in her class stood up without warning and vocally criticized her teaching methods and curriculum. Caught by surprise, the teacher allowed the student to draw her into an argument, and before long the entire class of students polarized on the boy's side. A power struggle quickly turned into a shark feed. The teacher ended up running out of the room in tears, prepared to resign and give up teaching permanently. Fortunately, the principal refused to accept the teacher's resignation. He held a conference with the teacher, several students, and their parents.

The parents supported the teacher and were able to apply enough pressure to force the students to stop attacking her. Within a few weeks, the students went back to adoring their teacher; but it took a long time before she regained her former confidence, and even then she admitted to having doubts.

When I observed that teacher's struggle, I felt sorry for her, but I didn't believe the same thing could ever happen to me. It didn't. Nobody ever stood up in my class, criticized my teaching, and stole my confidence. But just in case, I made an emergency meltdown plan and filed it away. A few years later, I took over a class from a long-term substitute who didn't want to be replaced and who worked hard to turn the students against me. She took another sub position at the same school and devoted her energy to sabotaging my class. I won't go into details, but I will say that those "regular" students were far more vicious and stubborn than any of the so-called at-risk, incorrigible, or behavior-disordered students I have ever taught, including delinquents who had spent time behind bars. When I realized that I was in the midst of my own shark feed, I pulled out my emergency disaster plan. Here's the plan, for what it's worth.

1. **Be professional.** Make sure your lesson plans (or a rough outline) are in order for the next few weeks. Check to see that your sub folder (see Chapter Four) contains lesson plans, roll sheets, and emergency evacuation information.

2. **Take a mental health break.** This is an emergency. Don't feel compelled to provide specifics. Just call the office, say that you are seriously ill and will be in touch when you are feeling better. If you have a spouse or friend who can call for you, even better. Pay at least one visit to a doctor, therapist, counselor, chiropractor, massage therapist, or other professional who can help you handle the stress, but don't make up a bogus medical condition. Stress is a serious problem in and of itself. Give yourself at least three days—a week would be even better.

3. **Do some serious self-reflection.** Do you really truly want to teach school? Or did you think you would enjoy teaching, only to find that you hate going to work? Do you struggle with teaching, but find enough joy and satisfaction that you are willing to work on improving your classroom management and leadership skills? Or do you have to admit that you just weren't cut out to teach, no matter how much you would like to?

You may conclude that you aren't the problem, that your entire school is out of control (and this does happen). If so, consider applying for a job at another school, working as a sub in your district or a nearby district, or taking a sabbatical. As one crusty old rancher I know used to say, "Don't blame yourself if you can't put out a forest fire by peeing on it."

**4. If you realize you don't want to teach, figure out how soon you can quit.** Do you have other options for earning a living? Can you afford to quit right now? If you can't quit right now, create a plan for updating your résumé and conducting a job search. Contact professional colleagues and ask them for general letters of recommendation. Don't whine about your job; just say that you are thinking of making a career change in the future. Focus on creating the life you want instead of hating the life you have. Just changing your focus will make it easier for you to teach until you can afford to leave. Knowing that you aren't stuck forever and you have choices will make a big difference. You may even find that once you've decided to stop teaching, you relax and enjoy yourself so much that you decide to stay.

**5. If you decide you do want to teach** (or if you have to teach until you can afford to quit), **prepare to make some serious changes in your classroom when you return.** Plan to change everything in your classroom—from the decor to the furniture arrangement, student seating, and even the rules and procedures. Also plan to change your attitude, your approach, your posture, even your tone of voice. Cut your hair. Get new glasses. Buy a suit or some other clothing that shouts "Power!" Check your local library or bookstore for books on power dressing; a black suit with a white shirt is the ultimate power outfit. If possible, visit a military training camp or a police academy—or watch video clips of their instructors in action. Learn how to stand like drill instructors stand, feet planted a few feet apart, shoulders back, chin up, arms loose at your sides. When you talk, don't move. When you walk, march. When you want to speak, plant your feet again, wait a second, then begin talking. Use your serious voice.

It may sound frivolous, but check your footwear. You may have to give up comfort for a little while. Find a pair of leather-soled shoes (boots are even better) that make an authoritative clunk when you walk, as opposed to the dainty click of high heels or the squish of tennis shoes. If your classroom is carpeted, make sure you leave the room once or twice during each class period so that students can hear you walking sharply back toward the room. When you enter, shut the door firmly behind you—not a slam but a nice, solid shut.

And, most important of all, call your department chair or one of your principals and request a meeting before you return from your "sick leave." (This isn't a lie. Mental and emotional stress do make people sick. They kill people.) When you meet, explain that you have been under too much stress in your classroom. Be honest. Tell them that you need help with classroom management because the students in your class are out of control. Ask her or him to be available to support you in person on the day you plan to return to work. Get a promise that if you call or send a student asking for backup, somebody from the admin staff will come to your classroom immediately and help you out.

**6. Change the look of your room.** Design an alternate arrangement of furniture. How you arrange it isn't so important as creating a new look. You want students to see immediately that things are different. Put your desk in a different corner. Shuffle some file cabinets around. Hang some new posters or artwork.

**7. Rearrange the student desks.** If you've been using a semicircle or U shape, move the chairs back into rows. If you've been using rows, find a different shape that will fit your room. Put some student desks very close to your teacher desk. Uncomfortably close.

**8. Create a seating chart.** Using one of the copies of your roll sheets that you keep at home for planning, create a chart that separates the strongest students from each other. Put a major power player nearest to your home base. Put another near the door, where he or she will have less distance to travel when it's time to step outside. Place that handful of good, decent kids near each other in the center of the room where they can offer each other moral support.

**9. Create a week's worth of lessons.** Create extremely interesting and challenging lessons, lessons that require students to do the bulk of the work. Place the focus on them, not on you. Search online, read magazines and journals, check the library and bookstore for ideas. The Web site www.teachers.net has a lot of good suggestions and links to other resources. If you have a wide range of ability levels in your classroom, consider a lesson that makes use of differentiated instruction such as a menu where students select from among several possible assignments. Your goal is to engage students so thoroughly that they forget to misbehave.

**10. Call on a Friday morning and tell the school you will be back on Monday.** Treat yourself to a movie or a special meal Friday afternoon. Try to relax because you will be working on the weekend (or Friday evening if you don't have weekend access—check with a secretary or custodian to make sure you can get into your room). Spend that Friday evening or weekend rearranging your classroom and getting things in order. On Sunday night take a long walk or get some exercise to help you sleep better. If you can't sleep, don't worry. You may be tired, but nervous energy will carry you through the day.

11. **Wake up an hour earlier than usual on Monday morning.** Do some calisthenics or yoga, meditate, or take a quick walk or jog—anything that will get your blood flowing and your heart beating a little faster than usual. You're in training for an important contest, so eat breakfast. Make sure you put some protein into your body. Put on your power clothes, grab your lesson plans, and get to school ahead of the early birds. Write the instructions for your first assignment on the board and station yourself in the doorway. Block the doorway so that only one student can enter at a time. When students begin to arrive, look each student in the eye, say, "Welcome to my new, improved classroom," and direct the student to his or her new seat. Don't discuss anything yet. If students ask questions, say, "We'll discuss our new plan later. Right now I'm busy and you need to get started on the assignment that is posted on the board."

12. **After everybody is seated, remind them to finish the assignment.** If they don't finish, collect the papers and slap them onto your desk. Then tell the students that you didn't like what was happening in your classroom, so you have done some serious thinking during your absence and have decided to make some changes. (If you have decided to stop teaching, don't tell them. It's not their business. Just tell them that you are still considering different options for your future and that you have a lot of options because you are a college graduate.) From now on, you are going to conduct things differently.

Remember to stand up straight, shoulders back, chin high, and plant your feet as you talk. This is one time you want to project your authority and power. If you don't know what to do with your hands, place your right hand over your left wrist and lightly grasp. Let your hands fall naturally in front of your body—or hold them behind you in the middle of your back, as though you were standing at military-style parade rest. This advice comes from a police academy instructor who teaches people to be calmly assertive when dealing with excitable people.

Don't shout, but use your most serious quiet voice. If anybody disrupts your conversation, don't hesitate. Tell them once that you want them to remain seated, be quiet, and listen. If they interrupt again, call whoever has agreed to provide emergency backup. While you wait for your backup to arrive, don't continue your discussion; fill out your referral paperwork. Then just stand and wait silently.

If it takes five, ten, or fifteen minutes for your support person to arrive, keep waiting silently. This will make the students uncomfortable, which is a good thing. They may mumble and whisper or talk out loud, but as long as they don't get out of their seats or start shouting obscenities at you, ignore them. Do not let them dictate your behavior. They have to get the message that you are in charge of your classroom and they will have to respond to your behavior. It's an important distinction.

When your support person arrives, ask him or her to escort your disruptive student to the office. Before they leave, ask your class, "Does anybody else want to go?" Most likely they won't.

After fifteen minutes, if nobody shows up to help you, alert the nearest teacher or staff member that you will be gone from your classroom for a few minutes. Then, turn to your disrupter and ask, "Would you like me to escort you to the office or would you prefer to sit down and cooperate? It's up to you." If the student sits down, say, "Thank you. Good decision." And continue your conversation as though nothing had happened. If the disrupter ignores you or chooses to continue the rude behavior, escort him or her to the office yourself. Don't make small talk. Just say, "Let's go," and start walking. If the student balks, don't argue, keep walking. Deliver the student and/or the referral to the office. (If the student has disappeared along the way or is lagging behind, just deliver the paperwork and let the administration handle the student.)

Inform whoever is present—the principal or the principal's secretary—that the student is interfering with your teaching and other students' learning and cannot return to your classroom until you have met with the principal and/or the student's parents. Then get back to your classroom. If your students are seated and reasonably cooperative, apologize for the delay and thank them for waiting. It not, insist that they sit and be quiet before you speak. Wait as long as necessary and look as mean as you can while you're waiting. Then finish your one-way conversation.

Tell your students why you have chosen to be a teacher. Explain that you want to help them be successful people and that you have made some changes in order to make that possible. Tell them everybody is starting with a clean slate, but that *you expect them to conduct themselves with self-control and self-respect.* Give them a long silent look after you say this. Make sure they get your message. Then start your first new, interesting, challenging lesson. And if you can find an opportunity to inject some humor into that first lesson, so much the better. Humor, especially unexpected humor, is the number-one persuader and a great tension reliever. There will definitely be some tension in your classroom.

There is an excellent chance that your students will cooperate—because this behavior is not what they expect and when the unexpected occurs, as I discussed earlier, the brain is caught off-guard and the cognitive gears slip a bit. This allows you to persuade people to cooperate who might otherwise be difficult to persuade.

Of course, there is always the possibility that you have more than one ringleader in your room. Or several. If your entire class gangs up on you—which occasionally happens—and you end up sending the entire class to the office, one at a time, go ahead and send them. That will get the attention of your administration (they shouldn't be surprised, because you warned them in advance that you needed their help). Something will happen. Either your administrators will support you or they won't. In the worst case, they may threaten to fire you. But if you have any record at all of asking for support prior to this meltdown and you can prove it, they will probably reconsider. If you truly believe you are going to be fired, you might tender your resignation "for personal reasons" before they have time to complete their paperwork. Even if you do get fired from a teaching job, it doesn't mean you will never get another one. It may be harder to find a job, but not impossible, especially if you stay in the same area where future employers will be well aware of problems in other schools.

This is the plan I used. It may not be the perfect plan for you, but it may give you some ideas. I'm not trying to be coy, but I have opted not to reveal the final resolution of my shark-feed situation because I don't want to unduly influence other teachers. Whatever you decide, good luck to you. Teaching can be darned difficult work, but if you make up your mind that you truly want to teach and you persist in trying to improve your skills, I believe your determination and sincerity will lead you in the right direction. It may take you a while. That's just fine. And it's perfectly normal. Even those "superteachers" at your school had to work at getting it right, although they may like to believe that they are "natural-born teachers."

## DISCUSSION POINTS

1. Articulate your own discipline philosophy in one or two sentences.

2. What classroom rules do you use (or plan to use)? Why these specific rules?

3. When and how should teachers present their classroom rules to students?

4. In small groups or in your journal, describe a time when you were disciplined in school as a child. How did this experience affect your attitude and behavior?

5. Working in small groups, create a good discipline plan for a specific grade level.

# The Three Rs: Reading, Reading, Reading

Children are not born with a natural aversion to reading. We know that. We see what happens when we introduce toddlers to books. They fall in love. They carry their favorites around and admire the pictures over and over again. They caress the pages with their stubby fingers. They gnaw on the edges of those beloved books as though they would like to eat them up. It isn't unusual for a child to request the same bedtime storybook fifty or a hundred or two hundred times.

Why, then, is reading such a problem for so many elementary and secondary students and their teachers? What turns so many little book lovers into such adamant book haters? Instead of speculating, I went straight to the source—real-life reluctant readers in my classes spanning the past two decades. Students from very disparate backgrounds and ranging in age from seven to fifty-eight. From struggling second graders, disenchanted teens, high school gangsters, English language learners, and adult basic education students to college freshmen and future teachers. Those reluctant readers taught me how to make reading less painful, and sometimes even enjoyable, for them.

## WHAT'S THE PROBLEM?

My first teaching assignment, while I was still a graduate education student, consisted of convincing a class of disenchanted high school sophomores to read and write. (I don't like the term *at risk* because, as one astute student pointed out, calling somebody "at risk" sounds like you don't think they can make it through school.) Those disenchanted students hated reading, which wasn't at all surprising, considering their abysmal reading skills.

The following year, as a newly licensed teacher, I taught two different classes, one a group of limited-English freshmen and the other a group of disenchanted sophomores. The non-English speakers were eager to learn everything, but the sophomores, of mixed ethnic backgrounds but most of them native English speakers, hated reading with a passion. And again—no big surprise—their reading skills were even worse than those of my students from the previous year.

How did these kids ever get to high school? I wondered. Didn't anybody notice that they can barely read?

One day, at the start of class, I asked, "How many of you like reading?" A few students raised their hands tentatively. Then I asked, "How many hate reading?" A sea of hands waved wildly, churning up the air with their negativity.

We then spent the entire class period discussing our feelings about books and reading. We talked about how we learned to read and how we came to love or hate reading. Many of those students admitted that during nine years of school, they had never read a single book.

As I got to know those students better, I found the answer to my original question: How did these kids ever get to high school? I realized how very talented they were at hiding their poor reading skills. Like blind people who develop more acute senses of smell or hearing, those poor readers had developed sharper skills in other areas to compensate. They were expert mimics. They convincingly parroted the comments and opinions of their literate classmates. They were excellent readers of body language as well, taking their cues from the slightest change in my facial expression or posture. And many of them had such well-developed memorization skills that they could repeat whole reading passages or long lists of definitions from our vocabulary lessons, word for word.

Those nonreaders had tap-danced their way through elementary school, struggled through middle school, and hit a wall at high school. They could no longer fake their way through math, because the problems were now too complex and abstract. And even the best memorizers couldn't memorize an entire biology text or a two-hundred-page novel. Suddenly they felt stupid. And, even worse, they knew their teachers would think they were stupid, even if their teachers were too polite to say so. Worst of all, their classmates who did know how to read thought they were stupid, and being polite was not high on their adolescent list of priorities. Understandably, many poor readers choose to nurture reputations as "tough" or "unteachable" because there is a sort of negative glamour attached to outlaw behavior. But there's nothing glamorous about being considered "stupid" or "too dumb to read."

I worked hard to convince those students that reading was a skill, not a natural-born talent, and that they were capable of learning. I offered the analogies of basketball and dancing, since many of them were NBA hopefuls and most of the girls spent their free time listening to music and practicing complicated dance steps in the back of the room.

"You can't sink a free throw if you never get on the court," I told them. "And you know even Michael Jackson had to practice moon-walking to get it down right." Because we had developed a solid rapport based on mutual respect and trust, those students agreed to give reading one more try. Together we created a new set of expectations and rules about reading. That group of sophomores, by the way, was part of the Academy program, a school-within-a-school for underachieving teens where I had the opportunity to work with the same students for their final three years of high school. And I am delighted to report that every one of those students eventually passed the standardized reading and math exams required to graduate. Eight of the first class of graduation seniors earned full scholarships to college, and the number of scholarships doubled for the second graduating class. But that's another story (see Chapter Eleven for a full update on the real students who were depicted in *My Posse Don't Do Homework*).

With each new high school class (and even with some advanced placement students, because some are reluctant readers in spite of their achievements), I kept the discussion about reading as one of the introductory activities. Later, when I began teaching college students and tutoring young children, I continued asking the same questions about reading: How did you learn to read? Did you ever enjoy reading? Why do you hate reading now? The same answers cropped up time and again. Following are the most common reasons those students offered to explain their aversion to reading:

1. Reading gives them a headache or makes their eyes hurt.
2. They fear they'll be required to read out loud and others will laugh at them.
3. They can't read so fast as their peers and they get left behind.
4. They always get put into the "slow" group, which makes them feel stupid.
5. They are too far behind to ever catch up.
6. They believe they have to finish every reading selection, no matter how long or difficult.
7. They expect to be tested on what they read—and to fail the test.
8. They have no interest in most of the material they are required to read.
9. They get lost and can't remember what they have just read.
10. If asked for their opinion of a book or story, they fear their opinion will be wrong.
11. They hate people telling them what to do all day long.

## WHAT'S THE SOLUTION?

I hope several possible solutions came to mind as you read the list of complaints and fears from those reluctant readers. The following suggestions are simply that—suggestions. Ideally, they will serve as springboards for your own ideas, using feedback from your own students. After all, reading is an individual activity, even if we learn it in groups. So individualizing our methods of reading instruction makes sense.

### 1. Reading Gives Them a Headache or Makes Their Eyes Hurt

Discuss scotopic sensitivity syndrome with your students (see Chapter Eight, on light and learning, for more information). Recent research suggests that nearly half of people who are labeled as learning disabled actually suffer from scotopic (light) sensitivity. People with light sensitivity find reading difficult and sometimes painful when the material is printed on glossy paper. Fluorescent lighting or other lights that cause glare on the page make reading even more difficult. High-contrast print, such as black letters on white paper, is the most difficult for light-sensitive people to read. Unfortunately, such high-contrast print is the most common format for texts and other school materials. I have even had students whose eyes turn red and teary after just a few minutes of reading. Even more sadly, many students who struggle with scotopic sensitivity find themselves placed in special education classes or programs for behavior-disordered children because they refuse to read or they misbehave in order to avoid having to read.

You may notice some students who lean over their desks and wrap one arm around their books and papers. They may not be trying to protect or hide anything; they may be trying to cast a shadow over their reading materials. Many students prefer to wear baseball caps with the brims low over their eyes for the same reason—to reduce glare, not to rebel. And it's possible that musicians and artists who wear sunglasses all the time, even indoors, are protecting their sensitive eyes, in addition to looking cool.

Quite often, scotopic readers love stories and enjoy hearing them read aloud. They participate in group reading assignments and may have excellent comprehension skills. When you ask those students to read on their own, however, their behavior changes dramatically. If you have students who are generally cooperative but start to wiggle and squirm as soon as you ask them to read independently, be alert for signs that reading is uncomfortable. They may squint, frown, rub their eyes, try to shade their books, hold their books far away or very near to their faces, blink rapidly, or lose their place repeatedly when reading. Often schools mislabel scotopic readers as dyslexic (they may or may not suffer from dyslexia, as well) and give them tutoring to provide strategies that don't work, because the glare and discomfort remain.

If you haven't heard of scotopic sensitivity, your best source of information is the Internet. Be sure to check the sponsors of any Web sites you visit to make sure that they are reputable. A number of universities and education organizations offer links and resources, as do independent consulting firms. Many Web sites will offer testimonials from people who have used transparent colored overlays or filters with great success.

Also be alert for new research on what is being termed vision therapy, vision convergence problems, or developmental optometry. Having 20/20 visual acuity doesn't automatically mean that a student has no vision problems. An August 2004 news release from the College of Optometrists in Vision Development reports that "because symptoms may be quite similar, visual disorders caused by faulty skill patterns may be misdiagnosed as learning disability or ADHD." The article reports that students who fail to respond to ADHD medication can sometimes experience dramatic improvement with vision therapy. To read more about vision therapy for problem readers, visit www.covd.org.

## 2. They Fear They'll Be Required to Read Out Loud and Others Will Laugh at Them

Consider making reading aloud purely voluntary in your classroom. Give students the option of reading to you silently so you can assess their skills and progress. In addition to easing some of the stress, letting students opt out of public reading may improve the attendance, punctuality, and morale in your classroom.

Let students volunteer to read out loud. Urge them to try. Don't allow other kids to laugh at the ones who do read, and beware the sneaky snickers. If you ask students to read aloud in your classroom, you owe it to your readers to make sure that nobody shames or humiliates them for trying. And if you have shy or timid students who never volunteer, work with them individually until they develop the confidence to read aloud (some kids will never volunteer, but that doesn't mean they aren't learning; and at least you won't have made them dread reading).

Many teachers insist that all students must read aloud. My response to those teachers is, "Why? What do you gain from forcing students to read aloud that is so valuable it outweighs their embarrassment, their stomach aches, their sweaty palms, their heartaches, and their reluctance to enter your classroom? Not to mention the fact that they may become lifelong nonreaders?" I would also ask, "If your current method isn't working, why not try a different approach?"

Some teachers call on students to read aloud as a way of keeping them awake or alert in class, but you could call on a willing volunteer who is seated next to your drowsy or daydreaming student instead. When his classmate begins to read, the daydreamer will tune back in without feeling embarrassment or hostility toward you.

And, finally, if you require students to read out loud simply because your own teachers required you to read out loud, I urge you to find some of your classmates who hated reading and ask how they felt. Most teachers enjoyed school. We enjoyed reading. We don't know how it feels to hate reading so much that we are willing to jeopardize our own grades—even drop out of school—in order to avoid reading out loud. We need to have more empathy if we truly want to help our struggling readers.

### 3. They Can't Read So Fast As Their Peers and They Get Left Behind

Because the imprint of the first experience with reading makes such an impact for so many years, I encourage elementary school teachers and reading instructors to allow students to read at their own pace, even if it means that those slower students don't cover so much ground as their quicker classmates. Parents repeatedly ask me to tutor young children whose teachers have claimed that a learning disability prevents their children from learning to read. Invariably, the real problem turns out to be speed. Those children simply can't read at the fast rate that their classmates do. But when they are allowed to read at their own individual pace, they do learn to read. Here are just two examples among many from my own experience.

The mother of one young girl asked me for help when Kayla's second-grade teacher called to say that Kayla was going to be placed in special ed due to a learning disability. Kayla had earned straight As in first grade, so her mother was puzzled by the teacher's belief that she couldn't teach Kayla to read.

"I'm not a reading teacher," I told Kayla's mother, "but I can give you my opinion for what it's worth." After working with Kayla for an hour on her spelling list and reading textbook, it was obvious to me that the problem was time. Kayla was in such a hurry to do everything quickly that she wasn't processing anything. When I asked her to slow down and spell the words on her list orally, she spelled nine out of ten correctly. When I asked her to write the same words, she scribbled half of them incorrectly. The same thing happened with her reading. When I asked her to slow down and read one sentence then tell me what it said, she was fine. But when I let her read without interruption, she began racing along, stumbling over words, and was unable to answer the most basic questions about what she had read.

"Why are you reading so fast?" I asked her. Her shoulders slumped and she sighed. "Because I have to go fast. That's how we do it at school."

"I don't care how fast everybody reads in school," I said. "I want you to slow down and read at your own pace. And one of these days, I promise, you'll read as fast as everybody else. Maybe even faster."

Kayla wasn't completely convinced, but she agreed to slow down. And her mother agreed to allow Kayla to skip some of her chores on their family's ranch so she could spend more time after school reading. In less than two months, Kayla went from failing grades back to straight As. She wasn't placed in special ed. And she did catch up with the rest of her class.

Another tutoring student, a precocious eight-year-old boy with an impressive vocabulary, sat down across the table from me on our first session and announced, "I'm the second dumbest kid in my class." When I asked him how he knew this, he said that the teacher posted their grades on the wall. I said I didn't believe the teacher would post their grades and their names. He said, "She didn't put the names, but she listed them in alphabetical order and I figured out which one was me. I'm the second dumbest." His solution to the problem was to demonstrate his intelligence by reading faster than everybody else in class. Unfortunately, in his haste, he skipped so many words that he had zero reading comprehension. After I convinced him to slow down, which took several weeks because he was determined to be the fastest instead of the dumbest, his reading skills improved quickly, and within a few months his grades improved to the point where he no longer needed tutoring.

Tennessee reading teacher Vicki Cline graciously agreed to critique this chapter. She filled me in on the speed problem. She says that some children become confused after taking the DIBELS reading test, in which they are instructed to read as quickly as possible and still maintain 90 percent comprehension. That makes perfect sense because even now, working with adults, I sometimes check for understanding, and students assure me that they understand the criteria for a specific assignment. We even go over written instructions together. But later on I realize they didn't fully understand. So it makes sense that young children would remember just the "fast" part of the instructions and form the impression that they were to read as fast as possible all of the time.

Since reading really is the cornerstone of academic success, we have to take special care to pinpoint the cause of reading problems. And the responsibility doesn't rest with reading teachers. We are all reading teachers, and we need to work together when we see a student struggling. Otherwise some of those students will completely lose confidence in their ability to learn or become behavior problems. And some poor little people will become victims of psychosomatic illnesses that literally make them sick when they have to face another day in the classroom. My youngest brother, who struggled very hard to learn to read, is a good example. He often vomited in the mornings before school because reading was such a traumatic experience for him. Nobody in the family realized he couldn't read, because the rest of us were all voracious readers. We just thought he preferred to play outdoors.

When my older sister and I finally identified his problem and worked together to help him learn to read, his illnesses gradually disappeared, as his grades rose from failing to above average.

## 4. They Always Get Put into the "Slow" Group, Which Makes Them Feel Stupid

I have a theory that is based not on research and statistics, but on thousands of conversations with students and teachers across the country. Since those conversations, I have come to believe that our first experience with reading influences our perceptions of our intelligence even as adults. Here's why. If you ask adults, "Do you consider yourself above average, about average, or below average?" most of them have a clear picture of where they fall on the intelligence spectrum. But what I find most interesting is that when I ask those same adults how old they were when they formed their opinions of their own intelligence, nearly all agree that they decided how smart they were during the first few years of school, when they were learning to read. Call them bluebirds and sparrows, stars and stripes, bears and bobcats, children always know who are the fast readers (translate "smart kids") and who are the slow readers (translate "dumb kids"). They know exactly where they fall on the reading-speed spectrum, and they believe this correlates to intelligence. Most of them will believe for the rest of their lives that they are smart or dumb or average, depending on how quickly and well they learned to read.

If teachers can find a way to group students that doesn't depend on their reading ability at least some of the time, I think they can avoid the situation where students correlate their intelligence to their reading group. Better yet, teachers can create classroom environments where students sincerely want to help each other and don't tease or torment the slower students. Sometimes students who process information slowly turn out to have much higher IQs than fast processors. Finding ways for slow readers to shine in other areas can be an effective way to help students understand that there are multiple forms of intelligence and that reading is one of many skills, but not necessarily an indicator of intelligence or ability to learn.

Just this past semester, in one of my courses for future teachers, I asked students to write about their memories of learning to read. Emily's journal almost made me cry. She wrote:

> My teacher separated the class into three reading groups by skill level. Although the groups were given nonjudgmental bird names, it was

quite clear that my group, the robins, were the lowest ... My group of robins were forced to read a series of unimaginative low-level books. All of these books were stored in an old dusty box and had to be read in order. They all had yellow covers and the illustrations were no more than simple black-and-white figures. The high-level cardinals, however, were allowed to choose any book in the room to read, including the beautiful story books on the shelves in the back of the room. I saw these as the "smart kids'" books and wanted desperately to read them. One book in particular caught my eye—a book of poetry with colorful pictures of fairies and forests. One day while the teacher was busy with another group, I snuck to the back of the room and pulled this book from the shelf. I was so engrossed in reading I didn't notice the teacher coming up behind me. I was punished for reading the wrong kind of book, embarrassing me in front of the class and creating an even more negative reading experience. I have been angry with Mrs. R for years for making me hate reading so much, but looking back on the experience now from a teacher's perspective she did have her hands full with a large class. I was later diagnosed with dyslexia and moved to a private school where a special program taught me the skills I needed to excel in reading and in other subjects.

Surely this teacher was the exception and not the rule. I have met hundreds of reading teachers, and they are a compassionate lot. I shared this student journal with you not because I believe most reading teachers punish students for reading "the wrong books," but because it demonstrates how clearly students remember their first experiences as readers, down to the color of the books and the dust on the covers. We owe it to our students to introduce them to books and reading in the gentlest, most encouraging manner. And we must never forget that we are creating future memories in our classrooms every single day.

### 5. They Are Too Far Behind to Ever Catch Up

When students read below their grade level, they don't understand that increasing their skills to the next level won't take a full calendar year. A ninth grader whose test score places him at fourth-grade level, for example, thinks he will run out of time before he can catch up with his peers. So first explain that a grade level in reading doesn't correspond to a calendar year. It is just a measure of how well a student reads a specific level of complexity in vocabulary and sentence structure. Encourage students to learn how to derive the meaning of unfamiliar words from the context of a sentence and to practice reading every day in order to improve their reading rate. One method I have used successfully is to photocopy a one-to-two-page-long generic magazine article or selection from a textbook. I distribute copies of the pages and ask students not to begin reading until my signal. When I say, "Begin," everybody starts reading. They read for one full minute until I say, "Stop." They circle the last word they read. Then I teach them how to count the words on a page without counting every single word. Count the number of words in four individual lines, then add the numbers and divide by four to get the average number of words per line. Then the students count how many lines they read, multiply that by the average, and get a word count for one minute. They write that number down in the margin, and I collect the papers. We put the reading-rate papers away for a month.

At the end of the month, we read the same reading-rate selection again and see how many words we have read. Students will nearly always improve if they have been making an effort in class. This shows them that practice doesn't make perfect, but it certainly makes improvement. We file those papers away and after another month, we try again with a new selection. We use a selection two or three times, then change it when it starts to sound familiar.

## 6. They Believe They Have to Finish Every Reading Selection, No Matter How Long or Difficult

Have you ever brought home a stack of books from the library or bookstore and then opted not to finish one or two because they just weren't so good as you thought they would be? Or have you ever put down a book halfway through and never went back to it because it just wasn't compelling enough to compete with the other activities in your life? I'm betting that you occasionally fail to finish something you start reading. That's why I suggest letting reluctant readers stop reading things they hate. Not forever. Just until they become good enough readers that reading isn't a dreaded chore. A challenge is good, but an impossible task is not. Forcing people who don't read well to finish reading materials that are too far above their ability level or that have no relevance for them turns reading into a chore instead of a means of gaining information, seeking new perspectives, or being entertained. One of the quickest ways to discourage poor readers from becoming good readers is to make them finish reading things that they hate.

Once students become good readers, they are usually more willing to read assigned materials. Good readers will tackle anything because they know that although sometimes reading requires real effort, they will be rewarded by gaining a new perspective, acquiring new knowledge, encountering an exciting but unfamiliar idea, experiencing a brain tickle, entering a completely new world, or simply enjoying the satisfaction of having conquered a difficult mental challenge. Poor readers don't experience those rewards, so you cannot convince them that reading is enjoyable until they learn to read well enough to forget that they are reading.

This suggestion may go against your teacherly grain, but I urge you to consider it: promise your students that you will expect them to read half of any article, novel, nonfiction book, essay, story, or dramatic play that you give to them. At the halfway point, you will take a vote by show of hands to see whether the majority of your class wants to finish the given selection. If more than half of the students vote against the reading material, put it away. Allow students to finish it on their own if they choose, but do not pursue the reading as a class. Ask students to write a brief critique of the selection, and then move on to the next activity (I suggest doing a nonreading activity next).

Let me explain why I make this suggestion. In one of my high school classes, students were reading the short story "The Birds" by Daphne du Maurier. When they saw the story listed in the table of contents in their literature textbooks, they were excited about reading it because it sounded scary, and some of them had seen the movie or heard about it. They looked forward to reading the story, writing their critiques, and then watching the film. Halfway through the story, I noticed that several heads were drooping and more than a few students were sound asleep.

After rousing the sleepers, I said, "I thought you guys were looking forward to reading this story. What happened?" They didn't know, but they were clearly disappointed with the story. Nobody wanted to finish reading, so I put the students in small groups and asked them to figure out why they didn't like the story so well as they had expected. In their critiques they concluded that the story was written in an "old-fashioned style," with stilted language and far too little dialogue. Some students argued that what might have seemed thrilling and scary when the author wrote the story was no longer frightening to people who had seen so many horror movies with incredible special effects. They thought the sentence and paragraph structure was too complex and contributed to the story's slow feel.

"Fine," I said, after reading their critiques. "Let's stop reading this story and find something more interesting."

"For real?" several students asked.

I said, "In real life, if you don't like something, you don't have to finish it. When you go to the library and check out ten books, you don't have to read them; you don't have to write book reports. You can read one chapter—or one page—from each book and then take them back. And you can keep doing that until you find some books you want to read. After a while you learn what appeals to you. Those are the things you read."

"That's cool," one student said. "But do we get to watch the movie anyway?"

"No," I said. "If we don't finish reading something, we don't watch the movie version, if there is one. We don't have a test. We write our critiques, have a short discussion, and then go on to something else."

Those students responded so enthusiastically to the "something else" that I made "read half–take a vote" my standard policy for reading with any group of remedial or reluctant readers. Of course, when I announce the policy students always grin and warn me that we aren't ever going to finish anything because they are going to vote it down. Especially Shakespeare, they say. But I have never had a class, regardless of how much they hate reading, who voted to discontinue reading *The Taming of the Shrew, Othello,* or *The Merchant of Venice.* (I will discuss my approach to teaching Shakespeare later in this chapter.)

I believe that one of the reasons this approach is so successful is that it gives students the feeling that they have a choice in what they read. And once they know that they can vote to stop reading a story or novel, they will often continue reading because they don't feel compelled to rebel just for the sake of rebelling. Once in a while, a group will start voting down everything, just to be obnoxious. In that case I assign a really long and difficult reading assignment, so that by the time they reach the halfway mark, they are more than willing to read any short selection I offer them. Because opting not to finish something doesn't mean we aren't going to read any more. Reading doesn't disappear. Giving up is not an option—for me or them.

### 7. They Expect to Be Tested on What They Read—and to Fail the Test

I know, I know, testing is important, especially today. So give the standardized tests when you have to. But if you have the choice between testing students about their reading or giving them an opportunity to honestly respond to their reading, go for the honest response. There will be plenty of time for testing once your students improve their reading skills and their self-confidence as readers.

Even at the college level, there are always a few reluctant readers in any group. They sometimes skip important reading assignments if they believe they won't be tested or required to write about or discuss the reading. Some teachers design quizzes to "catch" those students. That method works, but it doesn't motivate reluctant readers; it makes them even less inclined to read because their prediction has come true. They read something. They take a test. We can motivate many more students to read—at any age level—if we change our approach. We can still create assignments and activities that students won't be able to complete if they don't read, but we can design them differently, so they engage students in the reading instead of testing them.

In my opinion, the best way to overcome the read-and-test cycle is to break it completely. Read a few short things as a class. After each one, open the floor to comments. Ask, "So, what do you think about that?" Accept every comment as valuable. If nobody comments, say, "Well, let's let that one percolate for a while." And move on to the next activity. Let your students see that reading isn't a chore, a competition, or a test. It's a lifelong skill that we use to gain information, find a new perspective, and tickle our brains or our funny bones. As one of my former students wisely pointed out, "You don't have to discuss the crap out of everything you read. Some things you just read. That's it."

I'm not suggesting abandoning tests or assessments, just changing the format. For example, when reading as a whole group, we can stop and ask students to jot down their response to a single question about the reading assignment—Which of the characters is the most honest? Why in the world did he do what he did? What would you have done in that situation?—and give them credit based on the amount of thought and effort devoted to the answer, instead of whether the answer is "correct." Following this up with a quick discussion will give all of the students an opportunity to hear what other people think about the reading without putting them on the spot. This teaches them how to analyze a text without realizing they are learning. It will feel to them like you are just talking about the book.

Another option is to divide students into small groups and give them a set of questions to discuss about the reading assignment. Those students who didn't read won't be able to participate. Circulate the room and listen in on the group discussions. A few minutes into the activity, you might interrupt and announce, "It seems that some people didn't get a chance to do the reading. That will make it hard for you to contribute to the discussion. So everybody who didn't do the reading, please join me over here and we'll do a quick skim and discuss." Students who didn't complete the reading will now have to sit with the teacher and read, definitely more work than discussing your opinions with your peers. But then again, some students may welcome the opportunity to engage in some guided reading and discussion with the teacher, because that will give them a chance to discover "the right answers." Either way, you have a very different classroom dynamic than if you test and fail those students who struggle with reading.

Once you start thinking about nontesting options, you see the possibilities. You can interrupt reading periodically to ask students to give a thumbs-up or thumbs-down in response to a question about the reading. This engages them, gives them a chance to express an opinion without being singled out, and gives you an idea of who is getting it and who isn't. You can divide students into book groups, giving them several choices of books or stories to read, then let them create the plan for their group's discussion and the method they will use to present their views to the class. We can give students the choice of several projects (visual, auditory, and kinesthetic), such as designing a book cover with "blurbs" from book critics or readers, creating a movie poster with descriptions of the story, presenting a panel critique of the book to the class, or conducting a TV-show-type Q&A with the author.

When you do test students in a more orthodox manner, don't use the same format for every test. Instead of asking them to select the correct answer on a multiple-choice or matching quiz, try open-ended short essay questions or reading journals. Ask them to think of three good adjectives to describe a specific character and give examples of things those characters said or did to support the students' choice of adjectives. Ask them to rate the story's conclusion and explain why they give it a thumbs-up or thumbs-down.

## 8. They Have No Interest in Most of the Material They Are Required to Read

Scholars can be enticed to read anything in order to analyze and evaluate it; poor readers, struggling readers, and students who are still in the process of developing good critical thinking skills are harder to convince. But struggling readers will blossom if you give them material that is so interesting that they can't resist reading it. That's the trick: finding something so compelling that students forget they are reading.

You may have to abandon textbooks for a bit, even if they do contain interesting stories. Textbooks by definition are not interesting. (I sometimes make copies of a story or poem from the textbook and distribute it to students who enjoy it and are surprised to learn after the fact that it was in their textbook all along.)

Find some compelling magazine articles about people the same age as your students. Check anthologies for essays on controversial subjects such as gun control or immigration; most essay collections come complete with discussion questions and writing prompts. Look online for true adventure, crime, and sports stories and articles on topics of interest to young people—how to be popular, find a friend, get into college, or choose a pet, for example.

As you search for materials, keep in mind that boys often hate fiction. I don't know why they hate it, but many English teachers and reading instructors can verify this tendency. Many grown men prefer nonfiction as well. Check out the bookstore aisles. You'll find more men in the biography, science, military history, and do-it-yourself sections than in the literature stacks. Perhaps they simply cannot or will not suspend their disbelief long enough to become engaged in something that isn't real (unless it is science fiction). But boys will read nonfiction—about bugs, dinosaurs, race cars, computers, sports, spaceships, inventors, and dragons. If you allow those children Who dislike fiction to read nonfiction until they become good readers, they will be better able and more inclined to read fiction when you ask them to. Once they can read more easily, you will have done far more than help them improve their reading skills. You will have taught them that books can be enjoyable—and that we sometimes need to read things we aren't wild about in order to learn new information or develop new skills.

One way to engage students in a whole-group reading selection is to simply distribute the assignment without announcing that you are going to read. Let your students look the reading material over on their own. Some of them will begin reading immediately. Others will wait for your cue. If your quick starters begin making comments about the assignment, don't hush them up. Their comments will create interest and entice other students to read. Let them talk for a while, unless they begin shouting. Then ask them if they would mind backing up so that you can read the entire selection together as a class in order to discuss it afterward. (If some students ignore you and continue reading ahead on their own, let them go, as long as they are polite. They aren't holding anybody back, and they will probably reread the selection along with the class after they have finished it. It is very frustrating for fast readers to be held back. Many of them will shut down mentally or become disruptive out of boredom. So if you can give up some of the desire to control and let them read ahead, you will be doing everybody a service, including yourself.)

One activity that I've used with good success is the book exchange. I get a number of books from the public or school library on a wide array of topics, from spaceships to teen romance novels to horror stories. Then I place a book on each student's desk before class begins. Students read the books on their desks for five minutes, then give the book a rating of one to ten and jot down a few quick notes on an index card. They exchange books and read for another five minutes, then rate the book and take notes. They repeat this until they have read at least five books. If they like a particular book, they can keep the book. Students who don't like any of the books continue to exchange books until they find something they like. Some students may have to spend a class period (or two) in the library doing their own book exchange before they locate something irresistible. It's worth your time and theirs to allow them this opportunity. (If stubborn students refuse to find something simply to avoid reading, you'll be able to tell. In that case, I provide a book or article and insist that they read it for one session. I tell them that if they can't find something, I'll continue to provide different samples for them. That method always seems to inspire them to find something on their own. When they realize that they are going to have to read sooner or later, they give up and accept their fate. But if they have the option of choosing what they're going to read, there is a better chance they will learn to enjoy reading—or at least not hate it so much, which is still an improvement.)

## 9. They Get Lost and Can't Remember What They Have Just Read

Unfortunately, many students can read quite well without understanding what they are reading. They somehow missed the important point that when we read we must create some kind of mental reference. Without that reference, words are just words. One boy described his experience this way: "It's like I'm reading one of those signs in front of the bank where the letters move. As soon as I read the words, they disappear."

You don't have to be a reading teacher to give students some basic pointers on reading comprehension. First, explain that when we read, we create a mental picture of what we are reading. As we add details, the picture becomes more clear or changes to adjust to new or different information. If you lose the picture when you are reading, you are starting to lose your comprehension. Back up until you can see the picture again, and continue reading. If you do this as a class with a story or article, you can read a paragraph, ask students what they see, and discuss their different visions. This will help students who still don't get it to understand what you are talking about. Then read the next paragraph and stop again to ask students to describe their mental pictures. When I do this with a class, even with adults, they usually become very excited because they finally (some for the first time) understand what all the fuss is about and why some people enjoy reading. This exercise works far better than simply asking questions to check their comprehension after they have read a selection, because students with poor comprehension don't understand why they can't remember information and other students can.

Another option is to use books on tape, either commercial or homemade. I have made a number of tapes on which I read material for my classes. I play the tape in class, and the students follow along. This helps them learn pacing and phrasing, and it frees them to focus on maintaining a mental picture, instead of worrying about pronunciation. I ask them to listen to the entire selection once and then ask questions before we listen a second time. And, of course, we know that students learn better when they teach what they have learned, so asking students to read something and then give a summary to another student who hasn't read that selection is also a good activity.

If you detect serious comprehension problems, or if a student asks for more help, find out if your school has a reading specialist on the staff or as a regular visitor. If not, check with your local library to see if it has a literacy program, and encourage your students to attend the free sessions. Also, look for good Web sites devoted to reading. Do an Internet search for "online reading instruction," and you will find a plethora of books, articles, exercises, games, and instructional materials.

### 10. If Asked for Their Opinion of a Book, They Fear Their Opinion Will Be Wrong

So many students—most with tears in their eyes—have told me about the same experience: a teacher asked them to write their opinion about a book or story. The students worked hard on their essays and expected high marks for effort and content. Their teachers assigned either a D or F with no explanation or wrote some insulting comment such as "Wrong!" or "This is ridiculous!" in red ink across the top of the paper. In addition to doling out low grades and making students doubt their own intelligence, those teachers sent a clear message to the students: your opinion is worthless.

If you ask for an opinion, accept what you get and grade the writing on composition and content—not on whether the student agrees with your opinion. Certainly, you can appreciate the literary merit of *The Scarlet Letter* and

*Julius Caesar,* but sometimes young people simply aren't able to appreciate things we think they should appreciate. Instead of belittling them or lowering their grades when they don't get it, reward their honest effort and encourage them to develop their ideas logically and completely. If you allow your students to maintain their dignity and self-respect, they will continue to try and continue to progress. With advancing maturity and practice, their reading and writing skills will improve and they will be better able to appreciate literature that demands a more sophisticated approach.

Once they have a bit more confidence, you can teach your students the difference between a personal opinion (I don't like stories where animals get killed) and an academic critique (the characters in this story are unbelievable). First, teach them how to analyze the reading selections and articulate their personal opinions about what they are reading. Even little children will have an opinion about whether a story is interesting, informative, or exciting; whether characters are good or bad; whether descriptions paint vivid pictures; and whether the ending satisfies the reader. Prompt your students with questions: Why do they dislike certain stories and books? Is the vocabulary too hard? Can they give some examples of difficult vocabulary words? Are the sentences too long and complex or too short and choppy? Are the characters unlikable or unbelievable? Where does the plot become unbelievable? Is the pace of the story too slow or fast? Is it hard to tell who is talking?

When students can intelligently articulate their opinions, they are ready to learn how to analyze a story on its literary merits. ("Boring" and "stupid" are not acceptable adjectives for literary critiques.) Now students must use specific references to the material to make their point, using specific vocabulary and terms that you have taught them, such as *plot, dialogue, irony,* and *tone.* It may be helpful to teach these two different critical approaches as the "personal" versus the "professional" response to a book or story. You can personally like a book that you know isn't really written very well (characters are one-dimensional, the plot is predictable, and the dialogue is stilted), just as you can dislike a book that you know meets all the criteria for a well-written book (well-developed characters, snappy dialogue, great plot). The key to success—in school, at least—is to learn the criteria the "experts" use to evaluate books.

And one last thing that I think is very important to teach students who struggle to write acceptable literary critiques in school: once you get out of school, you can think whatever you like about any book, and nobody can give you a grade on your opinions. People can disagree with you all they like, but there's no report card in real life. You'll get to be the judge and the jury for all the books you read—or don't read. But don't give up on reading and deprive yourself of the many things that books can offer, just because your teachers don't always appreciate your brilliant opinions.

### 11. They Hate People Telling Them What to Do All Day Long

This is a personal issue, not a reading issue, but it often spills over into reading, so teachers can waste a lot of time and energy trying to win the battle of wills. Sometimes it can be difficult for people who enjoy reading (most teachers are book lovers) to empathize with people who don't. And many teachers worry about lowering academic standards. I'm not suggesting that we lower standards, but that we focus first on why our students don't want to read instead of on ways to convince or force them to read. In some cases, nonreaders simply need to assert their independence. They will resist our efforts to make them do anything, especially reading. In other cases, people have been taught through experience to hate reading. I liken people's attitudes about books to their attitudes about such things as dogs, horses, broccoli, or sex. If the first experience was enjoyable, people tend to look forward to future encounters. But if that first experience was traumatic, painful, or shameful, many people find it hard to forget. And if that painful first experience was followed by an equally uncomfortable third or fourth encounter, people understandably develop deep-seated aversions to specific activities.

If you work to establish good relationships with your reluctant readers before you ask them to read, you'll find them much more willing to work at things they don't enjoy. If you are thinking, "I don't have time for such nonsense," then consider the amount of time you waste on arguing with students or on discipline issues that arise from them not wanting to work. The time you spend creating a classroom environment where students feel motivated to cooperate will come back to you tenfold.

### AND NOW FOR SOMETHING COMPLETELY DIFFERENT

One elementary school teacher told me about a boy in her class who cooperated with all her instructions, but still couldn't seem to read. After vision tests and hearing tests and all kinds of interventions, she and the counselors were still stumped.

## Upside-Down Did the Trick

"Then one day I decided to turn his book upside down," the teacher said. "I don't know why. It just occurred to me to try it. And—bingo—he started reading. He had some kind of visual processing disorder or something. I never did quite understand, but he learned to read upside down. And later on, he turned the book around and started reading right-side up."

Reading upside down is a good example of a teacher using one of the most readily available and important resources any teacher can tap into—your own brain. Your own creativity and imagination. Don't be afraid to try something just because it seems silly. When you run into a problem that seems unsolvable, brainstorm every conceivable idea you can come up with. (The hardest part about brainstorming, as you know, is resisting the natural temptation to judge.) Brainstorm with another teacher—or with students. The more brains the better. You never know when you're going to hit on an idea that works. And even if it works for just one student, that's still a huge contribution to that student's life and education and tends to have a ripple effect. If you teach a student something that changes his or her life for the better, that positive change will affect the student's family and any future family the student may have. That's why the each-one-teach-one approach is so powerful. You don't have to save them all. If you save one, you're still a hero in my book.

## The Read Right Approach

At an education conference I happened to meet a teacher who had just tried a new method she read about in Dr. Dee Tadlock's book *Read Right! Coaching Your Child to Excellence in Reading* (McGraw-Hill, 2005). Tadlock was a reading specialist and the mother of a very bright young boy who couldn't read. When the teachers and reading specialists failed, Tadlock wasn't worried. After all, she was a reading specialist; she'd teach her son herself. When she failed, and her son gave up hope of ever learning, Tadlock gave up her job and went back to school to study the brain and how it learns. She developed her own approach to reading instruction and taught her son. She then wrote about her experience in the hope that her method might help others.

The teacher at the conference gave me a copy of *Read Right!* which I read on my return flight. Although the book is intended for working with beginning readers, I decided to try some of the suggestions for my own high school students—and they worked! The basic idea, as I understand it, is that our brains need to have an internal model of excellence to follow if we want to learn to perform a new skill with a high degree of excellence. Poor readers don't have that internal model. They hear other people read well, but they don't know how it feels to read well themselves. Excellent reading feels comfortable, sounds like normal conversation, and makes sense. Most of my remedial high school readers read in monotone voices, without inflection, or they read with inflection but without acknowledging punctuation or other indicators. They clearly don't understand what they were reading half the time. Even when they read as well as they can, they are nowhere near excellent.

So I followed the book's advice about giving feedback. I explained what I was trying to do, so my students wouldn't become frustrated or embarrassed. I would read a sentence from our literature book and ask a volunteer to read it out loud in the same manner that I did (some students opted to do this privately, but most were willing to do it as a group, since they weren't required to volunteer). Students had to read the sentences, not just mimic them or repeat what I had said without reading. Instead of praising them and saying, "Good, thank you," I would say, "That was not excellent. Try it again." The student would read the sentence again. If the second reading was better, I would say, "Better, but still not excellent." Then I would model excellent reading again. The student would try again. If they read excellently, I would say, "That was excellent." Now their brains knew what they were striving for. They had an internal standard of excellence and could make adjustments in order to achieve that standard again.

As more and more students take the chance and read out loud, others become braver. They want to know what excellent reading feels like too. This experiment has helped a good number of my remedial readers move up to the next level. It isn't my only tool, but it is a great addition to my teacher's toolbox. Obviously, I can't do justice to *Read Right!* or this reading approach in a few short paragraphs, but I mention it because it works well for me and it is based on common sense. Even if it doesn't work for you, it might spark an idea or lead you to another alternative approach. If we don't look for solutions, we'll never find them.

## SHAKESPEARE FOR RELUCTANT READERS

Before I ever mention Shakespeare to my reluctant readers, I make sure that they know I care about them and truly have their best interests at heart. I want them to trust me when I tell them we are going to read Shakespeare, and it isn't going to be painful. They won't have to memorize Shakespeare's birth date and birthplace, draw a picture of the Globe Theatre, or identify the speaker of random quotes from whatever play we have studied. (Later, after they have read some of his works, students tend to be interested in the historical details and I include them in our lessons and discussions, but not as test items.) There won't be a regular test at the end. I will just ask them to answer some questions about the play, but there will be no right or wrong answers. And they will be able to choose the format of their own projects, whether writing, drawing, or performing.

I promise my students that I will not make them hate Shakespeare. And I also promise that after we have read exactly half of the first play, we will take a class vote. If the majority of the students want to stop, we will close the books and move on to something else without any penalty, although I will ask for their reasons for not wanting to continue and we will not watch the movie version. (Before they begin, they always vow to quit reading halfway through, but I have never had a class that actually opted to quit; students always want to know the ending, because William tells a good tale.)

Why should they have to read plays by another "boring dead white guy" from the boring old literary canon? Because, aside from the fact that he was a white guy and he is dead, he was an intensely talented and prolific writer. Quotations from Shakespeare appear in so many aspects of world culture that being unfamiliar with his works puts students at a disadvantage in society (fickle men are often referred to as Romeos, for example; and people giving speeches sometimes begin by saying, "Friends, Romans, countrymen, lend me your ears"). In addition, every college student in the United States and Europe is expected to have read at least a few plays and sonnets at some time during high school if they expect to be considered well educated.

But Shakespeare is too hard to read, students usually protest. I agree that reading Shakespeare requires effort: some people spend four or more years in college studying his work alone. But difficult doesn't mean impossible.

"There is nothing wrong with your brains," I explain. "Ideas don't have grade levels. You can think about things just as well as the next person, even college students. Your reading skills may need some help, but that's why you have me. I will help you with the reading."

After I first mention Shakespeare to the class, I wait a week or so. Then one day I write several "backwards style" sentences on the board: "Where goest thou after class? He thinks to woo the fair maiden. 'Twere better, methinks, to run than to tarry." I ask my students to figure out the sentences and to try to write more of their own, to get them used to interpreting an entire phrase rather than word by word. Then I make a short glossary of words from the upcoming play, such as *marry, tarry, prithee, hence, 'tis,* and *whence.* (Students always raise a delighted ruckus when we get to the word *Ho.*) We make a poster of the glossary and keep it on the wall for reference. We add another chart with brief definitions of literary terms such as *irony, foreshadowing,* and *motivation,* which we include in the class discussions.

## The Art Part

Next comes the art part, to pull in the visual learners. On the board or on a large piece of paper I sketch a scene like the one in Figure 7.1 to represent the play and the main characters. If we are reading *The Taming of the Shrew,* I draw the two sisters, one smiling and one frowning, and the suitors standing in the street. Petruchio is about to enter town on horseback from one direction, while Lucentio and Tranio enter from the opposite direction.

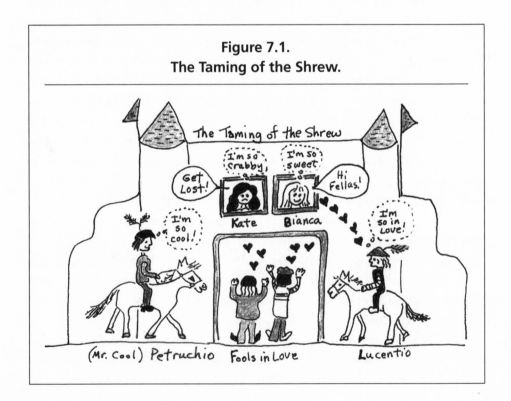

**Figure 7.1.**
**The Taming of the Shrew.**

**Figure 7.2.**
**Romeo and Juliet.**

Before we begin reading *Romeo and Juliet,* I draw two walled estates with a road running in front of them, as shown in Figure 7.2. I draw Juliet looking out her window and Romeo looking out his, with hearts connecting them. I draw two of the other main characters, Mercutio and Tybalt, fighting in the street. I use two different colors to distinguish the Capulets from the Montagues, which usually prompts a discussion of the similarity between the two ancient families and modern-day gangs, because of their fierce loyalty and willingness to die for the "family."

*Note to the artistically challenged:* As you can see, I never learned how to draw in perspective. Bad art is actually good in the classroom, because students love to improve on my drawings. Usually several students volunteer to correct my artwork or draw their own. Sometimes students discover new talents as they try to teach me to draw a horse or a castle or a fair maiden.

## The Ground Rules

Before we begin reading, we create a list of all the primary characters and post the list on the wall near the glossary, so that nobody will get lost during the reading. Then I explain exactly what I expect, as follows.

### Rules for Reading Shakespeare

1. Nobody is required to read out loud.

2. Nobody has to participate in discussions.

3. Points will not be deducted for quiet listening. Points will be deducted for sleeping, laughing at people who volunteer to read, or disrupting the class during reading.

4. In order to earn a passing grade for the unit, students must remain seated upright, awake, with books open to the page that we are currently reading. They must pay attention and ask questions if they become lost. And they must listen quietly, even if they choose not to take notes when we discuss the play at the end of each act.

## The Opening Curtain

We begin slowly. I explain the basic setup of the play. Then I read the first few lines and stop to paraphrase them. I read a scene, trying to add drama by using different voices for the characters. After a short while, I stop and ask students to help me out by reading a part. If nobody volunteers, I continue to read, stopping frequently to sum up the action. Occasionally I read an entire act by myself before students feel confident enough to try reading aloud.

In the beginning we do not spend the entire class period reading Shakespeare. We read one or two scenes, discuss them briefly, then go on to something different. After we finish reading one act, we make a set of class notes, using the board or overhead slides. I ask the class to state in one or two phrases the most important things that occurred in each scene. When we have finished reading the play, they have a complete outline of the plot, and I allow them to use their plot outlines during the postreading questions. (Those students who opt not to take notes are not permitted to copy other people's notes at the last minute. I don't force them to take notes, but I remind them that if they don't take notes, they won't have notes on hand when the questions begin. By the time we have read the second act, the holdouts have usually joined the note takers.)

## The Final Curtain

When we finish the play, we watch the movie version if one is available. Then each student completes the wrap-up questions, writes a journal response to the play, and chooses one of three projects: illustrate a scene from the play or make a poster to advertise it, write a magazine-style review of the play, present a monologue or act out a scene from the play (they have the option of rewriting the monologue or scene into modern language).

The wrap-up counts for 50 percent of the unit grade; the journal and project make up the other 50 percent. The wrap-up does not include lower-level thinking skills such as matching. Instead, students choose five out of ten questions to answer about the play. The questions require a basic understanding of the plot, character motivation, and setting. Here are some sample wrap-up questions:

Give one possible reason to explain Kate's behavior. Why does she act like a shrew?

If you had to marry one of the sisters, Kate or Bianca, who would you marry, and why?

What kind of person is Romeo? Give examples from the play to support your opinion.

Give an example of foreshadowing that occurs in *Romeo and Juliet.*

Why would a priest lie to the parents of some teenagers who weren't supposed to be dating?

Why do people feel they can't go on living after somebody they love dies?

How would you respond if your newlywed spouse treated you the way Petruchio treats Kate?

At the end, do you think Kate is really tamed or is she just pretending? Explain.

Students can't cheat or fake their way through the wrap-up, but if they have been conscious during the reading, they will be able to talk about the plot of the play and the characters. But instead of simply recalling information, they must analyze and evaluate what they have read. Invariably, after we finish the first play students ask if we can read more Shakespeare.

Reading Shakespeare this way takes more time, at least the first few times, but the payoff is huge. Students learn that Shakespeare is accessible, that the quality of his writing makes the effort worthwhile, and, most important of all, they learn that they are not stupid and can indeed read what the "smart kids" read. It's not unusual after reading the first play to hear students trying to use "old Shakespeare talk" in their conversations. "Yo, Tony, goes thou to lunchest?" or "Check out Tyrone—he be wooing and courting the fair Tyeisha." Because my postreading assignments focus on understanding the characters and their motivation along with student evaluation and analysis, students finish each project feeling that they have reviewed the play rather than being tested on it; methinks that difference be a huge one.

## USE MUSIC TO INTRODUCE POETRY

Because so many of my students hated reading or had negative experiences with English classes, I knew that if I announced that we would be reading poetry, I would lose them before we began. So I decided to sneak in the back door with a little rhythm and rhyme. In the movie *Dangerous Minds*, the producers took some liberties when they portrayed my approach. Yes, I did use song lyrics, but not Bob Dylan's "Tambourine Man." Instead, I typed out the words to the Public Enemy rap song "911 Is a Joke," Smokey Robinson's "Tears of a Clown," an English translation of the Hispanic folk song "Guantanamera," and the Garth Brooks hit "We Shall Be Free." When my students walked into class, I distributed the lyrics without saying anything.

"What's this?" they asked.

"Something I think is interesting," I said. After a few minutes, one of the kids said, "Hey, I know this song." Several private conversations sprang up around the room. Finally, somebody said, "Hey, Miss J, how come you gave us these songs?"

"I wanted to know if you think they are poetry," I said. (I love it when the kids play right along with my script.)

"Poetry?" a few kids mumbled. They shrugged and looked at each other. "Is this poetry?"

"You tell me," I insisted. "You know what a poem is, don't you?"

"Yeah," they said. "Poems rhyme."

"They got rhythm too," somebody else interjected.

"Right. Poems have rhythm or rhyme and sometimes both," I said. I held up the lyrics sheet. "So is this poetry?"

"You're the teacher," one girl said. "You tell us if it's poetry."

"You're the student," I said. "You tell me. Take your time. Think about it. Feel free to discuss it among yourselves. I'll wait." And I sat down with a very patient look on my face.

After a few minutes, one of the boys ventured a tentative "I think they're poems. They all have music, and music has rhythm. And most of them rhyme."

"I agree," I said. "I think many song lyrics are poetic, and the best songs are very good poetry. And I'm going to give you the opportunity to bring in your favorite song lyrics to share with the class." Several students applauded. Some cheered. Nobody protested.

"What if we don't have the words?" one girl asked.

"If you can't find the lyrics, you can check the Internet to see if you can find the words. Or you can listen to the song several times and write them down. I'll type them for you."

Those students were ready. Some of them opened their notebooks and began singing to themselves, jotting down song lyrics.

"But there is one condition," I added. "You will need to explain to the class why you admire your particular song choice as good poetry."

"That's it?" a boy asked. "We just have to say why it's a good poem?"

"Yes," I said. "That's it. One little condition. So who's interested?" Nearly every student raised his or her hand. "Good. But in order to explain why your song is good poetry, you're going to have to learn the language of poetry. If you'll bear with me for a week or so, I'll teach you how to talk about poems."

A few kids frowned, but before they could voice the suspicion that they had been had once again, I launched into my introductory lesson on onomatopoeia. Slam! Bam! Pow! Ping! Before they knew what had hit them, those students were reading poetry.

I'd like to share with you the results of that first poetry experiment with those antireading students. Everybody in that class, including me, expressed very distinct preferences for music. Before we started that project, I dismissed the idea that any student could find a poetic heavy metal song, but somebody did. Very few of those students had been introduced to jazz, and many of them later became big fans. And students who claimed they hated rap or country found themselves responding to the lyrics of songs when we read them without hearing the music. We discovered that it was often the beat we disliked, not the song itself. Students from very disparate backgrounds realized that they shared common emotions and dreams. Also I learned that filthy, disgusting, racist, sexist, or violence-promoting songs can't be passed off as good poetry. One young man (an angry young man who usually sat with his arms crossed and his mouth clamped shut during our class discussions) brought in a rap song filled with profanity and obscene language. Instead of dismissing his song choice, I asked him to tell me what he admired about that particular song as poetry.

"I like the beat," he said.

"We aren't looking just for good beats," I said. "We're looking for really fine words in this project. Which words in this song do you really admire as good poetry? Can you show me some internal rhyme or a metaphor? Maybe a simile? Some alliteration?"

He frowned at the lyrics he had scribbled on a sheet of notebook paper. "Well, I don't really like the words that much," he admitted. "But it has a really good beat."

"Then you need to find another song with words that you do admire," I said. The following day he brought another song. It wasn't exactly the kind of song parents would appreciate, but it wasn't vulgar and obscene, and because he was prepared to participate in his own learning for the first time, I accepted his contribution.

Two amazing things occurred after we completed that poetry project. First, my students didn't protest when I announced that we would be moving on to our textbooks to analyze and discuss classic poetry, including Shakespearean sonnets. Clearly, because they had analyzed and evaluated so many songs and original poems, they felt confident of their ability to tackle any poetry they might meet.

The second amazing thing was that my belligerent, pugnacious, disenchanted students unanimously elected "We Shall Be Free" as the best poetry of all the songs we read, which made me realize that instead of being amoral, apathetic young rebels, they were idealistic and hopeful children desperately in need of good adult leadership. For those who are unfamiliar with the song, here are the phrases that my students voted as best poetry:

> When the last child cries for a crust of bread
> When the last man dies for just words that he said
> When the last thing we notice is the color of skin
> and the first thing we look for is the beauty within . . .
> . . . then we shall be free.

## DISCUSSION POINTS

1. Describe your own early experiences with reading: How did you learn to read?

2. Which of the techniques you have used to motivate reluctant readers have worked the best?

3. What is your opinion of requiring students to read out loud in front of peers?

4. How can we use music and art to enhance reading for students?

5. What is your opinion on the use of sustained silent reading in school?

# Light and Learning

Alex Gonzales should have been my dream student: he was intel-ligent, witty, well mannered, likable, good-looking, responsible, and considerate of other students. He cooperated with the school staff and treated his parents with respect. His standardized test scores placed him in the top tenth percentile. Alex earned passing grades in every subject—barely passing. He refused to read one word more than the minimum required to pass any class.

## CAN'T READ—OR WON'T READ?

"I hate school," Alex told me when he applied for entrance into the Computer Academy, a school-within-a-school for at-risk teens at a high school south of San Francisco.

"But you are clearly intelligent enough to graduate and go to college," I said, thinking that perhaps some strong encouragement would boost his motivation.

"I'd rather go to prison than college," Alex responded. "But my parents want me to graduate, so I need to get into the academy."

As a student in my English class, Alex participated in discussions, wrote articulate compositions, and listened attentively to other students when we read aloud. During independent-reading assignments, however, Alex became the at-risk underachiever who had failed his freshman year in high school. He drummed on his desktop, hurled paper projectiles around the room, demanded bathroom passes, "accidentally" dropped his textbook onto the floor, picked fights with other students, and defiantly invited me to send him to the office—anything to avoid reading for more than a few minutes.

Because I had the same students for three years and because I spent the first year assessing their abilities and attitudes and helping them play academic catch-up, Alex had managed to squeeze by with minimal reading and a C in my sophomore English class. When Alex started his junior year, I focused on addressing those behaviors that kept him from enjoying the As he was clearly capable of earning.

Alex had joined the Computer Academy because he believed he could succeed in school with the help of our four-teacher team. He had signed a contract promising to stay off drugs, away from gangs, and in the classrooms where he belonged. He maintained that he wanted to improve his study skills and habits. He claimed he was willing to do anything to improve his chances of graduating—anything except read.

"I just hate reading," Alex insisted. "I've always hated it."

"But you enjoy listening to other students read," I said. "You always have comments on the stories. You add intelligent comments to our discussions. You like figuring out the motivation of characters and predicting twists in the plots."

"Yeah," Alex nodded. "But that's different. When I hear the stories, I like them. When I read them, I hate them."

Reading comprehension wasn't the problem, nor was vocabulary, phonics, or any other testable aspect of reading. Alex earned above-average grades on every achievement test. Later I learned that he forced himself to read in order to pass his exams, but at the time I began to wonder whether his previous teachers were right when they said that Alex's problem was power, that he had chosen reading as the one area where he refused to give up control. They believed that because he could read well when he wanted to, he simply didn't want to.

One morning I cajoled Alex's class into independently reading Act II of Othello—a difficult task for any group, but especially challenging for disenchanted, academically impoverished teens. Two minutes into the silent-reading period, Alex began his usual disruptive behavior. Out of patience I shouted, "Alex, would you just sit down and read your danged book?"

Alex slammed his book open and bent over it. Ten minutes later he walked to my desk and said, "This is why I hate to read." He motioned toward his eyes, which were red-rimmed and bloodshot. Tears streamed down his cheeks. I was astounded. I knew Alex hadn't been anywhere or done anything except read for those ten minutes.

"What happened?" I asked.

"I don't know," Alex said. "But this is what happens when I read. My eyes hurt."

"How long has this been going on?"

"Since forever."

That evening I called Alex's parents to make sure they had health insurance. I asked them to schedule an appointment with an eye doctor to have Alex's eyes examined. I accompanied Alex and his mother to the appointment because I was so concerned about his problem and I wanted to make sure the doctor took him seriously. After a complete exam, the doctor shook his head.

"Alex has a slight astigmatism," he said, "but there is nothing wrong with his vision. And I can find no medical reason for the bloodshot, watery eyes."

Back at school the following day, I asked my coworkers whether they had ever encountered a situation like Alex's. Some had, but none had an explanation or suggestion. After school I called Diane Herrera Shepard, a friend from Albuquerque who was living in a neighborhood near my school at the time and who worked as a tutor for learning disabled college students. I described Alex's situation to Diane.

"I'll be in your classroom tomorrow," she said.

Diane arrived with a briefcase packed with papers and 8-by-10-inch transparencies in an array of colors—shades of red, rose, peach, gold, gray, purple, green, and blue. She held out a paper on which a series of black Xs formed the shape of a pumpkin and asked Alex if he could count the number of Xs in the middle row of the pumpkin without using his finger as a guide.

"No," said Alex, "because the Xs are moving."

My students and I crowded around Diane. Some students quickly counted the Xs. Several other students agreed with Alex that the Xs were "wiggly." One student said the Xs looked like they were burning off the page. Another student remarked that it was hard to concentrate on the Xs because the page had so many "white rivers" running through it.

Diane placed a purple filter over the page and asked Alex if he could count the Xs. Without hesitating, Alex correctly counted the Xs.

"Cool!" he exclaimed. "How did you do that?"

Diane explained that black print on a white page creates very high contrast and that people with scotopic sensitivity syndrome (also known as Irlen Syndrome) find such contrasts distracting, uncomfortable, or even painful. Fluorescent lighting often increases the discomfort because fluorescent lights flicker and don't contain the full spectrum of colors that occur in natural light. By placing a colored overlay on the page or wearing specially created colored lenses, many people who suffer from scotopic sensitivity can read without eyestrain or headaches—even some who have a long history of problems with reading.

Diane distributed transparent overlays, and the students placed them over their textbooks, comparing the different colors. Placing a blue transparency over my own book made it much easier for me to read.

"Light sensitivity is a controversial subject," Diane warned me. "I offer this to students as a possibility. If it helps them, then I'm happy to provide whatever information is available."

I presented keynote speeches to over one hundred organizations over the two decades following Diane's visit to my classroom. During every presentation, I have mentioned scotopic sensitivity, and in every single instance multiple individuals have approached me following my speech to share their own stories about light sensitivity. Most recently, in Austin, Texas, after I addressed the annual conference of the Association of Texas Professional Educators, one teacher came up and hugged me.

"Bless you for telling that boy's story," she said. "You never know who it will help. My daughter is in the fourth grade, and we just got her some tinted lenses to wear while she is reading and it has changed her life. Before that, nobody knew what to do with her. She's been in every special ed program at the school, but nothing worked. Now she can read."

Because of those people and their stories, and because I have repeatedly seen dramatic and instantaneous responses to using Irlen filters and other transparent overlays in my own classrooms, I am now convinced that scotopic sensitivity does exist and that it may be responsible for many of the so-called learning disabilities in our schools. I believe that if we changed the lighting in our classrooms to natural daylight (by putting windows in our windowless classrooms) or replacing standard fluorescent lights with incandescent or full-spectrum fluorescent bulbs, we would greatly reduce both reading and behavior problems among students. I also believe that screening for scotopic sensitivity syndrome should be a regular part of every school health program and the first intervention for behavior problems that arise during reading activities.

## SEEING IS BELIEVING

In my own classroom, Alex's behavior changed dramatically from the moment he began reading with an Irlen filter. His reading problems disappeared, and he decided to go on to college (he currently works as an electronics engineer for a company in Silicon Valley). His grades improved in all of his classes, and he insisted that the purple filter was the key to his success. I still wasn't certain.

Four years later, after moving from California to New Mexico, an encounter with another student convinced me that scotopic sensitivity does indeed exist. Valerie Martin, a freshman in my reading class, displayed behavior very similar to Alex's. An intelligent, outgoing, articulate student, Valerie complained of headaches during every independent-reading assignment and became defiant and obnoxious if I demanded that she read silently for more than a few minutes. When I realized I might be working with another light-sensitive student, I was delighted to learn that one of the counselors had been trained at an Irlen center. The following week, when the counselor visited my classroom, fully one-half of the students in that class responded to the use of transparencies. Seventeen of thirty-four students had been labeled as suffering from learning disabilities or behavior problems—when in fact it appeared that their problem might actually be perceptual. This 50 percent response corresponded with Paul Whiting's research conclusions.

Valerie responded exactly as Alex had. The moment she received an Irlen filter (hers was such a dark purple that I could not read the print through it), she became the official reader for the class, insisting that she be given more turns to read aloud because she had not taken turns earlier. During class readings she often read aloud for twenty or thirty minutes without complaining of any discomfort. Her grades shot up to straight As in every subject.

"I'm so glad I found this out," Valerie told me, and she went on to say:

> But I'm kind of mad. I've been going to school for ten years, and all
> that time people have been telling me I'm crazy, lazy, stubborn, and

stupid. I used to think maybe I was crazy or something, because I would say reading made my eyes hurt, and teachers would say that wasn't true. They thought I was just trying to get out of work, and so did my parents. So everybody was mad at me all the time, even though I told them that reading gave me a headache. I was starting to think I might be stupid and crazy.

I can imagine how frustrating it must be for children to be told that their heads don't ache and their eyes don't hurt, to be accused of being lazy and stubborn. One of the most disheartening aspects of this situation is that when people who suffer from scotopic sensitivity concentrate harder on reading, their symptoms become worse. No wonder so many remedial readers also have behavior problems. Children's choices are limited. They can't demand to be taken seriously. But they can misbehave in school—because standing in the corner or sitting in detention doesn't make their heads hurt or their eyes ache.

After my experience with the remedial readers who responded so positively to using the transparencies, I started buying colored transparent overlays at the office supply store and distributing them to all my classes during the first weeks of school, as I briefly described scotopic sensitivity. Something very interesting happened in many of my remedial and at-risk classes. Students who were in the tenth or eleventh grade and reading at a fourth- or fifth-grade level, but who showed no signs of having light sensitivity would often grab an overlay and place it over the page and then invite me to teach them to read. One seventeen-year-old boy who had previously resisted any help decided he was ready to learn. Using the overlays allowed him to save face and accept reading instruction—something he had previously insisted was for "little kids" and "dummies."

"I'm not stupid, you know," he said. "I have a condition. That's how come I couldn't read before."

## SCOTOPIC SENSITIVITY

At the time I met Alex in the early 1990s, very little information was available on scotopic sensitivity aside from the fact that a psychologist named Helen Irlen had discovered a recurring visual perceptual problem during her work with adult students who had trouble reading. The patented Irlen filters and screening process were not readily available to the public. In order to get the filters, students had to have a vision exam to rule out normal vision problems, and then they had to be tested by a certified screener. Since then, the filters have been made available to the public, along with numerous articles and books offering advice and links to other resources.

You will find more sources of information in the Appendix of this book, but for a quick look I suggest visiting the Web site of the National Reading Styles Institute (NRSI; www.nrsi.com) or the Irlen Institute (www.irlen.com). Both sites have background information, testing kits, and overlays for sale. NRSI offers sample kits of small overlays as well as the standard page-size transparencies. The Irlen site includes an international list of certified screeners and a patented training program for screeners.

Despite numerous studies, there is no consensus among researchers about the cause of light sensitivity. Some believe the predominance of green in fluorescent lighting contributes to reading problems in rooms lit solely by fluorescents. (Full-spectrum fluorescents are now available at reasonable cost.) Others believe the sensitivity is caused by a vision convergence problem where the eyes don't work together as they should, or that the sensitivity may be linked to a deficiency of essential fatty acids or other nutrients. But there is general agreement that the following factors definitely affect light-sensitive people:

☐ **High-contrast print, such as black letters on white paper.** Many teachers report improved motivation and achievement when student assignments are printed on pastel-colored paper.

☐ **Lighting.** Given a choice, the vast majority of students choose to read under incandescent or natural light instead of fluorescents.

☐ **Glare created by lighting or text printed on glossy pages.** Some schools now allow reading visors to be worn in the classroom during reading assignments and during exams.

Charter and independent schools, colleges, universities, and various scientific organizations have welcomed the possibility that scotopic sensitivity screening may offer new hope for struggling readers. Sadly, U.S. public schools, with their bureaucratic maze of requirements and roadblocks, and thousands upon thousands of floundering readers have been slower to open their doors to screeners—perhaps because the schools' fluorescent lights are a primary culprit in the problem area of the reading department, and new lighting costs money. But now that word of mouth and personal anecdotes have the support of scientific studies that confirm the validity of using colored overlays to help poor readers, public schools are becoming more receptive to the idea. Many public schools now encourage their counselors and teachers to attend workshops where they can learn how to screen students, and some schools routinely refer parents to certified screeners as a standard intervention when reading problems arise.

At the University of Glamorgan in South Wales, light sensitivity is taken seriously enough to warrant the posting of this information on the university's student support Web site (www.glam.ac.uk), under the link titled "Support for Students with Disability and Dyslexia":

> Scotopic sensitivity syndrome (SSS) has a cluster of symptoms, and although little is known about the physiological basis of SSS, it is thought that it is due to the spectral modification of light. That is, individuals with SSS perceive the world around them in a distorted way as a result of sensitivity to certain wavelengths of light. This can lead to reading difficulties because those individuals do not see the printed page the same way as proficient readers do. For example, the page may flash, the words become blurred, move, change shape or reverse or the background may pulsate.

At Piedmont Community Charter School in Gastonia, North Carolina, scotopic sensitivity is a given. Principal Courtney Madden first used colored overlays when he was the principal of a public school. Madden used to gather groups of errant boys in his office every afternoon and have them read to him while using the overlays. "I was just piddling around, didn't really know what I was doing at the time," says Madden. "I had read about the overlays and got some samples, and they worked with those young fellows. So when we had thirty-six kids last year here at Piedmont who hadn't been able to make any progress in reading, I decided to try scotopic screening as one of many pieces to the puzzle. After using the overlays, all but two of those students passed the EOG [end-of-grade] exam."

In addition to providing overlays for use in school and at home, Piedmont Community Charter School provides a variety of colored papers for teachers to use in making assignments and worksheets for students who use overlays. The children's names are posted above the appropriate colors in the workroom. And because North Carolina has approved overlays for use during end-of-grade testing, students at Piedmont use the overlays during the testing itself.

"I know a lot of people are skeptical about the overlays," says Madden. "They want something real challenging and difficult as a solution to reading problems. And had I not experimented years ago, I would have thought, This cannot be. But those overlays have really helped some students who used to earn thirties and forties and are now making nineties and hundreds on their work. In one year our school went from 75 percent of our students passing the state test to 89.4 percent passing."

## SIGNS AND SYMPTOMS OF LIGHT SENSITIVITY

Light-sensitive students commonly exhibit the following behaviors:

- ☐ Red or bloodshot eyes after reading
- ☐ Rubbing eyes or repeatedly touching face while reading
- ☐ Fidgeting and squirming during reading or close-work activities
- ☐ Refusing to read or reading for very brief periods
- ☐ Squinting or holding book in awkward position
- ☐ Arching body over book or desk to create shadows
- ☐ Holding book beneath the desk or in lap while reading
- ☐ Complaining of headache or eye pain while reading
- ☐ Reporting that letters look "squiggly"
- ☐ Skipping words or lines while reading
- ☐ Frequently losing their place, even when pointing
- ☐ Reporting that words seem to be moving around

*Note:* Many light-sensitive students are mistakenly identified as dyslexic. Some students have light sensitivity along with dyslexia. In my experience, when students have both conditions, interventions for dyslexia are likely to be ineffective until the student's light sensitivity is addressed.

## SCIENTIFIC SUPPORT

When I began teaching, light sensitivity was a controversial subject, and not much information was available. Today an Internet search on "scotopic sensitivity syndrome" or "colored overlays for reading" brings up dozens of sites in a variety of languages, from colleges and universities that have conducted research, from people relating their own stories and successes, and from agencies that conduct testing and training for scotopic sensitivity. Colleges now routinely offer continuing education units for teachers and psychology professionals who want to learn how to screen students to determine whether they are good candidates for colored overlays or tinted eyeglass lenses. And, for the skeptics, scientific studies confirm the validity of using colored overlays as a tool for helping readers whose difficulties do not stem from visual acuity.

A good starting point for scientific research is this Web site hosted by the University of Essex in the United Kingdom: www.essex.ac.uk/psuychology/overlays/overlaysM1.htm. This site provides background information, links to further resources, and a brief review of some of the major studies involving overlays. A 1995 study by Tyrrell and colleagues, for example, confirmed a 15 to 50 percent increase in reading speed among students using colored overlays.

Paul Whiting, a professor of education at the University of Sydney, is one of the primary researchers in the field of scotopic sensitivity syndrome. Whiting has written several papers, including one published in 1993 in the *Australian Journal of Remedial Education* ("Irlen Coloured Filters for Reading: A Six-Year Follow-up"), in which he reports on a number of other published research papers.

Whiting's paper can be read in its entirety online at www.dyslexia services.com.au/Six-Year_Follow-Up.htm, but, briefly stated, he notes one obstacle facing researchers is that Irlen filters and formulas are patented and thus not readily available for trial by independent observers (fortunately, since the publication of Whiting's report in 1993, these filters have become more widely available). Studies scrutinized by Whiting involved a combination of Irlen filters, other filters, and commercial colored overlays. The majority of people involved in the filter-use studies reported improved visual perception of print, greater ease of reading, and improved written language skills. Whiting's conclusion states that the majority of people who use Irlen filters continue to report improvements.

Among the studies Whiting summarizes are the following:

- ☐ A study in Louisiana where over 90 percent of participants who used filters reported improved reading, with 49 percent reporting fewer headaches.

- ☐ An Australian study where 91 percent of participants reported improvement in overall ease of reading, 86 percent reported less eyestrain, and 85 percent experienced improved reading fluency.

- ☐ A three-year study conducted in four Western states where 86 percent of participants indicated that filters had been helpful.

Because my own experience coincides so closely with the ever-growing number of published research studies, it seems logical to me that all schools would test students' light sensitivity, just as we routinely check their vision and hearing. But logic so often gets lost in the convoluted bureaucratic shuffle. Testing students can be a time-consuming and frustrating process. In some school districts, parents or guardians must arrange for a vision exam to rule out problems such as nearsightedness before students can be screened for light sensitivity. If for whatever reason a parent or guardian opts not to have the vision exam, the student cannot be officially screened for light sensitivity. It might seem like a given that parents would agree to the vision and light sensitivity screening tests, but at one school I met a mother who refused.

She said, "I'm so sick of schools telling me that kid had problems because I drank when I was pregnant." I could understand her reluctance to have one more test added to the long list. So I simply provided her son with a transparency that I bought online. He found it helpful and used it in my class. Giving him the transparency prompted him to do his own research on the topic. He eventually convinced his mother to let him be tested and screened—he had no vision problems, but he did have light sensitivity and dyslexia.

Many schools lack the funds or personnel to attend training to learn how to screen students for light sensitivity. Also, some teachers and staff members may be reluctant to spend time or money on an approach to solving reading problems that is still controversial. And, sadly, one special education teacher who asked to remain anonymous confessed that she believes some special education departments will resist any intervention that could lead to reduced numbers of students in their programs, because they don't want their budgets reduced.

"They would rather hang onto their precious money than help our precious children," the woman said—which I hope is more a reflection of misplaced priorities and a depressed economy than a lack of ethics or empathy on their part.


## SHEDDING MORE LIGHT ON THE SUBJECT

As I reviewed the research for this second edition of *Teaching Outside the Box,* I found results of more research into the connection between light and learning. I also found research about the positive effects of lighting on elderly people's cognitive abilities and mental health. Below are summaries of some of the studies that reported significant, and sometimes dramatic, results.

## Better Grades, Better Attendance—and Fewer Cavities!

Physicians, teachers, social workers, nutritionists, and dentists in Alberta, Canada, led by W.E. Hathaway, collaborated on a two-year study funded by Alberta Education that involved elementary school students and four kinds of lights: "A Study into the Effects of Light on Children of Elementary School Age: A Case of Daylight Robbery." The results, reported in 1992, showed that students in classrooms with full-spectrum light learned faster, tested higher, grew faster, and had one-third fewer absences due to illness. Interestingly, they also had fewer cavities than expected.

According to the executive summary, the study was funded by the Policy and Planning Branch of Alberta Education in Edmonton and took place between 1987 and 1989, to replicate an earlier study that also showed positive results of full-spectrum lighting in schools. You can view the executive summary report for the Alberta study at www.netnewsdesk.com/lfh/index.cfm?fuseaction=ShowIssue& PID=740&ID=2367,0,9053.

## Sunnier Classrooms Equal Higher Test Scores

The Mahone Group, a consulting group based in California, used architectural studies, photos, and in-person visits to rate the amount of daylight available in more than two thousand classrooms in California, Washington, and Colorado. The school districts in the study had similar building designs and climates, and the 21,000 students in the study had similar backgrounds. The results? Students in the sunniest classrooms advanced between 18 and 26 percent faster in reading and between 7 and 20 percent faster in math over a one-year period.

You can read the highlights of the Mahone Group study, published in 2003, by following the "Schools" link on the Light for Health Web site (www.light-forhealth.com). You can also visit the Heschong Mahone Group Web site for executive summaries of a number of studies involving offices, classrooms, and lighting (www.h-m-g.com/projects/daylighting/summaries%20on%20daylighting.htm).

Of particular interest are three studies. The first, under the link "Daylighting in Schools: PG&E 1999," was funded by Pacific Gas and Electric and involved school districts in Seattle, Fort Collins, and San Juan Capistrano. This study found that students in Colorado and Washington classrooms with the most daylight had 7 to 18 percent higher test scores. In California, students in rooms with the most daylight progressed 20 percent faster on math tests and

26 percent faster on reading tests in one year than students in the classrooms with the least daylight. The second study, "Daylighting in Schools: Additional Analysis," funded by the California Energy Commission in 2001, continued the San Juan Capistrano study and identified a central tendency of 21 percent improvement in student learning rates between classrooms with the least and most daylight.

The third study details research involving over eight thousand students in grades three through six located in five hundred classrooms in thirty-six different schools in Fresno, California. Researchers made on-site visits to measure the light in every classroom during this study. They found that glare negatively affects student learning, especially in math classrooms, where instruction is often visually demonstrated. When teachers do not have control of their windows and lighting, student performance is negatively affected. Physical characteristics of classrooms, most notably windows, were as significant and of equal or greater magnitude than teacher characteristics, number of computers, or attendance rates in predicting student performance.

## A Room with a View Improves Grades

Another interesting study led by C. Kenneth Tanner, head of the School of Design and Planning Laboratory at the University of Georgia, analyzed the impact of the features outside a classroom on the grades of the children inside. After studying more than ten thousand fifth-grade students in seventy-one Georgia elementary schools, Tanner and his associates found that students who studied in classrooms that offered unrestricted views of gardens, mountains, and other natural scenery for at least fifty feet outside the classroom windows had higher test scores in language arts, science, and math than students whose classrooms offered views of parking lots and roads. The report, "Effects of School Design on Student Outcomes," was published in 2009 in the *Journal of Educational Administration*. The abstract can be accessed at http://assets.emeraldinsight.com/10.1108/09578230910955809.

At the Web site of the National Clearinghouse for Educational Facilities, a program managed by the National Institute of Building Sciences, you can follow the links to "Resource List—Impact of Facilities on Learning—Academic Research Studies" to find a number of studies and books about the relationship between student achievement and the physical environment of school buildings (www.edfacilities.org/rl/impact_research_studies.cfm).

## DISCUSSION POINTS

1. Share any experience you have using transparencies as reading aids.

2. Experiment with different colors of tinted transparencies placed over the page of a textbook as you read, then share the results of your experiment.

3. What can teachers do to improve reading conditions when their classrooms have only fluorescent lights or no windows?

4. What factors other than lighting can have a significant effect on student achievement and test scores?

# Foods for Thought

**A**mericans are too fat. We know that. We also know that childhood obesity and diabetes are running rampant in our schools,
along with asthma, allergies, attention deficit, and a host of other
learning problems. Fat and failure in school may be linked, according
to recent research. I had read some bits here and there about the
effects of nutrition on learning and behavior, and I was intrigued. But
after attending the 2003 European Council of International Schools
conference in Hamburg, Germany, I am convinced that nutrition and
neuroscience are going to change the way Americans view both eating
and learning. In fact, since then, I have read considerable new research
about the effects of nutrition on brain function and learning. It seems

that we chubby Americans may finally be getting the message that it isn't how much we eat but what we eat—more specifically, what we don't eat—that makes the difference.

In Hamburg I had the good fortune to hear Dr. Madeleine Portwood, an educational psychologist from the United Kingdom, present the preliminary findings from the Durham trial, a research experiment involving elementary school students whose behavior and academic achievement improved as a result of essential fatty acid supplementation. Before Dr. Portwood began speaking, I had been feeling a bit sorry for myself for having to spend the Thanksgiving vacation week away from my family. After hearing Dr. Portwood, I was thankful to be thousands of miles from home, sitting on a hard plastic chair in a chilly auditorium. And I was in a hurry to go home—not just to hug my family but to share what I learned with my fellow educators and parents and anybody else who would listen.

First, a disclaimer. I am not a scientist, a chemist, or a trained nutritionist. I have read extensively about diet and nutrition. Since I have no formal background in nutrition or neuroscience, however, I hope that the scientists and chemists among you will forgive me if I simplify enough to make a complicated subject more understandable to those of us who don't routinely ponder molecular structure and neurophysiological properties. I took copious notes while I was listening, and I have done my best to transcribe them accurately.

## THE BIG FAT PROBLEM

Fat is a dirty word in most Americans' vocabulary, and that is a big part of our problem. We need certain fats. Essential fatty acids (EFAs) are necessary for proper brain function and health. Omega-6 fatty acids and omega-3 fatty acids are both EFAs—essential in that the body requires them, but cannot manufacture them itself. Of the EFAs, the omega-3s are probably the most important because they suppress inflammation, which is the cause of many degenerative diseases. Very briefly, here's the difference:

> Omega-3s (alpha-linoleic acid or ALA) can be found in foods such as wild-caught salmon, mackerel, walnuts, flaxseed, and green leafy vegetables. Omega-3s are metabolized by the body into the two beneficial fatty acids,

eicosapentaenoic acid (EPA) and docosahexaenoic acid (DHA). You may notice that many nutritional labels now tout the inclusion of EPA and DHA.

Omega-6s (linoleic acid) come from plants and can be found abundantly in common cooking oils such as corn, sunflower, safflower, and soybean oil (but not olive oil). Most Americans have an abundance of omega-6 EFAs in their diet.

Omega-9 fatty acids are sometimes included in the mix, but they are not considered essential because our bodies can make them from unsaturated fats. Regardless of how they are labeled, omega-9s are required for proper brain function and health. Omega-9s are found in animal fats and olive oil, and the oil manufactured by human skin glands is the same fatty acid (oleic acid) that is found in olive oil.

## The Omega Ratio: The Most Important Piece of the Puzzle

Many nutritional supplements boast that they provide omega-3s or 6s, but most do not warn consumers that the *ratio* of omega-6 to omega-3 EFAs is the most important piece of the fat picture. The optimum ratio of omega-6 to omega-3 is two to one (2:1). Our brains can cope with a higher ratio—until it surpasses twenty to one (20:1). Then we have trouble because of the molecular structure and behavior of the EFAs. When omega-6s are present in much more abundance than omega-3s, the omega-6s will actually block the gaps between the molecules of omega-3s, interrupting or even canceling the transmission of electrical impulses in the brain, which directly relates to the ability to think, focus, and concentrate. In unscientific terms: *eating too much of the wrong kind of fat makes us stupid.*

**Foods with Omega-6-to-Omega-3 Ratios Below 20:1**

| | |
|---|---|
| Cream, butter, and canola oil | 2:1 |
| Soft margarine (not polyunsaturated) | 4:1 |
| Yogurt | 6:1 |
| Soybean oil | 7:1 |
| Olive oil | 11:1 |

So far, so good. We are still under the 20:1 cutoff point. But the typical American diet contains ratios of omega-6 to omega-3 EFAs that far surpass the optimum 2:1 ratio that nurtures our brains. Corn oil, perhaps the most widely used vegetable oil in the country, has an omega-6-to-omega-3 ratio of fifty-six to one (56:1). That is more than double the maximum ratio that the brain can handle without dysfunction. It gets worse. Much worse, as the following list demonstrates:

**Foods with Omega-6-to-Omega-3 Ratios Higher Than 20:1**

| | |
|---|---|
| Sesame oil | 144:1 |
| Polyunsaturated margarine | 370:1 |
| Diet spreads (70 percent polyunsaturated) | 370:1 |
| Sunflower or safflower oil | 632:1 |

During her presentation Dr. Portwood said, "Give a child a bag of chips fried in sunflower oil for lunch, and that child will be unable to learn in the afternoon." Sadly, many fast-food companies, in response to consumer demand that they stop using corn oil, have announced plans to switch to sunflower or safflower oil. And nearly every bag of chips in this country, even organic chips on the shelves of health food stores, list the oils used in their preparation as sunflower and/or safflower oil. If we can't cure our national addiction to fast food, we must convince food manufacturers to spend a bit more money and use cooking oils that have lower amounts of omega-6s. That might shift some of the expense burden from the health care industry to the food industry, and our health as a nation might improve, as well. Obviously, I am an optimist and a dreamer. So let's get back to reality and science.

### Americans Lead the Poor Nutrition Parade

Dr. Portwood said her research team was especially interested in the American diet because the United States tends to lead the rest of the world in diseases and problems such as attention deficit and other learning issues. She said that studies indicate 50 percent of children in the United Kingdom at age three now show signs of developing behavior and learning problems. Because the surge in attention and focus difficulties has been so sharp in the United States, and now in the United Kingdom, researchers do not believe the cause is likely to be organic (within the children). When a disease trend arises this quickly, scientists look to the environment for the cause of the problems. Nutrition is one of the key environmental factors that scientists study. Dr. Portwood said that 20 to 25 percent of neurobiological disorders are metabolically based, which means that they have something to do with the food we eat and the way our bodies respond to that food.

Corn appears to be a major culprit in the United States, not just because of the abundance of omega-6 EFAs in corn oil, but because of the high-fructose corn syrup that is so widespread in our diet. It is hard to find a cookie, cracker, or juice in the supermarket today that doesn't contain high-fructose corn syrup (HFCS; more on HFCS later in this chapter.)

Dr. Portwood didn't spend a great deal of time discussing HFCS because the focus of her research and presentation was EFAs, but she did say that the body can't break down high-fructose corn syrup and that its consumption may lead to weight gain and other health problems. The irony is that many American foods use HFCS instead of sugar and that many Americans have virtually eliminated fats from their diets in the belief that fats and sugars will make us fat. It may very well be the fat and sugar substitutes we eat that are doing the damage!

## MOTHER'S MILK VERSUS FORMULA

Dr. Portwood began her presentation about the Durham trial by summarizing the results of previous studies conducted to evaluate the effect of different formulas on infants' brain activity and IQ. These babies were not the victims of callous scientists; they were premature infants who had to be fed formula for their survival. The first studies compared two different kinds of formula, one with a superior nutritional content that resulted in significant differences in the infants' mental activity. Then scientists pitted their superior formula against mother's milk, believing that the formula would emerge as the winner. Not only were they wrong, but the babies who were fed breast milk (from their own mothers or from donors) showed significantly higher brain activity and IQs than formula-fed infants. These results led to more studies to find out what ingredients in mother's milk made such a drastic difference. The answer: mother's milk contains two kinds of omega-3 fatty acids: arachidonic acid (AA) and docosahexaenoic acid (DHA). DHA is the primary structural fatty acid in the gray matter of the brain and the retina of the eye, and it is important for the transmission of signals in the brain, eyes, and nervous system. Low levels of DHA have been linked to depression, memory loss, and visual problems. The infant formulas contained more linoleic acid and more alpha-linoleic acid than they did DHA and AA.

At specific times (seven, fourteen, and twenty-eight days), there was a dramatic increase in DHA (omega-3) in the nursing mothers' milk, which directly coincided with electrical activity in the cortex of the babies' brains. Further research revealed that the amount of DHA in mother's milk varied drastically depending on the mother's diet and how prematurely the baby was born. Babies born at six months had 50 percent of the DHA of full-term babies. Babies born at eight months had 80 percent of the DHA. This indicates that if the maternal diet is lacking in DHA, then proper levels of DHA will not be present at birth. If the level falls below 50 percent, children have metabolic difficulty breaking down omega-3 EFAs. And children with omega-3 deficiencies exhibit symptoms such as dry or itchy skin, eczema, asthma, lactose intolerance, sleep problems, bumpy patches on the backs of their arms, soft or easily broken nails, frequent urination, excessive thirst, dull dry hair, and allergies. But beyond physical symptoms, omega-3 deficiency has a major effect on children's behavior and learning, according to the research of Dr. Portwood's team and that of other scientists.

Repeatedly, researchers have concluded that omega-3 EFAs make it easier for signals to jump the gap between brain cells, which helps improve memory and concentration. Without enough omega-3s in the diet, the brain suffers and electrical activity slows down or stops.

Dr. Portwood's team designed the Durham trial to test the effect of EFAs on the behavior of two hundred children, nearly all of whom had problems with physical coordination. Eighty-two of the children had been clinically diagnosed as having attention deficit hyperactivity disorder (ADHD), and forty had reading problems such as dyslexia. Instead of taking a blood test, which would have involved needles and caused fear, the scientists devised a way to use a breath test to monitor the children. Each child was given six capsules per day of a supplement containing a ratio of 20 percent omega-6 EFAs and 80 percent omega-3 EFAs. No other change was made to the children's diets. The supplements were administered during the school day by school staff in a blind study, which means that nobody, including the researchers, knew which children were receiving the supplement and which were receiving placebos. Two months into the study, the results began to impress the parents, and eventually they impressed the scientists as well. The researchers found a dramatic drop in excitability and improved concentration among the students taking the EFA supplements.

When I returned from the Hamburg conference, I visited the Web site that discussed the research of Dr. Portwood's team (www.durhamtrial.org), and I did further research on the Internet and at the library to learn more about EFAs. After reading a number of studies and journal articles, I have come to believe that many of the health problems that plague Americans—ADHD, obesity, depression, and Alzheimer's—are directly linked to an overabundance of some fats and a deficiency of others.

## DOCTOR'S ORDERS

If you'd like to read about EFAs, a good place to start is the Web site of Dr. Thomas Greene, a Texas chiropractor who provides a good primer on vitamins, minerals, and EFAs, along with other nutritional information (www.dcnutrition.com/home.cfm).

If you can find a copy of Rachael Moeller Gorman's article "Captain of the Happier Meal" (which appeared in the May–June 2010 online issue of *Eating Well*; www.eatingwell.com), I highly recommend reading it. Joe Hibbeln, MD, is a captain in the U.S. Public Health Service and acting chief of the section on nutritional neurosciences. He is a specialist in mental illness and is most interested in the connection between low levels of omega-3 fatty acids along with high levels of omega-6 fatty acids and mental health—bipolar conditions, schizophrenia, depression, and so on.

Dr. Hibbeln's research record is wide-ranging, impressive, and very interesting. In 1995, he and a colleague published a paper in the *American Journal of Clinical Nutrition* (volume 62) that presented their theory: mental illness may be a result of omega-3 deficiency. According to the doctor, the American diet is too far out of balance; we eat ten to twenty-five times more omega-6s than omega-3s because of the prevalence of soybean, safflower, and corn oils. That imbalance, he says, may be the cause of many of the mental health problems that plague our nation. Dr. Hibbeln's current mission? To change the entire American military diet to include more omega-3 fatty acids and fewer omega-6s. He believes this change will reduce posttraumatic stress disorder and depression among veterans, which currently affects about 20 percent of troops who have been deployed. This is one scientist whose research definitely merits our attention.

## OTHER MAJOR NUTRITIONAL VILLAINS

Since the late 1980s, after realizing what a strong impact foods and nonfoods have on the brains and behavior of my students, I have continued to experiment, research, and read about nutrition and the brain. And for over three decades, two culprits continue to crop up time and again, whether I am reading magazine articles or major scientific studies: artificial sweeteners and high-fructose corn syrup.

### Aspartame

Aspartame and I came into conflict personally after I started dating a cowboy who was hooked on diet soda. (Aspartame is the main ingredient in artificial sweeteners like NutraSweet, Equal Measure, and Equal.) A nonsoda drinker until that point, I started drinking the occasional diet soda. Before long, I found myself craving them, just as my cowboy friend did. At the time, I was living in southern New Mexico, where hot is an understatement much of the time and crunchy-ice sodas, as my friend referred to them, tasted especially good. Before long, I graduated from twelve-ounce drinks to the typical forty-ounce bucket of chemicals, preservatives, flavorings, and artificial sweeteners that comprise most commercial sodas today. And within a few months, I started noticing some physical changes—brittle fingernails, a lot more hair than normal falling out and landing on my bathroom counters, a little spare tire around my middle, and chubbier than normal thighs. I didn't connect those changes to the diet sodas until I started having serious bladder issues. My bathroom trips became more frequent, and waiting wasn't an option. I had to go, and I had to go now. If not, my bladder ached. So I started asking questions and talking to people who shared similar stories, and a doctor suggested that I stop the sodas. I did. But giving up diet sodas turned out to be difficult—even more difficult than quitting smoking, which I had done several years earlier. Eventually I did quit, and within a few days my health started to improve. I ate more food but lost the extra weight. That's when I realized there was something shady in that soda, and my research led me to the culprit: aspartame.

Once again I was amazed at the amount of research and data that had been ignored or buried along the rocky road to governmental approval of food substances and additives. In 2010, aspartame can be found in over five thousand American foods and drinks, in spite of the mountains of paperwork and testimony from doctors and scientists who had warned the government about the dangers of artificial sweeteners in general and aspartame in particular. As I have said before, I am not a trained nutritionist, biologist, or chemist. But I am a reasonably intelligent adult and sufficiently educated enough to recognize baloney when I read it. And the soda company claims that the ingredients in their drinks are perfectly safe and harmless is baloney, in my opinion. Here's why I say that:

☐ Dozens of books written by medical doctors and scientists warn against consuming aspartame, citing the same basic fact: aspartame is composed of aspartic acid (40 percent), phenylalanine (50 percent), and methanol or wood alcohol (10 percent). None of these things are good for human bodies.

☐ There is general consensus that artificial sweeteners interfere with the body's delicate and critical insulin balance. One of the best of the many books I have read is the well-documented and comprehensive *Ultrametabolism*, by Dr. Mark Hyman, who writes about artificial sweeteners: "one of the side effects we know these sweeteners have is stimulation of hunger through the cephalic, or brain-phase, insulin-response. . . . Artificial sweeteners do not act as sugar does and do not balance your insulin. As a result, you end up with excess insulin in your body, so you end up eating more food to take care of this problem. This whole pattern disrupts your appetite control system in serious ways. What's worse, it can lead to insulin resistance."

☐ An Internet search for "safety of aspartame" calls up thousands of Web sites that repeat the same information from both sides of the fence. The food companies, the makers of aspartame, and the U.S. government health departments tasked with ensuring the safety of food additives all maintain that aspartame is safe. Doctors, neurologists, scientists, researchers, nutritionists, and over ten thousand American consumers who filed complaints about side effects after consuming products containing aspartame all maintain that aspartame is dangerous and possibly deadly.

☐ The studies funded by the food industry invariably show no danger posed by aspartame and other artificial sweeteners. But the vast majority of independently funded studies show just the opposite. Dr. Hyman's reference: "Of 166 studies on the safety of aspartame, 74 had at least partial industry funding, and 92 were independently funded. While 100 percent of the industry-funded studies conclude aspartame is safe, 92 percent of independently funded research identified aspartame as a potential cause of adverse effects."

☐ Dozens of doctors, including Dr. Joseph Mercola (www.mercola.com), include fact sheets and articles on their Web sites warning people to avoid aspartame.

☐ The Food and Drug Administration's own reports show that over ten thousand consumers complained of adverse reactions to aspartame (including seizures and death). In 1995, FDA Epidemiology Branch Chief Thomas Wilcox confirmed that aspartame was responsible for over 75 percent of all consumer complaints filed between 1981 and 1995 (*Food Chemical News*, June 12, 1995, p. 27).

☐ The U.S. Department of Health and Human Services released a list of ninety-two symptoms, including headaches, dizziness, seizures, nausea, weight gain, heart palpitations, depression, fatigue, irritability, vision problems, joint pain, and memory loss, in its 1994 list of Adverse Reactions Associated with Aspartame Consumption.

☐ In 2007, twelve U.S. environmental health experts asked the FDA to review potential health risks of aspartame because of recent studies linking cancer to aspartame. You can read a copy of the letter at http://cspinet.org/new/pdf/ aspartame_letter_to_fda.pdf.

☐ The clincher for me was reading the Congressional testimony of doctors and scientists who petitioned the U.S. government to disapprove aspartame because of previously documented side effects. Those health experts were successful in blocking aspartame's approval as a food additive until Arthur Hull Hayes was appointed FDA Commissioner by then–President Reagan. Shortly after aspartame was approved, Hayes left the FDA to work for NutraSweet's public relations firm, Burson and Marsteller, and subsequently refused all interviews.

One of the most well-known books on the subject of aspartame danger is Janet Hull's *Sweet Poison: How the World's Most Popular Artificial Sweetener Is Killing Us—My Story.* Hull was diagnosed with incurable Graves' disease in 1991. She claims that aspartame poisoning nearly killed her. Along with the story of her recovery through an aspartame detox plan, her book also contains a documented history of aspartame, government reports and senate hearings on aspartame safety, case histories, and a list of products containing aspartame.

To read about the history of aspartame approval and see a diagram showing the chemical structure of aspartame, visit www.associatepublisher.com/e/a/as/ aspartame.htm.

## High-Fructose Corn Syrup

You know something is up when food manufacturers spend millions of dollars on advertising campaigns and television commercials touting the safety of their products. The basic gist of the commercials is that person A warns person B not to eat high-fructose corn syrup (HFCS). Person B says, "Why not?" and person A has no answer. Gloating, person B then asks, "Because it's perfectly safe in reasonable amounts?" or some such question. A more factual comment from person B might be "because it won't kill you or make you sick immediately?"

HFCS is another one of those food additives (I hesitate to label it as food) that is at the center of years of controversy. Again we have government approval versus throngs of medical experts and consumers claiming that it may not be deadly in small doses, but that it should not be consumed regularly because it interferes with metabolism and can be linked to diabetes.

Once again, I can weigh in with my personal experience. Several years ago I mentioned to a friend that I had been getting depressed and feeling fuzzy-brained, but couldn't figure out why. Life wasn't especially difficult, and I was eating a 90 percent organic diet consisting primarily of vegetables, fruits, and high-quality protein. My friend said, "Maybe it's high-fructose corn syrup." I said, "I don't know what that is, but I don't eat it." "Oh, yes you do," he said. "Oh, no I don't," I insisted. Sounds like two little kids, I know. My friend then bet me one hundred dollars that if I read the labels on the packages of food and drink in my house, I would find HFCS among them. Certain that I would win the bet, I checked the labels. And there it was on the bottled iced tea that I loved so much. First ingredient—water. Second ingredient—HFCS.

My next step, as always, was to conduct my unscientific do-it-yourself nutritional study. I stopped drinking that iced tea immediately and replaced it with my own homemade iced tea, made from the same kind of tea leaves and sweetened with agave nectar or date sugar. Sure enough, the depression stopped, along with the fuzzy thinking. The way I tested for mental fuzziness was to log onto an Internet site where you can play Scrabble with word lovers from around the world. Those people know their game, and if you aren't mentally sharp they'll kick your dictionary. If I logged on and played after drinking the commercial iced tea, I couldn't concentrate so well and my scores were lower. I tried this off and on for a couple of weeks. The results were always the same. After drinking iced tea with HFCS, I simply couldn't think so well and my moods tended to swing from high to low.

My next step was to start doing research and asking everybody I knew about their experiences with HFCS. Folks at the health food store and the gym laughed and said, "You didn't know?" Internet searches revealed all kinds of warnings, many claiming that HFCS was responsible for everything from attention deficit disorder (ADD) to diabetes and fatty liver. And, once again, I read the same explanations over and over again, in article after article, book after book. Following is my understanding, stated in laywoman's terms, of course.

When we eat food, our bodies create insulin in order to carry the sugars (sucrose and glucose) in that food to our cells so it can be used. And our brains secrete a chemical called leptin that tells us when we're full, so we stop eating. Regular table sugar, sucrose, is a combination of glucose and fructose. Our bodies use glucose for energy and metabolism; it's one of the key building blocks of all carbohydrates, and if the carbs are of the complex variety, the glucose is slowly absorbed by the body as it should be. Fructose is most often found in fruit, and it's best eaten in the whole fiber-containing fruit package, rather than as juice because it is absorbed more slowly that way and contains more nutrients and fiber. Slower is better, when it comes to sugar absorption.

Fructose doesn't stimulate our bodies to create insulin, and it doesn't trigger our brains to release leptin. When fructose is turned into high-fructose corn syrup, it's absorbed much more quickly than other sugars and it ignores the insulin that our bodies create when we eat food. Unlike glucose, which needs insulin in order to be absorbed by cells, HFCS bypasses the insulin and goes directly into our cells, and that's where the damage begins. Inside our cells HFCS turns into carbon that is then made into cholesterol and triglycerides. It makes our cholesterol levels shoot up and can interfere with liver function, In fact, according to Dr. Mark Hyman, author of *Ultrametabolism,* it is "probably the biggest reason for the increase in cholesterol levels we have seen in our society over the last twenty years."

Here's an interesting tidbit from my reading: when researchers want to create diabetes in laboratory rats for experimental purposes, they feed them HFCS. It does the trick every time. The March 22, 2010, online version of *ScienceDaily* reports that Princeton University researchers confirmed that rats that had access to HFCS gained more weight than rats who ate sugar, even when both groups of rats ate the same overall number of calories. Not all calories are created equal, apparently. In addition to the weight gain, the HFCS rat group had fatter bellies and higher levels of triglycerides (blood fats). Male rats in the study fared worse than female. The males who has access to HFCS gained 48 percent more weight than the male rats who ate a normal diet, and they gained the weight primarily in their bellies. The online article includes a quote from psychology professor Bart Hoebel, a neuroscientist who specializes in appetite, weight, and sugar addiction: "When rats are drinking high-fructose corn syrup at levels well below those in soda pop, they're becoming obese—every single one, across the board. Even when rats are fed a high-fat diet, you don't see this; they don't all gain extra weight."

You can read details of the research and find links to other interesting studies on HFCS online at www.sciencedaily.com/releases/2010/03/100322121115.htm. And in the interest of fairness, you can read the Corn Refiners Association statement claiming that the Princeton researchers are off their rockers at www.corn.org/princeton-hfcs-study-errors.html. Given that the corn refiners have a huge financial stake in such studies, and the fatness of the rats, I tend to side with the Princeton guys. But you can decide for yourself.

Now, when you see those television commercials and person B asks why we shouldn't eat HFCS, you can impress your friends and family by answering the question: because research indicates that HFCS leads to increased appetite, obesity, high cholesterol, and high blood pressure.

### Bovine Growth Hormone

Common sense seems to be the key here. The point of bovine growth hormone (BGH) is to make baby cows grow and adult cows grow fatter. Aside from the fact that humans are not cows, hormones are delicate things. We humans have our own hormones, which regulate our intricate systems. Introducing bovine growth hormones may or may not be responsible for the early development of breasts and menstrual cycles of preadolescent girls, but since there is absolutely no nutritional requirement for humans to consume bovine growth hormones and there is so much controversy over the long-term effects of human consumption of BGH, it doesn't make sense to me to eat food that contain them if we can avoid them. I can't determine whether the scientists who conduct studies are funded or swayed by food companies or whether nutritionists are "health food nuts," but I can take a good look at a cow and see that our bodies are built very differently. And if you have ever had the dubious pleasure of driving past an overwhelmingly aromatic Texas or New Mexico feedlot in the summer sun where hundreds of cows stand hoof-deep in dungy dirt with nary a speck of grass in sight, you might begin to wonder whether humans have a lick of sense when it comes to the care and feeding of cows.

## WE NEED TO "USE OUR NOODLES"

I have read about so many scientific studies in which nutritional changes and supplements resulted in drastic reductions in violent and aggressive behavior, as well as dramatic decreases in ADHD symptoms and allergies, that I am thoroughly convinced: if we spent more time and money on nutrition instead of powerful prescription medicines that can have serious side effects, we would have much healthier children who would be better able to learn and behave in our schools. The only real question that remains is whether we value our children's health and mental well-being more than we value the goodwill of the insurance companies, pharmaceutical manufacturers, and test makers who reap billions of dollars in profits from the desperate parents and teachers of children who are unable to sit down, concentrate, and learn.

My thinking is that adults have the right to abuse their bodies any way they see fit—but children deserve a chance to grow up as healthy and strong as possible. Not just so they can support us when we are in our old age, but because it's the right thing to do. And I think it's a huge mistake to worry about every morsel we eat, because stress is a real killer. So, again, I hark back to the same idea: let's use some common sense. We can avoid artificial sweeteners, chemicals, colorings, and preservatives as much as possible. We can eliminate one food or food additive at a time and note any changes in mental clarity, mood, weight, sleep, and energy. We can try to do without added sugar. At first, food tastes bland, but eventually the natural sugars provide enough sweetener. Or we can use date sugar, agave nectar, stevia, xylitol, or local honey (raw honey should not be given to babies or young children). We can opt to drink water or herbal teas in place of commercial sodas. Even dedicated coffee drinkers who don't like the taste of plain black teas may like Teecino, which is made from a mixture of carob, chicory, and spices and brewed like coffee. My favorite teas are green chai, which has much less caffeine than black teas, and herbal spiced tea (Yogi Tea makes a great Classic India Spice blend), which is caffeine-free but bursting with flavor and aroma because of its roobois, ginger, cinnamon, and cardamom.

Most important of all, we can pay attention to what our bodies are telling us. If what we eat makes us sick, then we are silly to keep eating those foods. With the sky-rocketing cost of health care, it makes good financial sense to be proactive about our health and the health of our children. We can't count on doctors and health care experts to spoon-feed us every bite of information. We can learn the basics of how our metabolism works and the best natural sources of vitamins and minerals. We can take responsibility for our own health and retrain our taste buds. America tends to lead the way, and the rest of the world follows. We don't have to follow the unethical food companies and advertisers who are leading us towards obesity, diabetes, and learning disorders. There are ethical food and drink manufacturers in this country and legions of health advocates who read the research and distill the statistics and scientific studies and make that information palatable for us. We can chart our own course towards making healthier choices and raising happier, healthier, smarter children. As teachers—gatekeepers of information and influential role models for our nation's children—we should take our place at the head of the parade.

## DISCUSSION POINTS

1. What is your experience with the effects of nutrition on student behavior and learning?

2. How can we help children when their parents and grandparents practice poor nutrition?

3. Visit your local grocery stores—how many healthy snack products and drinks can you find (without corn syrup, artificial sweeteners, or artificial colors)? Consider making a list for your students or making this a class project so that they can take a list home to use for family shopping.

4. How can we incorporate exercise into our schools in addition to physical education courses?

# Top Twelve
# Motivational Strategies

Sometimes, in spite of your enthusiastic and student-centered approach to teaching, your students slump in their seats and yawn at you. You've spent hours creating interesting lessons, but they aren't interested. You are well educated and passionate about your subject, but your students don't appear to care one fig. They sigh and watch the clock. They daydream and tune you out. They roll their eyes at each other and shake their heads at your denseness.

These students are doing their best to convince you that they hate learning, that they don't care about school, that they are just too cool to be bothered. I maintain that they do care. Human brains are wired for learning. But sometimes young people focus so much on earning good grades (or resisting our attempts to teach them things they wouldn't choose on their own) that they lose touch with their natural creativity, imagination, and sense of play. You can reintroduce your students to the joy of learning. It can be done. In the words of my mentor, Al Black, "All you have to do is get their attention."

In the following sections you'll find twelve suggestions that may help you get your students' attention. These are not new ideas; there really are no new ideas when it comes to teaching. Find something new and if you go back far enough, you'll find that Plato or Dewey or Montessori used your "new" technique with their students. Some of these may be new ideas to you, though, and others may remind you of techniques you once used but forgot about as the administrative tasks associated with your job overwhelmed you and made you lose touch with the joy of teaching.

You'll notice that I don't mention offering rewards other than the satisfaction of learning and achieving difficult goals. Because of a scene in the movie *Dangerous Minds,* many people have the mistaken idea that I hurl candy bars at students in order to motivate them. That scene was concocted by a screenwriter who misinterpreted an anecdote from *My Posse Don't Do Homework* where I was trying to persuade a class of remedial readers to tackle Shakespeare. Those students were convinced that they were "too dumb" to read *The Taming of the Shrew*. I maintained that they were highly intelligent in spite of their poor reading skills. I insisted that somebody had to be willing to take a shot at interpreting the first few lines of the play. Nobody volunteered. I refused to give up. I stood and waited—for quite a long time—until a very shy student raised his hand and offered an idea. He wasn't right. He wasn't even close. But I had my hand in my pocket where I found a stray dollar bill. This wasn't planned. It just happened. I pulled out that dollar and handed it to the boy who had volunteered to think.

"Am I right?" he asked. "No," I said. "That dollar is for thinking, because you will never get the answer right if you are afraid to be wrong." Immediately, other students volunteered to think. Then they demanded their dollars. When I refused, they insisted that they should be rewarded for thinking. So I happened to have some candy bars on hand that I planned to use to reward the winners of the spelling bee. (During my first semester of teaching, I realized that candy was not the best or healthiest reward, so I stopped using it.) I gave a candy bar to the next thinker. Within thirty minutes, I had given away my lunch, my paper clips, my pens and pencils, and everything else I could find as thinking rewards. The students were thrilled because they received those gifts for thinking about Shakespeare. The following day hands waved as soon as I asked for volunteers, and they continued to wave throughout that school year—although I had made it very clear that there would be no more tangible rewards. Just recognition and occasional applause for really courageous thinking.

That said, I do sometimes offer rewards such as a homework lottery or stickers on papers or award certificates to motivate reluctant readers and unmotivated students (including adult students). Once they make a sincere effort and realize how good it feels to learn and to overcome challenges, they no longer need external motivators.

According to several articles on brain-based learning, external rewards can actually be counter-productive which is why I don't use them long-term. The arguments against them are convincing, and I believe the scientists who claim that our brains are wired for learning—that they actually create endorphins (the "feel-good" chemicals) when we learn something new. I believe that is why some students like school immediately and keep on liking it. Their brains got the message and it actually does make them feel good to learn. But other students, for myriad reasons, didn't have those positive experiences. Those are the students who may need external motivators.

For some students, one bribe is enough to get them started. Others need a few positive experiences—or a few years' worth of positive experiences—before they learn to love learning. But once that internal motivation machine kicks on, it keeps running.

## 1. HELP STUDENTS BELIEVE SUCCESS IS POSSIBLE

Brains, like engines, don't operate at peak efficiency when they are low on fuel, clogged by dirty oil, or missing small but critical parts. If your students are all well fed, adequately parented, emotionally well adjusted, and well educated prior to entering your classroom, you probably won't face any serious problems when you try to motivate them to learn. But not many teachers are fortunate to face such a class. It's much more likely that some of our students will come to school hungry, tired, emotionally distressed, and ambivalent about education. Don't despair. What you bring to your students is just as important as what your students bring to your classroom.

We have all heard the statistics, and we have learned from our own experiences that the teacher's attitude toward his or her students is the primary factor in student success. When we believe that students can succeed, they can. But our belief is only half of the solution to the problem of poor performance. Our belief alone isn't enough; we must convince our students that their success is possible.

If students themselves don't believe in their ability to learn, it doesn't matter how intelligent they are or how easy we make the material—they will not succeed. The sincere belief that success is possible is the key that unlocks the door to learning.

How do you convince students that success is possible? Some people suggest that you provide an easy exercise or activity that guarantees success for every student. I disagree with that approach. Usually such success experiences are far too easy and therefore defeat their own purpose. Instead of convincing students that they are capable of achieving, easy assignments and esteem-boosting activities may send the message that students aren't capable of handling truly difficult challenges. In the words of a former student, "You give us easy assignments because you think we're too dumb to do hard stuff."

So instead of creating an easy task, it might be better to assign a truly difficult task and then help your students complete it. When you introduce the task, explain that it is difficult and that you don't expect anybody to do it perfectly—including yourself. Tell them you are going to tackle this project because you believe they are intelligent and that you know they can learn because you see evidence of many things they have already learned: they can read and dress themselves, they know their own addresses and phone numbers, they can play musical instruments and a hundred different games, they know the words to a lot of songs, they can fix meals, and they know how to operate machines and kitchen gadgets and computers and VCRs.

Where do you find the challenging assignment? One good place to look is at your own school. If you teach second grade, for example, ask a fourth-grade teacher for a sample vocabulary lesson. Tell your students that they are going to do an assignment that kids two whole grades ahead of them are doing, just to see what those kids are learning. And if they do a good job, they will earn extra credit. If you teach middle school or high school, find a college textbook that has an interesting essay. Tell your students that they are going to read something that college students read; show them the textbook so that they can see that you are telling the truth. Explain that their brains work just as well as the brains of college students, but they don't challenge their brains the way college kids do. Assure them that if they don't know all of the words in the essay, you will help them because that is your job. Then read the essay aloud in class, discuss it, and ask your students to write their responses to the reading. When they finish this project, some student will very likely say, "That wasn't so hard." And this is your cue to respond, "Of course it isn't, because everybody in this class knows how to think, and thinking is the key to learning. We have good brains in this room, so let's use them."

## 2. ADJUST THE ATTITUDES

### The Student Perspective

You could ask your students how they feel. Some of them will be eager to tell you, especially if they are younger, but many older students opt to observe instead of participate in class discussions; they don't want to talk about school. They don't want to write essays or paragraphs about school either. But most of them will be willing to give you a few comments if you insist. Go ahead and insist, because you want maximum input from them on this topic. Distribute index cards and ask your students to write down their thoughts about school in general and your subject(s) in particular. Visual learners will respond better if you write your questions on the board.

Tell your students that they earn credit for cooperating and that everybody who fills out a card will earn the maximum grade. Make sure that they understand that names are optional, so they can freely state their opinions without fear of offending you or feeling vulnerable. (If you walk down the rows and collect the cards in order, putting each one on the bottom of the stack, making a point of not looking at the cards, you will still be able to figure out which students said what, just in case you find any extreme comments that need your attention.)

Some groups will go to town on this project, but others will require a little prompting. You might print your questions on the board and then write your own answers.

Q: What do you like the most about school?

A: I like learning new things.

Q: What is your favorite subject?

A: I like English and gym because I like to read and run. I like to exercise my brain and my body.

Q: What is your least favorite subject?

A: I don't like math because it's really hard and I never get all the answers right.

Even if your students decide they are more interested in reading your answers than writing their own, you will probably be able to engage them in a conversation about school, which was your goal in the first place.

This next step is optional, depending on your students. If they are reasonably well behaved and paying attention, you might consider reading a few comments from the cards after you have collected enough that students won't be able to identify the author. Read comments that you think might elicit a response from others: "I hate writing because I always run out of stuff to say," for example, may prompt a discussion and alert you to the need for a lesson on prewriting and developing ideas.

Whether you discuss the cards or not, thank your students for taking the time to share their opinions. Take the cards home and read them carefully. Look at the spelling, sentence structure, vocabulary, and handwriting for clues to student personalities and areas of difficulty. Look for areas of common concern and specific problems that you can address in the future.

### Your Own Perspective

After you have adjusted your students' attitudes, it's time to adjust your own. You may think your attitude is just fine, but if you are having a problem with discipline, motivation, or participation, then you may be part of the problem. Perhaps you aren't prepared when class begins, so students follow your disorganized example. Or maybe you believe you are treating your students with respect, but you have a hidden agenda to save them from themselves—and they have detected your patronizing attitude. Instead of focusing on how to fix your students, find ways to fix yourself. For example, if students constantly shout out answers instead of raising their hands before speaking, have you taught them the procedure you want them to follow? Do you ever respond to the shouters? Perhaps you have created the problem or contributed to it in some way.

How much do you listen—really listen—to your students? And how do you respond to their comments? Do you always have the last word? Do you correct their grammar when they are talking passionately about something? Do you imply that your values and standards and lifestyle are superior to theirs? Do you belittle their ideas or brush off their concerns as trivial? Do you use a dismissive or singsong tone of voice? Even if you think you are always courteous and respectful, try setting up a tape recorder near your desk and taping your class for thirty minutes. You may be surprised to hear the tone of your voice or the way you speak differently to different students. (I have tried this myself and was unpleasantly surprised.)

Many teachers have trouble getting students to talk to them. The same students who talk each other's ears off may suddenly become tongue-tied if you ask them to talk to you. Or you may have one or two students who dominate every class discussion. In order to involve everybody in your class, I suggest that you try beginning each class period by asking, "Who has a question? You can ask me anything about anything. If I don't know the answer, I will find out where we can locate the information."

Students don't automatically respond to this approach. It may take several days or weeks of asking this before somebody finally responds. Once somebody responds, others will follow. But you may have to do a lot of prompting to get that first response. You might find that if you ask your own question and answer it out loud, students may respond. You might say, "I was thinking about reality TV shows last night. And I wonder if those shows could really be called reality because the people know they are being filmed, so they probably don't act like they would if they weren't being filmed. Some of them act like they are just picking fights with each other because they know they will get attention and more people will see them." If nobody comments, just say, "Well, that's what I was thinking." Then start your lessons.

The next day you might say, "Who has a question? Anybody? Let's wait a minute to see if anybody has one." Wait a full minute to see if anybody can think of one. Watch the clock for a full minute. If nobody speaks, say, "Well, I was just wondering what happens to change our society so drastically. At one time the only people who had tattoos were bikers and ex-convicts and people who wanted to make a statement. Today tattoos are like jewelry. I wonder what happened to change that." Then wait a second to see if anybody responds. Choose a student who seems to be considering your comments and ask if he or she has a comment. If not, start your lesson.

Continue each day asking your own question for two or three weeks, even a month if you can think of enough comments. If nobody ever responds, then you might want to consider trying a different approach. But don't give up easily. And don't think your students aren't interested. They will be listening, even when they pretend they aren't.

Although this technique works very well for me, it wasn't originally my idea. A few years ago I attended an awards ceremony for a student who had won an essay contest. He wrote about his teacher: "Our teacher used to come in every morning and say, 'What do you want to know?'" The boy told me, "Nobody ever answered him, but he kept asking. Finally, after a really long time, I asked him a question. The next day I asked another one. Pretty soon other kids were asking questions, and we started talking about all kinds of stuff. And after a while, we got to like school again. That teacher showed us that we had forgotten how to dream. He gave that back to us."

After meeting that student, I tried his teacher's approach. It worked so well that I have continued to use it in every class, regardless of my students' age or academic background. One of my former students, a young man who was in my class in 1993, recently sent me an e-mail in response to my request for advice to teachers who want to connect with students. Alex wrote:

> I liked when you took time to have class discussions at the beginning of class for a few minutes. Sometimes you would focus on one student, and the rest of the class was paying attention because they knew they might be next. I did not feel pressure when you asked me a question because at the end, no matter what our response was, you always made us feel good for responding. You listened to us. After that warm welcome to class, it did not matter what kind of hard work you gave us. We tried our best to do the work.

One more tweak to your attitude may be in order. If you earned consistently high grades in school or if you haven't been to school for a while, try taking a very difficult class, one that you will have to struggle to pass. If you are creative, for example, enroll in statistics or advanced mathematics. If you are scientific-minded, try an art class. Your goal is not to earn an A, but to remember (or find out for the first time) how it feels to be intelligent yet unable to easily grasp a new concept. Some teachers find that an academic adjustment enables them to better empathize with their students.

## 3. ALTER STUDENT SELF-PERCEPTIONS

After you have adjusted the attitudes, in your classroom, students may be receptive to a perception shift as well. We can't make students care about getting an education. But if we can somehow convince them to care about themselves, they will begin to care about school. The tricky part is figuring out how to shift their self-perceptions. If only we could say, "I think you are an intelligent, capable person" and have the student say, "Oh, you're right. I guess I am intelligent. So I think I'll start taking my education seriously and make some plans for my future." Ho ho ho. We have to be just a bit more subtle and a lot more patient.

Subtle and patient don't come naturally to me. I have to work at them. When I first started teaching, I thought I could muscle students into accepting my point of view. In a passing conversation, I once asked a high school junior what he planned to do after graduation.

"I'll probably go to prison," Julio said.

Surprised, I asked him if he was in trouble with the law.

"No," he said.

"Then why would you go to prison?"

"Because that's where all the men in my family go."

"Well, you don't have to go to prison. You're going to graduate, and you already have a job waiting for you."

"You don't understand," he said. "The men in my family always end up in prison."

"You don't understand," I said. "You don't have to go to prison."

Neither of us understood. Of course, I was upset by this conversation and determined to change Julio's mind. I never could. And he did eventually go to prison after graduation. But a couple of years later, one of his friends called me and said, "Julio is out on parole, and he has a good job, and he just wanted you to know he's doing all right."

That phone conversation was my wake-up call. I realized that Julio had been listening to me, and he was also right. But I hadn't listened to him. I heard the words, but I didn't realize he was telling me that he felt hopeless to change what he believed was his destiny. I needed to change my approach. Instead of trying to bulldoze students into accepting my perception of their talents and potential, I needed to find a way to help them change their perceptions of themselves as hopeless losers or powerless pawns—a subtle but powerful difference.

First, I had to figure out how my students perceived themselves. I began by asking the group general questions when I felt they were in a comfortable and talkative mood.

"How many people plan to go to college?" (Some hands waved.)

"How many would like to go, but you don't think you can do it?" (More hands.)

"How many people here think they will end up on welfare someday?"

"How many people think they will travel all over the world?"

"How many people see themselves having pretty good jobs?"

"How many think they will probably go to prison?"

"How many people think they will be married and have a family in ten years?"

"How many people think there's a good chance they will be dead before they are thirty years old?"

I didn't respond individually to students during these quick surveys, but I did make notes of the students who raised their hands in response to the negative questions. Then, during the normal course of a school day, I created opportunities to tell those students how I saw them and the possibilities for their future. For example, I might say, "Do you know how much artistic talent you have? I could see you as an architect or a graphic artist someday." To kids who are especially interested in computers, I might say, "You have such a good imagination, I bet you'd make a great video game designer. I could also see you working as a systems analyst, helping people figure out what kind of computer system they need for their business."

I persisted in telling students how I saw them every chance I got. And it worked. Eventually they began to see themselves as people with talents and skills. Sometimes I would ask them to humor me and try a visualization experiment. I'd ask them to close their eyes and imagine themselves getting up in the morning, getting dressed, grabbing their briefcase and a cup of coffee, and driving to work in a spiffy car. Then they enter the reception area of a big company, greet the receptionist, and head for their office, where they turn on the computer and check their mail. "Can you see it?" I'd ask. Most of them couldn't, but one or two could.

Another day I might ask them to imagine that they get up very early, eat a hearty breakfast, and grab their toolboxes. They jump into their pickup trucks and head off to a construction site where they will install kitchen cabinets in a new housing development. A few more seers.

These scenarios were very helpful, I think, because most students have no real idea of what occupations actually involve, other than the most familiar ones—doctor, lawyer, or teacher. They may hear about other jobs from the counselors and see people portraying different occupational roles in movies, but they don't know what those people actually do on the job. I try to give them details, so they can imagine what it might be like to work as an X-ray technician, a hotel manager, a bartender, a restaurant owner, a construction supervisor, an engineer, a dental assistant, a veterinarian, a sports promoter, a tailor, a shoemaker, or a security guard. I encourage them to think of themselves in a variety of situations until they find one that feels right for them.

This may seem like New Age hocus-pocus, as my father likes to say, but it isn't. When you tell a student, "I see you as an intelligent, talented person," that student can no longer think of himself only as a stupid or untalented mess. Even if he rejects your idea, it's now in his thought repertoire. He won't change his perception immediately, but we do know that once you introduce a new idea to a brain, it can't go back to its former state. The seed of that new idea will grow, even if it isn't watered.

Another way I tried to change students' perceptions of themselves was to ask other adults to tell them for me. I invited a handwriting expert to analyze my students' handwriting and focus on their positive traits (this was a huge hit and a great motivation to do a lot of writing beforehand so the expert would have many samples). Local businesspeople were very willing to come to our classroom and conduct mock interviews with students—and give positive feedback and constructive criticism about their interviewing skills. My students would not attend job fairs at school because they felt too insecure to put themselves out there, but they were very excited about having our own job fair inside the classroom, where they felt safe. Parents and relatives of students came to our class to share their experiences in creative pursuits and various businesses. Among our visitors was an amateur photographer, a sculptor, an office supervisor, and the manager of a day care center. Those people invited my students to think about their futures, and most of those students accepted the invitation.

## 4. CATCH KIDS BEING GOOD

Children crave attention. If they can't catch our attention by behaving well, they will misbehave, because they know that we won't ignore them when they do wrong. And we teachers know we should focus on the positive, but we still tend to accentuate the negative in school. It seems to be the default setting of adults. We spend much more time and effort trying to stop bad behavior than we do rewarding good behavior. We remember having to ask a student to sit down or be quiet, but we forget how many times that same student participated and cooperated and acted like a decent human being. With practice and persistence, we can change our default setting to the positive. We can learn to notice when children are behaving. There are many more opportunities to catch them being good than there are to catch them being bad. If we want children to be kind, considerate, compassionate, generous, and honorable, we need to notice and thank them when they do act in those ways. We don't have to give them candy or points, but we do need to give them acknowledgment for cooperating and praise when they excel.

If you'd like some suggestions for ways to start catching your students being good, visit Dr. Mac's behavior advisor Web site at www.behavioradvisor.com/CatchGood.html. Here you'll find fifteen descriptions written by teachers about working with real students and keeping an eye out for good behavior.

One way I remind myself to catch students being wonderful is to take three blank index cards to class every day with the names of three students written on them. During that day I make sure I notice when those students do something kind or admirable—lending somebody a pen, offering to collect papers, picking up litter from the floor and placing it in the trash, erasing the board without my asking, helping another student complete an assignment. The specific act isn't important, as long as it is honestly spontaneous. I take a minute to write notes that I hand to students at the end of class. The notes aren't long: "Thanks for helping to keep our classroom clean today. I appreciate you" is enough. Don't be surprised if a student confides that yours was the first positive note any teacher ever wrote to him or her. It's enough to make a grown woman cry.

## 5. REACH OUT TO PARENTS AND GUARDIANS

Parents and guardians are used to receiving phone calls from school staff and teachers complaining about unexcused absences, tardiness, missed assignments, bad attitudes, and disrespectful behavior. Often they become defensive because they believe teachers are blaming them (and sometimes we are) for their children's misdeeds. But they are equally responsible when their children behave respectfully and decently. So we need to call and let them know that we appreciate their efforts.

When a student in your class behaves especially well, call the parent or guardian and say, "I just wanted to thank you for doing such a good job of raising your son [daughter]. I know that kids don't behave well by accident. They were taught by their parents. I wish all my students were as well behaved as yours. Thank you for making my job easier." Better yet, write a note instead of calling. Positive notes from teachers are often displayed proudly on the front of the refrigerator in the student's home and may result in special privileges for the student—which may come back to you in the form of increased cooperation and undying loyalty from that student.

In addition to creating a good relationship with parents and improving student performance, good-news phone calls let the students know that you and their parents are working together. Sometimes children try to play their teachers and parents against each other, but if you make the first contact a positive experience, you won't fall prey to that scam. And if you should ever need to call those same parents or guardians because of a behavior problem, you will find them much more receptive than they might have been otherwise.

I've found phone calls so helpful that whenever I have a new group of students, I take home my roll sheets and call four or five parents each night. I write notes to those I can't contact. I introduce myself, provide my phone number and e-mail address, and ask them to let me know if they need any help from me during the year. I also find something good to say about their child, even if it takes some serious effort to find that good thing. If just one or two parents respond positively to my overture, it's very likely that their children will respond positively as well. And all it takes is a few individuals to get the good behavior ball rolling in your classroom.

Another very effective strategy is to write notes home to the parents and guardians of your worst-performing students. Yep, those little stinkers who make you want to quit. They expect bad news, and so do their parents. So if you write a positive note (it has to be true, so you'll have to work to catch those students doing something good), you are bound to get everybody's attention. One mother called me, in tears, and said, "I have two children in your school, and in ten years I have never heard a good word about either one of them." I had both her children—they were twins—in my class and I could see very clearly why nobody had ever praised those rambunctious ill-mannered children, but I didn't tell her that. I said, "Well, they certainly have a lot of energy and they are basically good kids." It was true. They weren't murderers or child molesters or drug dealers or bullies. They were just ordinary obnoxious teenagers. But those positive notes made a huge change in their behavior. The terrible twins didn't become scholars overnight, but they toned down their behavior in my class because they wanted the rewards and love that they received at home in response to my positive progress reports.

## 6. BE YOUR OWN GUINEA PIGS

One of the most effective methods I have ever used to motivate students—including adult university students—is to use our class as guinea pigs to test various theories or research that we have read. For example, most recently one of my classes of future teachers was discussing an article from a pop psychology magazine that summarized recent research into the value of making mistakes. According to the article, people retain information better if they make mistakes while they are learning. We decided to create a way to test that theory. Our method was very rudimentary and would not meet scientific standards, but that wasn't the purpose of the exercise. My goal was to get those students to seriously consider the value of making mistakes and to think of ways they could incorporate mistake making into their classrooms.

That class is a good class. They come on time, they read the assignments, they willingly participate in discussions. But occasionally I'd notice somebody checking the clock or gazing out the window, disengaged from the current activity. During our mistake-making exercise, every single student was fully engaged for the entire activity. They were so enthusiastic that they bubbled. It wasn't a "fun" activity. I gave them two lists of difficult words (*jacamar, baggala, inchoate,* and *icteric,* for example). For the first list, they had to write definitions for each word, making them up if they didn't know them. Then I gave them the correct definitions to compare with their versions. For the second list of words, I simply gave them the definitions to copy down. We put the two word lists away until the end of the class, almost three hours later. Then I gave them both lists of words and asked them to write down as many definitions as they could remember. Our results upheld the research—we all remembered many more of the words from the first list, where we had corrected our mistakes.

Nobody wanted to leave the room that day. They wanted to discuss ways to teach their students how to make mistakes and learn from them.

My high school students were just as receptive to being guinea pigs. Spelling tests were not popular, as you can imagine, among my remedial reading classes. But when I suggested that we try various strategies to test their effectiveness, everybody became interested in taking those tests. First, we pretended we were in kindergarten. We chanted the words together, slowly, out loud. We did this Monday through Thursday and took our test on Friday. We recorded the results. The following week, we tried air-writing with our fingers to learn the words. Again, we practiced for four days and then took the test. Overall we tested six different methods, including flash cards, word lists, and pretests. During those months, nobody complained about having to study spelling words. They were so interested in seeing which methods worked best that they forgot they were supposed to hate spelling.

In the same class, we also used ourselves as test subjects for reading experiments. We all read the same passage for one minute to see how many words we read. We marked them and put the passage away for a week. Then we read several articles to practice our skills. The following week we read a similar passage to see if we read any faster. Most of us did. We used this method for a month and then tried something else. The activities themselves weren't important—it was the idea that we were testing our brains to see what made them work best. The focus switched.

Instead of viewing assignments as work, we began to see them as tools for learning. What a novel idea!

## 7. REQUEST FREQUENT FEEDBACK

Students are far more likely to cooperate when they have the opportunity to provide feedback to their instructors about the level of difficulty, specific or optional requirements, and the time allowed for completing their assignments. Of course, it's important to remind students that you, the teacher, make the decisions about what and how you teach, but that you appreciate their input and will not retaliate if they provide honest, constructive criticism. Some students may need a reminder that constructive criticism offers a thoughtful suggestion for improving something. (If you get some ridiculous or mean-spirited comments, don't reward the students who wrote those comments by responding to them; file their worthless feedback in the trash can during a private moment.) Thank the students who provide honest feedback and tell them you will consider their comments as you plan future assignments. Depending on your students' age, maturity, and personalities, you may decide to allow them to provide anonymous feedback. I usually make names optional (and most students do include their names because they want me to know that they gave a thoughtful response).

Monthly feedback works for some teachers; others like to wait until the end of a unit or the end of a quarter or grading period. I prefer frequent feedback because in my experience, students' morale improves when they know I care about their feelings.

Whether you allow students to comment on your teaching style or methods is up to you. Some teachers prefer to stick to questions on lesson content and format, activities and projects, quizzes and tests. If you ask open-ended questions, be sure to allow ample space. Students tend to write very brief answers when the spaces are small. For younger students, I provide a form where all they have to do is check the statement that they agree with for each activity or assignment, such as "give me more," "it's okay," or "forget about it."

## 8. CHART STUDENT PROGRESS

Ironically, the students who claim to care the least about school are the same ones who complain the most about the bad grades they earn. During my first year of teaching, I had one class of accelerated and one class of remedial English students.

The college-bound students accepted their first-quarter grades with a few sighs and moans, but the self-proclaimed too-cool-for-school remedial students spent an entire class period arguing about their grades. Some begged; others demanded an audit of my grade book or questioned my sanity.

When the deluge of complaints after report cards subsided, I tried holding individual conferences to keep students informed of their progress. Next I tried giving students periodic written progress reports. Twice each month, while they were busy working, I would circulate through the room and hand them slips of paper showing their current grade. I would stop by the student's desk and place the paper face-down.

"Good work," I'd write, or "You're moving up. Hang in there." To failing students I'd write, "Your grade is not passing right now, but if you want some help, let me know. I'm glad you are in my class." Regardless of the grade, I shook the student's hand. Some kids preferred not to shake, because they didn't want to give the impression that they cared about school. To them I'd give a quick and silent thumbs-up. When semester report cards arrived, moans and groans were down by about half, but clearly the other half of my students believed that I had somehow robbed them of their due.

The first day of the second semester, I offered my students a deal. Everybody who came to class every single day (no unexcused absences), earned at least a C on every classroom and homework assignment without copying, cooperated with me and participated in every lesson, and earned a C or higher on every quiz would earn a passing grade, even if they flunked their final exam.

"What are you trying to do, psych us out?" one boy asked. Ryan was one of the brightest, least motivated young people I've ever had the pleasure of trying to teach. He earned an A on every assignment he did, but he did only half the assignments, so he ended up with 50 percent and an F on his report card. Ryan wasn't the only underachiever in his class. Failing grades, missing credits, truancy, and bad attitudes were much more common than good attitudes and high grades.

"Absolutely," I told Ryan. "I am trying to psych you out. I don't believe it's possible to come to class every single day, honestly try to learn, complete all your assignments by yourself with a passing grade, and still fail to learn what I'm teaching. Anybody who does all those things and who has a functioning brain will pass. You all have functioning brains, so that's the deal I'm offering you. Why not try it?

You have nothing to lose, and you might find out that you're a lot smarter than you think you are."

Ryan took me up on my offer and started doing all the assignments. His grades were at the top of the class, but he couldn't believe he was passing. Every day he'd ask to see his grade in my grade book. It didn't matter that I told him every day that he was passing. He had to see it for himself, in writing, on the page. Soon other students started joining Ryan, clamoring to see their own grades. As a self-defense tactic, I created a wall chart for Ryan's class that turned out to be an excellent motivator, even for my most unmotivated students.

On a large sheet of poster board (I could have used a blank page from my grade book, but back then I didn't think to make a copy of the book before entering grades), I printed the names of the students in Ryan's class down the left-hand side of the sheet and divided the rest of the sheet into small squares. I made sure to leave enough squares to list each assignment, including homework, quizzes, exams, and special projects. Above each square, I wrote the name of the assignment, using abbreviations such as w/s for worksheet and T for test (Sp T-1, for example, meant spelling test number one). If a student completed an assignment with a passing grade, he or she earned an X in the square for that assignment. I drew a green box around the square for students who failed or were absent. If the student made up the assignment before the deadline (which I wrote just below the name of the assignment so that there would be no doubt about due dates), I placed an X in the box to show that the student had completed the assignment with a passing grade. I put a big red zero in the box for any assignment that was incomplete or failed and no attempt was made to bring the failed grade up to par. Figure 10.1 shows a sample of the progress wall chart I used.

The chart didn't contain any grades, because I don't think it's a good idea to humiliate students or try to create competition for grades as a motivator. Some people simply can't spell, for example, and though spelling doesn't indicate intelligence, poor spellers who are constantly compared to others feel like failures. I wanted my students to compete with themselves to make sure there was an X in every box.

"If you have all Xs, there is no way that you can fail my class," I assured them. "The quality of your work will determine whether you earn an A or a D, but if you do the work, you're going to pass this class."

## Figure 10.1.
## Progress Wall Chart.

X = done    □ = missing    ⊠ late    ⊙ = no credit

| Deadline Name | 9/1 Journal | 9/4 Spelling | 9/11 Reading | 9/17 Vocab | 10/3 Spelling Quiz | 10/7 Essay | 10/17 Project | 10/25 Group Report |
|---|---|---|---|---|---|---|---|---|
| Chavez, D | X | ⊙ | X | X | X | ⊠ | X | X |
| Cohen, P | X | X | X | X | X | X | X | X |
| Dexter, L | ⊙ | X | X | ⊠ | X | X | X | X |
| Farley, M | X | X | X | X | X | X | □ | X |
| Haqq, K | X | X | X | X | ⊠ | X | X | X |
| Hong, S | ⊠ | X | X | X | X | X | X | X |
| Jones, J | X | X | X | X | X | X | X | X |
| Langley, A | ⊠ | X | X | X | X | X | X | X |
| Martin, F | ⊙ | ⊙ | X | X | ⊠ | ⊠ | X | X |
| Martinez, R | X | X | ⊠ | X | X | X | □ | X |
| Porter, L | X | X | X | X | X | X | X | X |
| Quintana, K | X | X | X | X | X | X | X | X |
| Ross, P | ⊠ | X | X | X | ⊠ | X | X | X |
| Stango, J | X | X | X | X | X | ⊙ | ⊠ | X |
| Tano, F | X | X | X | X | X | X | X | X |
| Wildhorse, A | X | ⊙ | ⊙ | X | X | ⊠ | ⊠ | X |
| Young, T | X | X | X | X | X | X | X | X |

Even my most unmotivated, apathetic students couldn't ignore the string of red zeros placed beside their names. They didn't rush into my room and run to check the chart as most students did; they shuffled in, yawned, sidled a few steps until they could check the chart while pretending to glance casually over their shoulders at something more compelling. During the first report period that I posted the chart, the students in my lowest-achieving class complained that it wasn't fair that they couldn't make up all those missed assignments. I made a super-duper, incredible, one-time offer: a three-week grace period during which students could make up any missing or failed work. After that, deadlines would be nonnegotiable.

It worked. A few red zeros remained on the chart when the next report cards came out, but every single student passed my class.

When my other classes saw the progress chart for Ryan's class, they demanded similar charts for their classes. Even the good students who routinely took home report cards filled with As and Bs wanted tangible proof of their progress and of the demands

I would make of them. That's when I realized that many unsuccessful students give up because they can't visualize themselves making real progress toward the end of a quarter or semester. To them, school is an endless journey made more difficult by mountains of paperwork. When they see visual proof that they are succeeding, they stop pretending that they don't care. They may not become scholars, but they begin to believe that they may actually survive school and eventually graduate.

## 9. GO RIGHT-BRAIN

Brain dominance is one of those topics that goes in and out of favor, depending on the latest scientific research (and perhaps, who funds the research). But based on my own reading and experiences as a teacher, I believe the basic concept is sound.

The idea gained popularity in the late 1950's when doctors learned they could help prevent severe seizures in epileptics by severing the connection between the two hemispheres of the brain. This led to all the other research because it clearly demonstrated that the two hemispheres process information differently.

The left brain monitors the areas for speech, understands the literal interpretation of words, recognizes words and numbers. It is analytical and performs arithmetic computations. Arousing the brain's attention to deal with outside stimuli is a left-brain specialty.

The right brain gathers information more from images than from words, looks for patterns, interprets language through context—body language, emotional context, tone of voice—rather than through literal meanings. It specializes in spatial perceptions, recognizes places, faces, objects, relational and mathematical operations such as geometry and trigonometry.

People tend to be right- or left-brain dominant, just as they are right- or left-handed. But logic is not confined to the left hemisphere just as creativity is not restricted to the right. Because the two hemispheres do not function independently, it is impossible to educate only one hemisphere. It is possible, however, to design activities that are designed to encourage right- or left-brain brain activity. Turning a drawing upside-down, for example, and trying to copy it will engage the right hemisphere rather than the left.

Research into brain dominance most likely inspired the creation of the Brain Gym exercises which have been so successful in helping preschool children develop early literacy. Toddlers who can't crawl or who have poor eye-hand coordination usually have trouble learning to read. The exercises are simple, but they involve moving the arms and legs so that they cross the median of the body. This is also used often by physical therapists. When people's coordination improves (tapping the right knee with the left hand, for example, and vice versa) other positive changes occur. Children who learn how to crawl more gracefully are more likely to be able to learn to read.

Although making generalizations can be dangerous, I believe it would be safe to suggest that the majority of teachers are left-brain dominant (detail-oriented) thinkers. Left-brainers like school, because their natural preference coincides with the left-brain paradigm of most traditional school systems. Unfortunately, the majority of students may not be left-brain dominant. For the sake of argument, let's assume that half the students in a given class are right-brain ("big-picture") dominant thinkers. They think differently from their left-brain teachers, and they often become discouraged or uninterested in school because they are made to feel unintelligent by virtue of the way their brains operate.

If you are unfamiliar with the subject of brain dominance, you can find an excellent introduction to the topic in David Sousa's book *How the Brain Learns* (Corwin Press, 2006). Chapter Five of that book, on brain specialization and learning, provides an overview of hemisphere dominance, along with notes about interesting research on gender, language acquisition, and learning to read. And Daniel H. Pink's bestseller *A Whole New Mind: Why Right-Brainers Will Rule the Future* (Riverhead, 2006) presents an interesting case for the importance of cultivating the brain's right hemisphere, inside and outside the classroom.

### Take a Brain Dominance Quiz

Teachers can take a brain dominance quiz that offers tips for teaching at www2.scholastic.com/browse/article.jsp?id=3629.

Students can take a similar test designed specifically for them at homeworktips .about.com/.../brainquiz/bl_leftrightbrain_quiz.htm.

### Add Some Right-Brain Activities

You can change the dynamics in your classroom by adding some right-brain activities and educational games. If you do an Internet search for "wacky wordies" and "right-brain games," you will find many resources.

To get you started, here are two brief examples. Exhibits 10.1 and 10.2 contain some word puzzles that I like to use to identify my right-brain students. Don't read the answers immediately. Instead, read the directions and try to solve each puzzle. If you are a left-brainer, this may be very frustrating for you.

## Exhibit 10.1.
## Wacky Wordies.

*Directions:* The words in each box represent a popular phrase. The placement, size, and shape of letters inside the box give clues. For example, the word "pigs" when printed three times in small letters inside the box would represent the phrase "three little pigs."

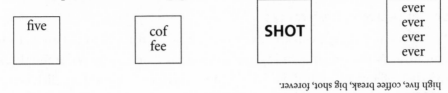

*Answers:*
high five, coffee break, big shot, forever.

## Exhibit 10.2.
## Right-Brain Word Puzzles.

*Directions:* Each group of words shares a common trait (but not common definitions). Only one answer shares that same trait. Figure out the common trait and select the correct answer.

| 1 | 2 | 3 | 4 | 5 |
|---|---|---|---|---|
| sexes | golden | tea | modem | youth |
| level | tallow | eye | willow | usher |
| redder | clamp | sea | domed | item |
| a. dined | a. trace | a. wee | a. clash | a. water |
| b. mom | b. crawl | b. ate | b. winter | b. there |
| c. start | c. oven | c. you | c. tablet | c. hero |

*Answers:*
1. mom: the word spells the same forward and backward
2. trace: remove the first letter to form a new word
3. you: sounds like a letter when you say it (tea, eye)
4. tablet: the word begins and ends with the same letter
5. hero: the word begins with a pronoun

If you do this exercise with your students, you may find that the students who enjoy it most are those who do not have the highest grades in your class. The left-brain dominant scholars sometimes become very upset because they are used to being smarter and faster than their classmates. Your right-brain dominant students will enjoy being the "smart kids" for a change. (And be prepared: sometimes students may figure out alternative answers that aren't on the answer list, but are equally correct.)

## Look at Learning Preferences

After you do your right-brain activity, tell your students that you would like to help them identify their own learning preferences (and be sure to write the three primary preferences on the board for your visual learners): auditory (listeners), visual (lookers), and kinesthetic (movers). Then ask your students to think about how they approach a new game. Do they like to have somebody explain the game and the rules and give them verbal instructions? Do they like to watch other people play for a while and then jump in themselves? Or would they prefer to just get into the game and learn as they go along?

Another example that helps students identify their learning preferences is to give them directions. For example, tell them to imagine that they have asked you how to get to the post office. First, say, "You exit the school and turn right. Go two blocks and take the next left turn. Go up the hill and around a curve, then take the second right. After the second stop sign, turn left and then make an immediate right into the parking lot." Ask how many students feel confident that they can get to the post office after listening to your instructions. Those who raise their hands are your auditory learners (probably a small percentage of students).

Next, draw a map on the board or distribute copies of a map you have drawn. Use the same instructions that you gave verbally. Next, ask how many students feel confident that they can get to the post office. Probably more than half your class will raise their hands; these are your visual learners.

Watch for students who are frowning at the map or turning it sideways. Perhaps they are tilting their heads. Ask, "If I drove you to the post office right now, how many of you would be able to retrace that same route, even if we drove it only once?" Those frowning students (your kinesthetic learners) will shoot their hands into the air, relieved to learn that there is a third alternative.

I would also suggest, if you have time, that you teach your students how to ask for help from their teachers, tutors, or parents. Students who become confused often say, "I don't get it." And teachers repeat what they have said, either more loudly or more slowly. But that response will help only auditory learners. Auditory learners do need to say, "Could you please repeat that?" or "Could you please explain that to me again, a little more slowly?" Visual learners need to say, "I can't quite picture that. If I could see a drawing or a graph or video or something, I think I could understand it better. Maybe an example would help me." And your kinesthetic learners need to say, "I learn by doing things. Could you walk me through a couple of examples step-by-step, so that I can practice doing them and get the hang of it?"

And, of course, teachers need to remember that different students learn in different ways, so we need to vary our methods of instruction to incorporate visuals and movement, as well as listening activities. When you discuss a new concept, for example, be sure to provide some kind of visual to accompany your verbal introduction. And make sure that you walk students through several examples. Your kinesthetic learners need to do the examples themselves, however. Copying your work from the board isn't enough for them; they need to do the work themselves with your guidance.

Many researchers suggest that teachers should encourage students to strengthen their weak areas. A visual learner, for example, may need to work on developing better listening skills, because not every idea can be easily pictured. Likewise, an auditory learner might benefit from working on kinesthetic skills such as eye-hand coordination. But it is helpful to know a student's preference, so that when problems arise during instruction you can use examples that favor the student's strengths and help them move forward.

## 10. MAKE MISTAKES MANDATORY

Have some fun making mistakes. We often tell children that mistakes are OK because everybody makes them, but we then turn around and punish students academically for being less than perfect. Imagine that your supervisor expected you to perform eight out of every ten tasks perfectly. Few salespeople can boast a 70 percent success rate; most would be happy with 50 percent or even lower. Baseball players are considered top-notch if they can hit more than 30 percent of the pitches thrown at them. Yet we expect children to perform with 70 percent accuracy when they are working with unfamiliar material and learning new skills. How unreasonable can we get?

Of course, we have to have tests, exams, and other measures to assess how well students are learning, but if we want children to be interested in learning, we must allow them to make mistakes without embarrassing or penalizing them. For example, instead of grading a regular classroom assignment as soon as students finish it, why not let them keep their papers while you go over each item and discuss the correct answers, possible answers, and common mistakes? Let students explain how they arrived at their answers, both wrong and right, and then allow them to redo the assignment before they turn it in. Their comprehension will improve, and they will be much more likely to remember the information if you correct any misconceptions immediately than if they have to wait a day or two (or six) to see how well they did. In the meantime, that misinformation percolates in their brains and may work its way into their long-term memories.

In subjects such as math, this is especially important. If you simply present the lesson and then instruct students to complete an assignment, some students will get about half the answers right and it may appear that they understand. But those correct answers may be accidental or the result of faulty logic. Correcting faulty logic is important for long-term student success. My eight-year-old nephew, for example, looked as though he understood the concept of carrying numbers to another column when adding three-digit numbers. He got about 60 percent of his math problems correct. Because he got that many problems right, his teacher and his parents thought Anthony was simply being lazy or trying to work too fast. When he did his math homework at my house one night, I asked him to explain each step he made. When he carried a number, it was often incorrect, because, as he explained, "If the number is ten or higher, you write a number up here and keep going." When I asked him how he knew which number to write up there, he said it didn't matter. You just put a number. When I showed Anthony how to correctly carry a number, he was thrilled and his math grades immediately began to improve. I could see how his teacher might have missed Anthony's faulty logic because it certainly looked like he knew what he was doing and if you asked him, he would assure you that he did.

Celebrate mistakes, even yours. When you make a mistake, ask the students to give you a round of applause for demonstrating that although you are an educated and undoubtedly intelligent teacher, you are also a human being. Don't worry that students will lose respect for you when they learn that you aren't perfect. On the contrary, they will respect you more for admitting your mistakes and helping them learn from theirs.

During class discussions, when a student offers an incorrect answer or idea, instead of simply saying, "Wrong" or asking another student, try saying, "That's an interesting idea. How did you arrive at that conclusion?" or "I hadn't thought of that. Could you explain your thinking?" Not only does this teach students that mistakes are acceptable, but you may identify misinformation before it solidifies in a student's mind. For example, if a student identifies 0 as an improper fraction, that student may not understand the basic principles of fractions. If you ask how she arrived at that answer, you may be able to adjust her thinking and set her back on the right track.

I have to admit that I have been guilty of hiding my mistakes. During my first years as a teacher, when one of my wonderful activities bombed in class, I would collect the papers and throw them away after students left the room. Usually the students forgot about the fiasco, but if anybody asked, I'd say, "Oh, I haven't had a chance to grade those papers yet." Eventually they would forget about the exercises that didn't work, but I didn't. After one of our discussions about mistakes, I realized how hypocritical it was for me to encourage my students to make mistakes and then hide my own. The next time an exercise failed miserably, I stopped the students and told them what I had hoped the activity would teach them. Then I asked them to form small groups and discuss the assignment. They could either fix the assignment so that it would work or decide it wasn't worth saving. In every case the students came up with a more challenging and complex assignment than I had. And in addition to the academic lessons, they learned that teachers aren't perfect and that mistakes really can be stepping stones to improvement. After more than a decade of teaching, my lesson designs have improved and I don't have many flops, but when I do, I share them with students. Surprisingly, revealing my mistakes doesn't diminish students' respect for me; their respect actually increases.

## 11. CONNECT THROUGH PRIVATE JOURNALS

If you use journals but your students aren't writing very much, there is a reason. I could suggest a few possibilities based on my own students' comments about journal writing: you don't read the journals; you grade entries on spelling and grammar, which inhibits expression; you don't allow enough time, so they feel rushed and unable to think; you allow too much time, so they procrastinate and lack focus; or your prompts are not inspiring.

Inspiring prompts are a must if you expect journal writing to produce results. Prompts such as "Write a letter to Abraham Lincoln" or "Write your own obituary" may sound interesting to adults and may appeal to more scholarly students, but they won't work for students who aren't excited about school or are frightened by death. If you want students to write a letter to somebody, choose a person (or let them choose a person) they would actually consider talking to in the first place. Most children wouldn't be inclined to talk to a dead president or a historical figure. They would, however, talk to their parents, relatives, teachers, principals, and friends. If you use letter writing as a prompt, assure your students that you will not send their letters off and that students can destroy them as soon as you have recorded their grade for completing the writing assignment.

Letter writing can be a great catharsis for students who are distracted by emotional stress or too keyed up to focus on school. You can use journal writing to teach students that writing down their feelings, especially when they are angry, helps dissipate pent-up energy and may help them calm down.

For teachers who haven't used journals or haven't used them successfully, my high school students created the following list of dos and don'ts:

- Read the journals. If you aren't going to read them, don't ask us to write in them.
- Make at least one comment on every page.
- Don't mark all the spelling and grammar errors—just circle a couple.
- Give good prompts. Give us choices or let us make up our own.
- Show us some good journal entries that other kids have written.
- Read some journals out loud, anonymously.
- Let us know when we write something especially good or original.
- Let us use our journals as rough drafts for essays and big assignments.
- Make journal writing a regular activity, at least once a week.
- Let us use swear words sometimes, when we are really mad.

If you have a problem coming up with good prompts, do an online search for journal writing. There are a number of good Web sites on which teachers share their own prompts for various age levels. It's important to choose something that your students might actually care about. Unless I am using the journal-writing exercise to help students think of comments on a story we have read in class, I always include this as the final prompt: "Tell me what's on your mind (if it's something truly important don't tell me what you're going to have for lunch)."

Recently a teacher e-mailed me to say that she had decided to use journal writing as the starter activity for the first ten minutes of every class, but that her students balked at the assignment. I advised her to continue with the journals so that her students wouldn't think that they could make her give up any activity they didn't feel like doing. I also suggested that she require journals for two or three weeks and then stop for a few days. A few weeks later, she sent me an e-mail that said, "I did it. Now my students are complaining that they never get to write in their journals. They liked having that quiet activity to help them calm down and focus."

When working with reluctant writers, it may be helpful if you make the journals anonymous to everybody but you. Create a code, using letters or numbers to identify journals by class, but don't label them in alphabetical order. Randomly code them so that if they are lost, nobody will know whose journal they are reading.

I also offer students the option of writing the required number of pages in their journals, showing them to me for credit, and then destroying them if it makes them feel too vulnerable to have those words in print. And for seriously reluctant writers, I give them the option of writing what they have to say and then folding the page in half so that what they have written is not visible. I then check to see that they have written a page or two or whatever the assignment was, but I don't read what they have written. I give them credit for doing the assignment and respect their request for privacy. Only once did I break my promise not to look. I had a student who made it clear that he didn't like teachers, including me, from the moment he entered my classroom. I worked hard to connect with him, but he wasn't having it. He rarely wrote more than a sentence. One day, he wrote and wrote and wrote. I was so excited. I couldn't wait to read what he had written. But when I got home and took out the bin of journals to grade, I saw that he had turned down the page in his journal, indicating that I was not to read it. I couldn't resist. I opened the page. He had torn out the pages of writing and on the page that remained, he had written, "I knew I couldn't trust you, you f**king liar." He was right. He couldn't trust me. I had to work hard to regain his trust—it took two years. Fortunately I had the same students for three years, so I had that time. But he taught me a very valuable lesson: *don't make promises to students unless you know you can keep them.*

## 12. INTRODUCE ETHICS

Children have an innate sense of justice, but they also tend to view themselves as the center of the universe, which can cause problems because they are unaware of the effects that their actions have on other people. By introducing students to sociology and psychology, you can help them see the bigger picture and realize that they each play a small but important role in a large society. Our goal as teachers is not to impose our own values and ethics, but to encourage students to explore, form, and articulate their own.

I first introduced an ethics exercise to a class in which negative peer pressure was causing a lot of stress and behavior problems. I wanted my students to realize that each person has an individual code of ethics, even if he or she isn't aware of it. I thought that if they could articulate their values and morals, they would be less likely to succumb to negative pressures. For the first experiment, I used something relatively impersonal but universal—money. I asked students to select their best answers to the questions shown in Exhibit 10.3 in their journals.

---

**Exhibit 10.3.**
**Ethics Exercise.**

**Ethics Exercise: Too Much Money**

In your journal, answer the following questions.

1. If a clerk or waiter gave you back too much change, would you return the money or keep it?

   a. Yes, I would definitely keep the money.

   b. No, I would never keep the money.

   c. Maybe I would keep the money. It would depend.

2. If you answered a or b above, please explain.

3. If you answered c in question 1, what would affect your decision—the amount of money, whether anybody else would know, or something else?

4. If your answer to question 3 depends on the amount of money, where would you draw the line? What amount would it take before you felt it necessary to return the money?

---

After students wrote their answers, I took a quick survey and tallied their responses to question one on the board for each category: yes, no, and maybe. Then we had a class discussion about the topic for ten minutes. Next, students formed groups of three to five people and discussed the questions for another ten minutes. After their small-group discussions, students returned to their desks and wrote down their thoughts about the discussions, particularly if they had changed their minds. I asked those who had changed their minds to write the reasons. Finally, we took another quick vote to see if people had changed their views. Many more students had joined the "no" group, those who would return the money. Students enjoyed seeing where they fell along the ethics spectrum, and many of them expressed admiration for the students who originally said that no, they would never keep the money. Those students were steadfast in their refusal to compromise their ethics.

You can slant ethics exercises to fit your subject. In a social studies class, for example, after conducting the exercise about whether to keep money that doesn't belong to you, the teacher could assign the project of researching crime statistics for ten, twenty, and thirty years ago and have students chart the trends. Math students could figure the percentage of people who would keep or return the money and the percentage of people whose votes changed after the discussions. Computer classes could generate charts or tables to display voting results. Art students could make drawings or posters expressing their feelings about money and greed. English composition students could write essays about their thoughts on ethics in general or stealing in particular.

With a bit of practice, you will be able to design ethics and sociology activities that are appropriate and effective for your students. I suggest beginning with journal writing so that students can think about their own ideas first, before being influenced by others.

## DISCUSSION POINTS

1. How can we discover what students think of themselves if they are reluctant to talk?

2. What are some ways we can "catch students being good"?

3. Try to create your own Wacky Wordy puzzles.

4. Take a brain dominance quiz. How might your preference influence the way you teach?

5. Do the Too Much Money ethics exercise with a group of teachers. Share your thoughts about how to design and present such activities for students at your school.

# The Posse Update

**P**eople often ask what happened to the students who were depicted in my book *My Posse Don't Do Homework* and later portrayed in the 1995 movie adaptation, *Dangerous Minds,* starring Michelle Pfeiffer. I'm delighted to report that many of those students still stay in touch, sending me occasional progress reports about their educations, their jobs, and their families. Many of them are parents, and many of them are delighted to report that they now make more money than I do—they don't know how much I make, exactly, but electronics engineers, software developers, and video game designers tend to make a bit more money than teachers do. I am happy for them, and I like to tell them how happy I am because if I ever become a destitute bag lady, I will have so many doors where I can go knocking for handouts!

Seriously, I am immensely proud of those students, who overcame tremendous challenges—including poverty, physical abuse, and neglect, along with learning disabilities and language barriers—just to finish high school. Established in the early 1990's and funded by a government grant, our school-within-a-school computer academy enrolled fifty at-risk high school sophomores who became a cohort and studied with a team of four teachers for the three years until they graduated. When the first fifty became juniors, a new group of sophomores enrolled until we reached our capacity of two hundred fifty at-risk students. Eight students in the first class of graduates from our program earned full college scholarships. Sixteen graduates took home scholarships the following year. And the program continues to thrive—but now, instead of being dubbed by students as the program for "losers," it has a long waiting list of students from all backgrounds who hope to participate.

## WHERE ARE THE *DANGEROUS MINDS* KIDS TODAY?

In 2004, twelve years after the first program graduates hugged me goodbye, I visited California on a quick business trip, and one of my former students arranged a mini-reunion. What a thrill to see those smiling students and their spouses and children. Even more thrilling to learn what they were doing with their lives. In that small group there was a school secretary, a nurse, an insurance agent, two electronics engineers, a delivery truck driver, a software developer, an office manager, a Realtor, a mortgage loan officer, and a professional musician. They filled me in on the occupations of the students who couldn't attend the reunion: a FedEx supervisor, a UPS truck driver, a big rig driver, a grocery chain produce manager, a dental hygienist, an ESL teacher, an art instructor, a lactation coach, a systems analyst, a navy journalist, a corporate executive, a day care center manager, a rancher, two music producers, and two football coaches. (One of these coaches had been drafted by the San Diego Chargers and tried out for the team—he didn't make the team, but that didn't diminish our pride in his accomplishment. We all recalled our steadfast belief during high school that he was good enough to play with the pros.)

Here is a quick peek at the current lives of some of the key players from the movie adaptation of the book—Raul, Gusmaro, Callie, and Emilio—along with a handful of their classmates. These students are a representative sample of the students in our program and the hundreds of thousands of struggling students in similar programs throughout this country. Their stories and their lives inspire me to continue believing in the potential of America's "disenchanted" students. And I hope their stories inspire other teachers to continue believing and inspire other young people to continue striving.

### "Raul"

Raul attended college for a year before leaving to work at a family business. (And, yes, he did repay me for the jacket on the day he graduated from high school at age twenty-one.) At last report, Raul found himself on the wrong side of the law and is temporarily a guest of the U.S. justice system. But his wit and sense of humor remain intact. I have several manila envelopes filled with letters and photos from Raul, and regardless of the circumstances of his life his letters always end with a smile, a hug, and a plan for the future.

### Oscar ("Gusmaro")

Oscar started working as a receptionist at the Stanford Linear Accelerator Center during high school, stayed on with the lab full-time after graduation, and was promoted to a job in quality control. Although he steadfastly refused to attend college (he never learned to like school, even when he earned high grades), he had a knack for computers and soon he found himself facing the delightful dilemma of having to choose between two good job offers. A year or so later, I saw him at a book signing in Palo Alto. Oscar arrived a bit late and breathless.

"Hey, Miss J," he said, grabbing me in a hug. "Sorry I'm late. A cop pulled me over because I'm driving a shiny silver SUV, and you know I'm not supposed to be doing that in this neighborhood."

Seeing my dismay, Oscar patted my shoulder and reassured me.

"I'm cool," he said. "I know he was probably just pissed because I drive a lot better car than he does." He laughed. "And I make a lot more money than he does. I probably make more than you, too."

He then filled me in on his job. We reminisced about his first job in high school, when he resisted going for a job interview because he didn't want to talk to "white guys wearing three-piece suits." He insisted that they wouldn't like him or hire him, although they had specifically requested that our students apply for their positions. I asked him how he felt about his job now.

"Those guys are all right," he said. "They don't have no fashion sense and they tell stupid jokes, but they're okay."

About two years after that meeting, Oscar phoned me to discuss a problem. His new job was on the other side of the freeway and a world away from his neighborhood in East Palo Alto. He had the opportunity to buy a house near his work.

"But my homies say if I leave the neighborhood I'm a back stabber," he said. "What do you think?"

I asked him how much time he spent with his high school friends. Very little. I asked him if he wanted his daughter to grow up in East Palo Alto. No. His wife thought they should move. What did his parents and siblings think? They said they would support any decision he made.

"Real friends don't hold you back," I told him. "They lift you up. Just like your family does. I say go for the house. And if your EPA homies are true friends, they will come visit you. And you will visit them. If they turn out not to be real friends, then you'll have to make new friends. Your concern now should be creating the best life for your family."

Oscar bought the house and later called to let me know he was happy with his decision. We lost touch for a few years, but then I received an e-mail from him after my novel *Muchacho* was published. He deemed it a "pretty good book," which was high praise from him, and he thanked me for "turning him on" to *The Four Agreements,* which he and his daughter were reading together. Today Oscar works as a computer technician for a company in Silicon Valley and is happily married.

Oscar's success alone would have been enough to make my entire teaching career worthwhile, but last year I received an e-mail from Shirmel ("Callie," in the movie, who got pregnant and had to fight to stay in school). I had often wondered what happened to Shirmel and I was thrilled to find out.

### Shirmel ("Callie")

"Sorry it took me so long to earn my business degree," Shirmel's e-mail read. I nearly fell off my chair laughing. As I read more of her message, the laughter turned to tears. She had married her high school sweetheart, a young man who lived on the edge and was killed when their third child was young. Shirmel raised her children alone as a working mother, and when her sons were in middle school one of them became involved in some dangerous business and was shot—but fortunately not killed.

"My girlfriend called me and said, 'Have you had enough?'" She continued:

> I said yes and moved to Georgia, outside Atlanta, and started going to school. And I just finished and I wanted to let you know because you always gave me support. Now I have a good job at a big non-profit organization. I have a lot of school loans to pay back and I was going to get two jobs so I could pay them back faster. But my daughter is starting middle school this year, and I remembered that my mother worked at night when I was in middle school and that's when I started stepping out. So I decided I'm just going to work one job. We don't have too much money, but I know where my daughter is at night.

Recently I reconnected with Shirmel, who has grown into a beautiful and successful businesswoman and parent. Her most recent e-mail concluded with a note about realizing that after age thirty she realized she couldn't eat and drink everything she wanted to if she expected to maintain her trim figure: "This year I began participating in a couple of 5K runs. I'm no Flo Jo, but I'm happy with at least being able to place second and third in my age group. In October I will be flying to California to run in my first half-marathon."

I can see Shirmel in my mind, running like the wind, with a smile on her beautiful face.

## Jose and Juan ("Emilio")

And whatever happened to Emilio? In my book, Emilio's character was actually a composite of two boys—two very different boys with the same basic bad-ass attitude. He didn't really die as he did in the movie (one of my biggest complaints about the discrepancy between my book and the film adaptation). The first Emilio, as I think of Jose, spent four years in the Marine Corps before settling down with his wife and two daughters. We had a short but sweet phone conversation about what he called his "new, improved life."

The other inspiration for the Emilio character, Juan—who is the bigger and more belligerent of the two—spent his high school graduation week in jail after threatening a teacher who taunted him. (Because there were witnesses to the event who heard the teacher's remarks, Juan was permitted to finish his class work in jail and take his tests at school so he could graduate.)

About a month after graduation, I received a phone call from Juan, who was working as a baggage handler at San Francisco International Airport. He told me that the handlers worked in shifts and that some of the groups, including people from his shift, had started breaking into passengers' bags and stealing cameras, electronics, and money. He said his supervisor was getting suspicious and he was worried because he didn't want to get arrested. I suggested that he request a transfer to a different shift, one that wasn't stealing.

"Give your supervisor a meaningful look when you ask for the transfer," I said. "He'll know why you're asking, and you won't have to spell it out." He called me a few days later to tell me he had been transferred and things were going well. But he called again a few weeks after that.

"I got a problem," he said, to open the conversation. "My new boss is a pain in the ass. He keeps dogging me, so I might have to hit him."

"Absolutely not," I said. "You don't hit your boss at work. Period."

"Okay." Juan promised not to hit his boss. Two days later, another call. This time from a jail cell.

"Don't freak," Emilio said. "I'm not going to be here that long, but I didn't want you to hear it from somebody else." It turned out that he had hit his boss after all.

"But you promised you wouldn't hit your boss," I said. Juan had very strong ethics, and once he'd given his word he usually didn't break it.

"I didn't hit him at work," Juan said. "You said I shouldn't hit him at work. So the next time he started dogging me I asked him what time did he get off work. He told me and I told him I'd see him outside the parking lot. Then I hit him. It wasn't at work."

Fortunately, the boss didn't carry a grudge, and Juan's job was waiting for him when he returned to work. We had another conversation, this one more specific: "No hitting bosses ever, under any circumstances, in any location. If you hate your job, quit and find another one. But don't ever hit the boss." I haven't had a phone call from him since. I take that as a good sign.

### Heidi

When our new three-year program was offered to struggling high school freshmen, Heidi was one of the first to apply, and she walked into my classroom as one of the most highly motivated and mature teenagers I have ever met. Many of the girls in our three-year program found the boys a bit hard to handle, but Heidi met them eye to eye and convinced them to treat her with respect. A motivated student from day one, she set her sights on working in the dental field—and she made it happen. Today Heidi is a registered dental technician living in Foster City with her husband and son.

### Octavio

Like Gusmaro, Octavio enjoyed working as a dishwasher at Stanford University because he worked with a crew of boys from his neighborhood that had grown up together, spoke the same language, and shared the same disinterest in academics. But he didn't hesitate to accept a job outside his comfort zone—and he has remained a loyal employee of Stanford for the past seventeen years, rising to his current position of facilities dispatcher. A new father, Octavio continues to demonstrate the same outgoing personality, quick to find the humor in any situation and ready to embrace new challenges and new experiences.

### Eric

Definitely not interested in school when he entered our program, Eric eventually realized that he could choose the direction of his life instead of letting life take him for a ride. A few years ago Eric tracked me down and sent me an articulate and heartfelt note of thanks for believing in him when he had lost faith in the value of an education. Highly intelligent and multitalented, Eric still takes his time analyzing situations before forming his opinions. He divides his time between his two very different occupations: independent hip-hop artist and fraud detection specialist.

### Shonta

Shonta's smile is unforgettable. She is proof that a glowing face is not just a literary cliché. Shonta really does glow. Although it's been nearly two decades since she graduated from high school and we haven't seen each other since, I immediately recognized her when I saw her photo on Facebook. We quickly caught each other up on our lives. In one e-mail, she wrote: "I'm a case file coordinator for Ohlone College, taking courses to lead to social worker licensure. I have fallen in love with cultural anthropology, . . . but I am a practical person and I have yet to come across a job posting for an African American female Indiana Jones. LOL."

### Nick

To a stranger, Nick may have looked like a typical "at-risk" teenager—rebellious, nonconformist, not very impressed with high school and its attendant requirements. But a second look reveals a different Nick. For example, after the Rodney King trials, student unrest and cultural clashes became more common at our multiethnic high school. Nick was the target of an attack by a group of African American students, some of whom were classmates. But instead of seeking revenge, Nick and those boys, along with several of their classmates, formed a student-only organization with the goal of promoting racial harmony. Although as adults we were excluded, we were impressed by the compassion and tolerance of those young people. A session drummer and aspiring electrician, Nick continues to espouse the same agenda today: let's all just get along.

### Isabel

Like many of my first "limited English" students, Isabel moved to the United States from Mexico with no English speaking or reading skills, but with a solid elementary school education in Spanish. And, like many of her classmates, Isabel insisted that she could not read or write the materials I presented in class. Every time she said, "I can't," I responded with, "You may say you don't *want* to do something, but don't tell me you *can't* do it." Isabel took those words to heart and after three years in our high school program for at-risk students, she not only graduated with a high GPA, she earned a college scholarship. Now a proud graduate of the Heald College accounting program and mother of a gorgeous fifteen-year-old daughter, Isabel works as a school secretary in the same neighborhood she lived in while attending high school.

## MY TAKE ON THE MOVIE

First, I'd like to say that Michelle Pfeiffer is not only a fine actress, she's a fine person as well. She read my book and she spent three days in my classroom with my students, getting to know them and observing their interactions with me. She got it right. After watching the movie, one boy said, "It creeped me out, you know, seeing her do the exact same things you do, like push your hair a certain way or give that hard look that makes you shut up and sit down."

Michelle's visit transformed our classroom—not physically, but mentally. Prior to her visit, we were dubbed "the dummies," and even our own students bought into that negativity. But her stardust remained after her visit, and it gave our room a new stature. Suddenly everybody wanted to be part of "that cool program." For that, and for her compassion and generosity, I am eternally grateful.

But my Hollywood experience made me seriously reflect on the idea of authors selling the rights to their books to movie production companies. Mine was a frustrating and expensive lesson. I stupidly signed away the opportunity to be involved in the script development, and I signed for a percentage of the net profit before I learned that there is no such thing as net profit in Hollywood. For a long while, the money (or lack of it) was my focus. Then I finally accepted that, yes, the producers took advantage of my naiveté. But commercial movie producers are in the business of making money. And I could have called the Authors Guild or contacted other authors and asked for advice. But I didn't. I signed the contract. I also realized that if I had needed to be a millionaire, I never would have become a teacher in the first place.

The real issue here, I think, is whether or not to hand over your creation, your vision, to somebody else, who has his or her own vision. When an author writes a book, whether it's fiction or nonfiction, that author has a clear vision of the events and characters in the story. Every reader creates his or her own image of the story, which may or may not match the author's. Movie producers tend to create very clear visions of their own—and their visions are influenced by every previous producer's visions. Unless an author is absolutely certain that the producer's vision and the author's vision reside somewhere in the same solar system, the author shouldn't sell the rights to her work. Period. If it's purely a matter of money, then the author should sign the contract, cash the check, and never look back. If artistic integrity or clarity of vision is the key factor, the author should say, "Thanks, but no thanks," and put that book back on the shelf.

Despite my whining and moaning, and despite the ethnic stereotyping and emotionally manipulative moments, I believe *Dangerous Minds* is a good movie. It touched people's hearts. It inspired a lot of people to become teachers or to become the teachers they always wanted to be. It encouraged many students—students who might otherwise have dropped out—to stay in school. It produced

Coolio's incredibly beautiful song, "Gangsta's Paradise." And it gave a lot of talented but unknown actors a chance to star in a movie with Michelle Pfeiffer. I have to credit the producers for that.

When I was whining about the inaccuracies one day to my friend, Tawana, she said, "I don't care. That movie spoke to black people. We saw ourselves portrayed on screen, and we're hungry for that—whether that portrayal is accurate or not. Black kids need to see themselves reflected in our society."

Tawana's comments made me step back and see the bigger picture, instead of taking the experience so personally. She was right. *Dangerous Minds* is a good movie, in spite of its stereotypes and imperfections, because it touched people's hearts. It inspired people to follow their hearts and their dreams. And it shined a bright light, for a few moments, on a group of students who deserved their fifteen minutes of fame and so much more—the "unteachable" students who turned out to be so talented and intelligent and who taught me how to be a good teacher.

# Twenty Years from Now

Twenty (or even forty) years from now you may not remember your students, but they will remember you. They may not remember the lessons you taught them, and they may have forgotten your face, but they will remember quite clearly the way you made them feel about themselves. They'll remember your criticisms and your compliments—often word for word. I once complimented a bank teller on her beautiful handwriting. She blushed. Thinking she might have misunderstood, I repeated my comment.

The teller looked down at her hands and said, "My second-grade teacher used to hit my knuckles with a ruler because my handwriting was so bad. I loved my teacher and I wanted her to like me, so I sat at my kitchen table every day for months and wrote my letters over and over."

"Well, she must have been pleased to see how beautifully your handwriting turned out," I said.

"I never did meet her standards," the teller said, "but I kept practicing, even after I left her classroom. When I was in the fourth grade, I went back and showed her how nicely I could write."

"Certainly, she praised you for working so hard," I said.

The teller sighed and shuffled through the deposit slips on the counter.

"She didn't remember me." After a moment she forced a smile. "But that was a long time ago, wasn't it?"

Hundreds of other people have written to tell me about their teachers. Clearly, time doesn't seem to diminish people's recollections of their experiences with teachers as it does with other memories. Although age may allow people to put their childhood experiences in perspective, it doesn't necessarily dull the memory—or the joy or pain, as the following excerpts from readers' letters demonstrate.

> One instance really sticks out in my mind. My eighth-grade teacher asked us to write our opinion on a certain subject. I do not remember the subject or how I responded; however, I do remember the teacher practically snickering, the red F for failure, and the comment, "This is not the correct answer," written at the top of the first page. When I questioned the grade, reiterating the fact that she wanted my opinion, she just laughed and said she felt I was wrong. . . . I'm forty-two years old now, and I just learned in the past three years that my opinion is valuable and I am worth something.
>
> —**Diane, St. Albans, West Virginia**

> I remember my first-grade teacher, a woman I can still envision after all these many years, who taught me to read, a habit which has brightened my life for over fifty years since then. I remember a very demanding teacher from whom I took a class in Old English when I worked on my first undergraduate degree—how troublesome he was, how wise he was, what a great gift he gave me in demanding excellence. We have remained friends over the ensuing years. Many teachers stand out like bright stars in my sky.
>
> —**Arthur, Suffield, Connecticut**

My mother and father were divorced when I was about nine or ten, and my mother had only an eighth-grade education. We worked very hard to survive, and I can still remember vividly the stiffness of the shirts I wore made from feed sacks. It was through the help and encouragement of coaches and teachers with the love, compassion, and commitment such as yours that I continued my education. I received an athletic scholarship to college and enlisted as an airman basic in the U.S. Air Force in the middle of my junior year. I then entered the flying training program and graduated with wings and a commission on the same day. I spent twenty years as a fighter pilot and four years in the Pentagon, rising to the rank of colonel. I completed my bachelor's degree under the bootstrap program and my master's degree at night school. I also completed the War College national security management program. I am now vice president and general manager of an aviation company. I am not telling you these things to brag, but to let you know that successful lives and careers often begin by warm and loving teachers.

—**Bud, Springdale, Arkansas**


I am a twenty-four year old female. School was the enemy to me. I was bullied and tormented. I got into a lot of fights and started running with gangs. In the first two fights, I was defending myself, but I still got into trouble for it. Then one day I finally snapped and beat the crap out of the school bully. The other kids at school gave me more attention than the school staff did. Then my rep was made, and I did more than live up to it. The vice principal tried to reach out, but was convinced by the school board that I was a "danger to other children" after my third fight. If I had had just one teacher who cared, I would have actually gone to high school instead of having to get my GED at seventeen.

Most gangsters I grew up around were just like me: lonely, feeling there's nothing out there, no place to fit in, and no one who wants to give them a chance or view them as a person. Most kids who were as bad as me don't recover enough to be able to tell the system that they are all backwards and retarded! Most slip into drugs, prison, or worse, then they have kids of their own who never relate to their teachers either.

—**Dana, Pleasanton, California**

## THE GOOD NEWS

Now for the good news. For every negative letter I receive about a teacher, I receive a hundred positive ones, which confirms my belief that there are many more good teachers than bad. Some years ago, while visiting New York City, I had the good luck and pleasure to meet Bill Parkhurst, a broadcast journalist and author. The conversation turned to teachers at one point, and Bill told me a truly remarkable thing. As a research project for a true crime novel he was writing, Bill had spent a year working closely with a private detective so that he could write more accurately and realistically about the detective in his book.

"You'll be interested and surprised, I think, to know the most common reason that people hire private detectives," Bill told me. "It isn't matrimonial surveillance, as many people think. I interviewed over 150 detectives, and every time I walked into an agency one of the first things I'd hear would be somebody asking for help in locating a former teacher. People want to find their teachers and thank them."

Bill was right. I was interested and surprised to learn that so many people go to so much trouble to track down their teachers. And I was delighted, because I know that for every person who hires a detective, there must be hundreds of other people who are considering the idea—which means that teachers in this country are doing their jobs, educating and inspiring children, despite all the bad press about the failures of our schools.

Of course, there is no way to tell what your students will remember about you, but perhaps you will see something of yourself in these excerpts from three of the many letters I've received in response to *My Posse Don't Do Homework* and "The Girls in the Back of the Class." The first one is from a man who took his teacher for granted:

> Dear Miss LouAnne,
>
> I really don't know where to start. Last night I read the *Reader's Digest* and I found your story "The Girls in the Back of the Class." I usually can't read anything longer than a paragraph, but I used my whole lunch hour reading and thinking about that story. I know you don't know me. As you can tell, my English is not that great. I even hate to write. But I felt the need to write to you. Don't ask me why. Maybe it's because you made me cry. I never cry. Only when somebody in my family dies.

After I read that story I went outside. It was a cold and dark night. I work on a loading dock from 9:00 p.m. until 7:00 a.m. I walked and walked where no one could see me and I cried. I cried hard. I had a teacher just like you in high school who did everything she could to help me. She must have said to me, "You can do it" a hundred times a week. She got me to believe in myself so good that I thought I could do anything.

The main reason I wanted to write to you is because I really didn't know how my teacher felt about me. Reading your story gave me some insight—ooh, big word. I know that y'all are two totally different people, but I bet you she felt the same way about her students as you did. As I read, I saw myself in the story a lot of times. I was selfish. I only cared about my feelings. Now I know that she really cared, and I wish I had just one more chance to tell her thanks.

See. There you go again, making me want to cry. But really I wish that I could hug her real tight and tell her thanks for everything. She played a very important role in forming the foundation of my life.

—Rick, Abilene, Texas

The second letter is from a young woman who wrote from Germany, where she was attending medical school. Her letter is about a teacher she met when she came to the United States as an exchange student during high school.

Dear LouAnne,

When I came to the U.S. as an exchange student, I was put into English-as-a-second-language classes. That day I decided not to like the teacher. This teacher was just as stubborn about keeping me in the ESL program as I was about trying to get out. I finally gave up, not knowing that this would save my life.

I was sure she would hate me for making all this trouble. I expected her to reject me, but instead she kept asking me how I was doing and how things went. For a long time I was suspicious of her behavior toward me, since back then I could not imagine that somebody was truly interested in me and my life. I still remember the day when she offered me to talk to her. She was sitting at her desk and when I was leaving the classroom she called to me. She said that she would always be there if I wanted to talk. I had never heard that before. At that point I had a choice. I could take advantage of her offer or reject it. I figured I had nothing to lose, since I would leave the States anyway once the school year was over, so I took the risk and started to open up bit by bit.

In an environment that was filled with respect, understanding, and love, I was able to tell her things I had denied for a long time. By the end of the school year, the teacher I had once decided not to like became the most important person in my life, and she still is today. She was the first person who told me she loved me and cared about me. She always believed in me and my abilities. Though she was on the other side of the world, she helped me get through one of the hardest times in my life. Shortly after I returned to Germany from the U.S., I was diagnosed with cancer. I had a tumor at the ovary. I had surgery followed by chemotherapy, which was hell. What kept me going through this treatment was the knowledge that somewhere out there was somebody who loved me and respected me for the kind of person I am. At times when I was about to give up, she was there in my mind and reminded me of my strength that I have inside of me.

When there is somebody who loves you and cares about you, you can handle almost everything in life.

—Liesl, Dusseldorf, Germany

And the last letters came from a young man in India who has written twice to tell me about his wonderful teachers—a college professor and a high school teacher. This is the first letter he wrote, when he was still in high school.

Dear Madam,

I am a sixteen-year-old boy and my name is Jaskirat, but you can call me Anu, as I am called at home. The day I read your article I am desperately wanting to contact you. The reasons are many, but the main one is that I had a teacher very much like you and I adored her very much, but after teaching us for a few months she went to Canada. I was really shocked, but I could do nothing. I lost her, maybe forever, but her sweet memories shall remain in my heart for all the remaining days of my life. As I went through your article I could see her in you. I began to think what is the magic in the people like her that they make such long-lasting impressions on the minds in such short periods of contact. The day the results of our tenth standard exam were reported, I stood there with tears in my eyes and hoped that she could know that I, an average student for others, had topped in the whole class with 91 percent marks in her subject (general science).

I am writing this letter to you because I wanted to tell her how I felt about her and express my gratitude, but I could not and so I want to tell it to you because I find you just like my good-natured, sweet, loving young madam. I want to be your friend, maybe because my feelings require an outlet which I am not able to express to very many people. I hope you will accept my friendship. I promise that I will not bother you much.

With love and affection, yours faithfully,

—Anu, Modeltown, India

Several years later, I received another letter from Anu. He wrote to tell me about another teacher, a college professor who took him under his wing and helped him during his difficult freshman year. "Thanks to that professor and other caring teachers, I graduated with high marks," Anu wrote. "I thought you would like to know this."

Someday the students you are teaching now will want to thank you for helping them, although you may never know. And it won't be your A students who will wish they had thanked you; most of them will have thanked you already. The ones who will wish they could thank you will be those difficult students, the ones who sometimes make you want to give up teaching. The irony is that those difficult kids are the very ones who need you to love them the most. In some cases, you may be the only adult who does love them.

On behalf of those students who won't be able to find you or will be too embarrassed to admit how slow they were to appreciate you, I would like to thank you for being a teacher. Thank you. Thank you. Thank you.

—Anu, Modeltown, India

## DISCUSSION POINTS

1. Describe your own best and worst teachers. How will they influence the way you teach?

2. What do you want your students to remember about you twenty or thirty years from now?

## APPENDIX

It's difficult to choose from among the hundreds of books on my shelves and the dozens of "favorites" among the Web sites on my computer, but I think the following are among the best sources of information and inspiration for teachers (and parents who home school or want to know more about how children learn). The Web sites and books chosen for this list emphasize the sharing of information above selling products. Many of these resources have direct links or suggestions for further reading . . . and so the sharing continues. If you find something helpful here, please pass it on to others.

## MY EXCELLENT-ELEVEN BOOK LIST

*Right-Brained Children in a Left-Brained World: Unlocking the Potential of Your ADD Child,* by Jeffrey Freed and Laurie Parsons. New York: Fireside, 1998.

I frequently recommend this book to parents, teachers, and anybody who works with children or adolescents. A former teacher who now works as an educational consultant, Freed devotes his time solely to helping students who have been labeled ADHD. Because he has seen positive results from his methods, Freed maintains that most ADHD children are actually gifted. He discusses diets and medications, but his primary focus is on techniques for helping young people acknowledge and use their talents.

*Brain-Compatible Strategies,* by Eric Jensen. Thousand Oaks, CA: Corwin Press, 2004.

> This eighty-four-page book is packed with hundreds of suggestions and strategies based on principles of neuroscience to turn your classroom into a fun and brain-friendly place. Jensen is the author of several excellent books for teachers and is a staff developer and member of the Society for Neuroscience.

*Teaching with the Brain in Mind,* by Eric Jensen. Alexandria, VA: Association for Supervision and Curriculum Development, 1998.

> This book may be a few years old, but it's still in my top ten. The scientific but accessible explanation of how our brains work make it a valuable resource for teachers. It's immensely helpful to understand how emotion, stress, rewards, and movement affect memory, attention, meaning, motivation, and learning.

*Teach Like a Champion: 49 Techniques That Put Students on the Path to College,* by Doug Lemov. San Francisco: Jossey-Bass, 2010.

> This book offers practical strategies along with specific instructions for implementing them. A great resource for teachers who want to know exactly what to do and how to do it, using proven techniques such as cold calling, maintaining 100 percent participation, and checking for understanding. The book comes with a DVD that features clips of teachers using the techniques at Uncommon Schools across the country.

*How the Brain Learns,* 3rd ed., by David Sousa. Thousand Oaks, CA: Corwin Press, 2006.

> I use this book in my own classes for future teachers. Beginning with basic facts about how our brains work, this book presents research on the brain and learning (brain hemisphere dominance, language acquisition, windows of opportunity, and memory and retention), and suggests practical applications for use in the classroom.

*Read Right: Coaching Your Child to Excellence in Reading,* by Dee Tadlock. New York: McGraw-Hill, 2005.

> Reading specialist Dee Tadlock became frustrated when nobody could teach her intelligent son to read. So she quit her job, went back to college, and studied the brain. Then she developed her own method of teaching reading, which has won many awards and devotees. Tadlock's premise is that readers must have a very clear idea in their brains of what good reading feels and sounds like so that their brains can make adjustments as they learn. This book

is definitely worth a read for any teacher or parent who is interested in ideas for helping struggling readers.

*Tools for Teaching,* by Fred Jones. Santa Cruz, CA: Fred Jones & Associates, 2000.
This is one of my favorites of all the manuals and advice books for teachers, because Jones knows his stuff. In his preface Jones says that this book is "the culmination of all that I have learned about managing classrooms," and he has done an incredibly thorough and entertaining job. Illustrated by Jones's son, this full-color manual is a keeper.

*The Highly Sensitive Person,* by Elaine Aron. New York: Broadway Books, 1997.
Teachers tend to be nurturers by nature, and many teachers are highly sensitive. Aron provides suggestions for handling overwhelming stimuli. Even the not-so-sensitive can benefit from some of her suggestions. This book includes suggestions for teachers who work with sensitive children. (Teachers who find those suggestions helpful may also want to check out Aron's other books.)

*The Curious Incident of the Dog in the Night,* by Mark Haddon. New York: Doubleday, 2003.
This delightful novel can double as a learning text for teachers and a great read for young adults. Teachers who find it hard to empathize with autistic or emotionally distant children may gain some insight. And students will enjoy reading about this fifteen-year-old autistic boy who can do complicated mathematical equations in his head, but can't understand even the simplest human emotions.

*It's So Amazing! A Book About Eggs, Sperm, Birth, Babies, and Families,* by Robie H. Harris. Cambridge, MA: Candlewick Press, 1999.
This has to be one of my all-time favorite books. Michael Emberley's illustrations are absolutely wonderful, and they depict children and adults of every shape, size, and color. Narrated by a bird and a bee, this would be a great book for children who have questions about where babies come from. I think it would also be perfect for teen sex-education courses as well; older students will probably enjoy reading about a potentially embarrassing subject in a factual book that is also amusing and fun.

*Practical Classroom Management,* by Vern Jones. Boston: Pearson, 2011.
This guide for classroom teachers earns an A+ for its focus on creating positive teacher-student relations rather than punitive discipline techniques that so often backfire, especially when used by inexperienced teachers. Excellent advice

in every chapter, from Working with Parents to Increasing Students' Motivation to Learn. And every chapter concludes with an impressive list of recommended reading. The author, a former junior high school teacher and vice principal, is now chair of the Teacher Education Department at Lewis & Clark College. He knows his stuff!

## RECOMMENDED WEB SITES

*www.learner.org*   A wonderful resource for both teachers and learners. Funded by Annenberg Media, this Web site contains over 2,000 online videos about teaching and learning, divided into subject area such as Arts, Language, Science, Social Studies, and Math. Teachers can search by grade level or subject and many of the videos have additional resources and links.

*www.sitesforteachers.com/index.html*   Pages and pages of links for lesson plans, Internet study, songs, clip art, social networks—all for teachers.

*www.busyteacherscafe.com*   Web site for K–6 teachers with themes, strategies, and resources such as printables for reading, writing, math, and Spanish. Customizable calendars, behavior charts, and classroom newsletters.

*teachers.net*   Chat boards, lesson plans, projects, blogs, articles by Harry Wong and others, job listings, printables for teachers of all grade levels and subjects. If you have a great lesson plan, you can submit it here.

*www.theteacherscorner.net*   Free resources for teachers. Printable worksheets, daily writing prompts, pen pals, job listings, collaboration projects, message boards, and more.

*www.schoolrack.com*   Free services for K–12 teachers, including free Web sites for teachers.

*www.educatorpages.com*   This site lets teachers build their own free Web sites with unlimited pages.

*www.behavioradvisor.com/CatchGood.html*   Unfortunately, the main Web site requires registration and is heavily devoted to advertising. But, fortunately, you can read this excellent article "Ways to Catch Kids Being Good" without signing up. Here you will find direct links to real-life experiences of teachers who extol the rewards of focusing on what kids do right instead of what they do wrong.

*www.positivediscipline.com*   The nonprofit Positive Discipline Association is based on the work of Austrian psychiatrist Alfred Adler, who believed that all human beings are equal and worthy of dignity and respect. This program promotes and encourages the development of life skills and respectful relationships in families, schools, businesses, and community systems. Jane Nelsen and Lynn Lott have built on Adler's work. Although this Web site heavily promotes the association's books and speakers, it does offer a number of intelligently written and helpful articles (see link at the top of the page) for teachers and parents, including "18 Ways to Avoid Power Struggles" and "How Do You Motivate a Teen?" Well worth a look for adults who are seeking successful approaches to discipline. Includes some free videos that are also available on YouTube.

*www.accelerated.org*   Educators who need proof that it's possible to create a successful school will find inspiration on this Web site. Two idealistic young teachers in inner-city Los Angeles started a charter school in 1994. Every child at The Accelerated School is treated as a gifted child—and they live up to the high expectations. The school's curriculum incorporates culture, fine arts, and physical activities such as yoga, and the combination seems to work. Attendance averages in the high nineties, test scores in reading and math continue to climb, and the school continues to expand into additional sites.

*http://homepage.smc.edu/zehr_david/brent%20staples.htm*   This Web site provides the full online text of Brent Staples's brilliant essay, "Just Walk on By: A Black Man Ponders His Power to Alter Public Space," which first appeared in print in *Ms.* magazine in 1986. Born into urban poverty, Staples earned his doctorate in psychology before becoming a respected journalist who serves on the editorial board of *The New York Times.*

This essay is a must for any teacher who has tried to repair the damage to self-esteem and confidence that young black males suffer when they realize that many people fear them for no reason. Staples's illuminating and inspiring essay may not heal the hurt, but it will show young minority males that they are not alone. It may also help them learn to cope with a widespread and demeaning prejudice that so many Americans seem unable or unwilling to overcome.

*www.adbusters.org*   This is a great Web site for older students and teachers who are seeking thoroughly thought-provoking articles to spur class discussions, research, and essays. The site's spoof ads for tobacco, fast food, and fashion will definitely appeal to kids who are beginning to realize how advertisers manipulate them.

Beware, though, that this site is sponsored by creative folks (this Canadian-based group describes itself as "a global network of artists, activists, writers, pranksters, students, educators, and entrepreneurs who want to advance the new social activist movement of the information age"), and they occasionally use four-letter words.

*www.bbc.co.uk/learning*    If you visit only one Web site today, make it this one. Make sure you have a little time to spare, because you will want to stay a while. Hosted by the British Broadcasting Corporation, this site allows visitors of all ages—preschool to adult—to go to school online. The home page provides a selection of topics ranging from religion and ethics to art and design. The section of free online courses is also worth a look. My favorite section is under the education and teaching subject listing, which brings up several choices, including "BBC Schools—Teacher Resources." Teachers have the option of choosing by age group: preschool, ages four to eleven, eleven to sixteen, or sixteen and up. Each age group offers lessons, games, and quizzes, without the annoying commercial pop-up ads that plague American educational games online.

This site clearly is devoted to learning, and exploring all of the associated links and lessons would take months or years. ESL teachers may find that the spelling and reading games for ages four to eleven are perfect for both beginning and advanced English language learners. On the main page here, you'll find many choices including Adults, Schools, Parents, Teacher, Distance Learning (free online courses), and Learning Subjects. Teachers will find the Learning Subjects links the most helpful, I think. If you select English, for example, you'll find links for primary school literacy, word skills, world service for English-language learners, and much more. The BBC Primary School-Literacy link is one of my favorites. I love the animated games in the Magic Key, Bitesize Literacy, Little Animals Activity Centre, and Words and Pictures, where Salty Sam helps young learners sort out word sounds in colorful postcards and Colin the Clam plays a fun phonics game. Bitesize Literacy offers selections in phonics, rhyming words, spelling, using pronouns, use of punctuation, synonyms, alphabetical order, and so on. Bitesize Maths gives you choices of games for addition and subtraction, telling time, number sequences, length and weight measurement, money, place value, and more. If you only check out one Web site, make it this one. If you don't have Adobe Reader on your computer, this site connects to a link at BBC Webwise that will help you install it.

*www.englishpage.com*    This is another good resource for language teachers, including ESL. Weekly grammar lessons, vocabulary builders, grammar tutorials, and a host of quizzes and games make this site a winner. The online dictionary is also a valuable resource, especially for low-income students who may not have good dictionaries at home. The highlight of this Web site is the online reading room, which offers a wealth of free reading from newspapers in the United States, United Kingdom, Canada, Australia, New Zealand, South Africa, and India, as well as several popular magazines and full online text of classic novels, from *Alice's Adventures in Wonderland* to *This Side of Paradise*.

*www.EdibleSchoolyard.org*   This eye-appealing Web site offers a superb model for any school, but especially for science teachers who want to give students an unforgettable hands-on experience. The Edible Schoolyard is a nonprofit program located on the campus of Martin Luther King Jr. Middle School in Berkeley, California. The cooking and gardening program began with a collaboration between world-famous chef Alice Waters and the school's former principal, Neil Smith. The school cleared more than an acre of asphalt parking lot, planted a cover crop to enrich the soil, and refurbished the school's abandoned cafeteria kitchen in 1997 to create a kitchen classroom for students.

Today the school's organic garden is integrated into the curriculum. Students are not only skilled gardeners and junior botanists, they are also talented chefs who enjoy the fruits of their own labor. Students attend garden classes where they learn the principles of ecology and respect for all living systems. They plant crops; monitor compost; and harvest their own flowers, fruits, grains, and vegetables. This Web site offers advice and guidelines to teachers who want to start their own projects, along with a variety of links and resources for more information.

*www.eslcafe.com*   Dave's ESL Café is a great site for English as a second language learners, but the grammar quizzes are just as useful for native English speakers. Most of the material is too advanced for most elementary students (except for grammar whizzes), but the site has quizzes on a number of subjects, including geography and American idioms, as well as links to a wide variety of other online sites. The "Pronunciation Power" link under "Stuff for Students" in particular is especially helpful because it allows students to listen to the proper pronunciation of words as many times as necessary.

*www.funbrain.com*   This fun, kid-centered site has some excellent educational games such as Grammar Gorillas and Spell Check, and a great selection of math and reading games. Math Arcade challenges students with twenty-five games.

*www.pbs.org/wgbh/pages/frontline/shows/medicating*    Direct link to the PBS *Front-line* documentary *Medicating Kids: A Report on Parents, Educators, and Doctors Trying to Make Sense of a Mysterious and Controversial Medical Diagnosis—ADHD.* The program interviewed children on medication, their parents, teachers, and experts with vastly diverging opinions. This was the program that publicized the connection between the organization Children and Adults with ADHD (CHADD) and the pharmaceutical corporation that funded the group's pro-Ritalin videotape. As of June 2011, the entire program can be viewed online in five separate chapters. There is also a follow-up posted about the four children and their families who were the subjects of the documentary.

*www.borntoexplore.org*    One of the most comprehensive and competent sites for parents who struggle with the ADHD issue, Born to Explore! The Other Side of ADD is hosted by an environmental scientist who home-schools her two children. Her Web site posts information about "creativity, learning styles, and giftedness to counter the idea that all those kids labeled with attention deficit disorder actually have something wrong with them." This site has nutritional and scientific information, links to an array of resources, book reviews, inspirational quotations, articles, and essays including one entitled "The Problem with CHADD" that provides one of the more balanced critiques of the organization.

*www.blockcenter.com*    Web site hosted by Dr. Mary Ann Block, author of *No More Ritalin* (Kensington Books, 1996). Block is a licensed osteopathic physician who entered medical school in an attempt to learn how to help her own sick child when traditional treatments failed. Her method focuses on underlying causes of ADD/ADHD such as hypoglycemia, allergies, environmental factors, and hyperthyroidism. She provides actual case histories, provides dietary guidelines, gives a good list of resources and explains how to enhance the learning process. Block has developed a series of programs and materials that visitors can purchase for in-home use. She also provides a bibliography of scientific research on ADD/ADHD.

*www.methylphenidate.net*    This site will lead you to the Web site Death from Ritalin, which sounds a little melodramatic until you learn that it was created by a couple whose young son died after taking Ritalin. They include the date of death, the doctor's name, and this statement from their son's death certificate: "Death Caused from Long-Term Use of Methylphenidate (Ritalin)." They list a number of important pieces of information that they believe are being withheld from parents who must decide whether to medicate their children. Worth a quick read, at least.

# INDEX

## A

accelerated.org, 283

Accountability, 6, 14

adbusters.org, 283

Adjective game, 113–114

Adler, A., 283

Administration, meeting, 87–89

Adult education, 13

Agave nectar, 228

Agenda: daily, 64–65; optional, 28–29; posting, 63–65; values/ethics and, 29

Air cleaners, 48

Air-filled balloons, as opening activity, 95

Alpha-linoleic acid (ALA), *See* Omega-3 fatty acids

Alphabetical seating, 57

Alzheimer's disease, 220

Antibullying resources, 146

Appearance, 21–22; checking, 86

Arachidonic acid (AA), 219

Aron, E., 281

Artificial sweeteners, 221–224, 228

Aspartame, 221–224

Assignments for Rude People folder, 73–74

Association for Supervision and Curriculum Development, 98

At risk, use of term, 172

Attendance monitor, 124

Attention deficit hyperactivity disorder (ADHD), and omega-6/omega-3 EFAs, 220

Attitude adjustment, 235–238

Auditory learners, 185, 252–253

## B

Bathroom breaks, planning, 26–28

bbc.co.uk/learning, 284

Bean bag game, 95

Behavior cards, 155–156

behavioradvisor.com/CatchGood.html, 241, 282

BigHugeLabs.com, 50

Bingo-style game, as opening activity, 94

Black, A., 28–29, 232

Block, Mary Ann, 286

blockcenter.com, 286

Bloom's Taxonomy of Cognitive Domains, 129–132; revisions of, 131–132; school applications, 130; terms used in, 131–132; using, 130–131

Body language, 154

Books on tape, 188

Boot camp instructors, and teacher-vs.-student attitude, 98–103

Born to Explore! The Other Side of ADD (Web site), 286
Bovine growth hormone (BGH), 227
*Brain-Compatible Strategies* (Jensen), 280
Brain dominance, 249–253; quiz, 250
Brain Gym exercises, 249
Brodeur, K., 124–125
Bullies, identifying, 144–146
busyteacherscafe.com, 282

## C

Calendar, 64–65
Call-and-response, 95; creating, 85–86; as opening activity, 95
Cameron, C., 140–142
"Casual remarks" to children, 42–44
Chants, to get students' attention, 116
Chill-Out Pact, 86–87
Classroom: agenda, 63–65; calendar, 64–65; checklist, 88; environment, controlling, 24–26; feel of, 49; look of, 49–50; paperwork, 67–68; preparation of, 46–67; private zone, 60–61; rules of order, 65–67; seating, 52–59; sensory details, 47–52; storage, 61–63; supplies, 61–63
Classroom preparation, 46–67, *See also* Self-preparation; agenda, posting, 63–64; paperwork, 67–80; private zone, establishing, 60–62; rules of order, 65–67; seating, psychology of, 52–59; self-preparation, 80–89; sensory details, 47–52; supplies and storage, 61–63; wastebasket, 63
Classroom procedures, 115
Classroom zones, 154–155
Clear instructions, providing, 96–97
Clothing, 21–22; checking, 86
Codell, E., 10
Community colleges, continuing education programs in, 12

Complainers/groaners. teachers as, 6–7
Comprehension, reading, 187–188
Consequences, assigning, 150
Contract with student, creating, 159
Controlling the classroom, 24–26
Covering curriculum, 40–42
Cowboy philosophy, 140–142
Crates for student folders, 71–72
Crazy quiz, as opening activity, 95
Critical thinking, 129, 131, 185
Cultural differences, in discipline, 147
*Curious Incident of the Dog in the Night, The* (Haddon), 281
Curriculum, covering, 40–42

## D

Daily agenda, 64–65
Daily lesson folders, 68
*Dangerous Minds* (movie): author's take on, 268–270; posse update, 261–268
*Dark into Light* (Craig Cameron video), 142
Date sugar, 228
"Daylighting in Schools: Additional Analysis," 213
"Daylighting in Schools: PG&E 1999," 212–213
Death from Ritalin (Web site), 286
Delegation of authority, 123–124
Depression, and EFAs, 220
Desk: keeping off-limits, 61; teacher's, 60–61
Detention, 162–163
Diagnostics, 120–121
Disciplinary referral forms, 72–73
Discipline, 135–170; allowing students to back down gracefully, 149–150; antibullying resources, 146; asking student to step outside the classroom, 156–157; assigning consequences, 150; behavior cards, 155–156; body

language, 154; bullies/outcasts, 144–145; calling the culprit, 159; characteristics of successful policies, 146–153; in the classroom, 136; classroom zones, 154–155; code, designing, 83–85; consequences addressing specific behaviors, assigning, 150; contract, creating, 159; cowboy philosophy, 140–142; cultural differences, 147; and cultural differences, 147; defining your philosophy, 136–137; detention, 162–163; emergency meltdown disaster plan, 164–165; expectations of future behavior, 150–151; experts, consulting, 163–164; good behavior, 152; humiliation, 139; humor, using to defuse tension, 155; ignoring the offender, 154; making student accept responsibility, 149; making students accept responsibility, 149; in the military services, 135–136; modeling behavior expected from students, 147–148; nonverbal messages, sending, 154–155; perpetrator, removing, 160–162; policy, 136–138; positive feedback, providing, 151; positive techniques, 138–139, 138–140; practical advice, 153–162; punitive techniques, 138; quick chat, conducting, 156–157; record keeping, 163; reinforcements, sending for, 160; removing the perpetrator, 160–162; repeated misbehavior, identifying the reason for, 151–152; rewarding good behavior, 152; rewiring your connection, 158; rules vs. procedures, 142; seeking solutions vs. assigning consequences, 150; sending students to the principal, 152–153; separating the child from the behavior, 148; silence, 154; solution seeking, 150; steps to improving, 153–162; student contracts, 159; student transfer, requesting, 160; successful policies, characteristics of, 146–153; teacher's journal assignment, 137–138; time-outs, 157; wiping a student's slate clean, 151

Discipline with Dignity program, 164
Disposable gloves, 63
Disrespect, 14
"Do-Now" activity, creating, 108–111
Docosahexaenoic acid (DHA), 217, 219–220
DonorsChoose.org, 46
Double semicircle seating, 55
Dutton, K., 97, 99

**E**

EdibleSchoolyard.org, 285
educatorpages.com, 282
"Effects of School Design on Student Outcomes" (*Journal of Educational Administration*), 213
Ego needs, 128
Eicosapentaenoic acid (EPA), 217
Electronic grading, 75–76
Emergency meltdown disaster plan, 164–170; addressing the class on your return, 168–170; changing the classroom on your return, 166–167; confronting the students, 168–170; mental health break, 165; planning on quitting, 166; preparation for, 165; professionalism, showing, 165; quitting teaching, 166; rearranging student desks, 167; return-day activities, 168; returning to the classroom, 168; seating chart, creating, 167; self-reflection, 165–166; student desks, rearranging, 167; tell the school when you'll be back, 167; treating yourself well, 167; week's worth of lessons, 167

Lott, Lynn, 283
Love and Logic program, 164

## M

Madden, C., 208–209
Mahone Group, 212
Makeup work folder, 70
Martin, Valerie (student), 205–206
Maslow, A., 126–128; hierarchy of needs, 126–128
Master lesson plan draft, 76–79
Master teacher, and student teaching, 11–12
"Me" dolls, creating, 94
*Medicating Kids: A Report on Parents, Educators, and Doctors Trying to Make Sense of a Mysterious and Controversial Medical Diagnosis-ADHD*, 286
Mental health break, 165
Mental illness, and omega-3 deficiency, 221
Mercola, J., 223
Metacognition, 129–132
Methods of instruction, varying, 253
methylphenidate.net, 286
Misbehavior, 24–26
*Miss J's Welcome Handout*, 80–83
Mistakes: making mandatory, 253–255; teacher's, 14
Mobile classrooms, 56–57
Modified U seating, 54
Moeller, R., 221
Monthly feedback, 245
Mother's milk vs. formula, 219–220
Motivational quotations, 50–52
Motivational strategies, 231–259; attitude adjustment, 235–238; believing in success, 233–234; catching kids being good, 241–242; ethics, introduction of, 258–259; frequent feedback,

requesting, 245; mistakes, making mandatory, 253–255; parents/guardians, reaching out to, 242–243; private journals, 255–257; right-brain dominance, 249–253; student progress, charting, 245–249; using class as guinea pigs, 243–245
Music: in classroom, 47–48; using to introduce poetry, 198–200
Mutual respect, 14
*My Posse Don't Do Homework*, 107, 173, 232, 261, 274

## N

Name cards/file folders, as opening activity, 94
National Clearinghouse for Educational Facilities, 213
National Reading Styles Institute (NRSI), 207
Negatively stated rules, 144
Nelsen, J., 283
"Night Walker" (Staples), 31–32
Noise Meter, 116
Non-teaching jobs, 12–13
Nonverbal cues, 115–117
Nonverbal messages, sending, 154–155
Notes: to parents/guardians of worst-performing students, 243; positive, 242
Nutrition, 215–229, 216–219; arachidonic acid (AA), 219; Aspartame, 221–224; bovine growth hormone (BGH), 227; coffee, 228; corn, 218–219; docosa-hexaenoic acid (DHA), 219–220; essential fatty acids (EFAs), 216–217; fat, 216–219; high-fructose corn syrup (HFCS), 218–219, 224–227; metabolism, 228; mother's milk vs. formula, 219–220; and neurobiologic disorders, 218; omega-3 fatty acids, 216–217;

Progress Wall Chart, 247–249
Punishment, humiliation as, 139–140
Punitive disciple techniques, 138

## Q

Questionnaire, as opening activity, 94
Quick chat, conducting, 156–157
Quitting teaching, 166

## R

Rain stick, 116
Raw honey, 228
*Read Right! Coaching Your Child to Excellence in Reading* (Tadlock), 191–192, 280
Reading, 171–200; aloud, 176–177; battle of will, 190; and being put in the "slow group", 179–180; below grade level, 180–181; books on tape, 188; comprehension, 187–188, 202; correlation of intelligence to reading group, 179–180; finishing reading selections, 181–183; and lighting, 174–175; material of interest, 185–187; opinion, 188–190; opinion of reading selection, 188–190; out loud, ridicule caused by, 176–177; read right approach, 191–192; reading specialist, 188; scotopic (light) sensitivity, 174–175; Shakespeare, 192–193, 192–198; speed, 177–179; and student's assertion of independence, 190; students' aversion to, 172–174; testing, 183–185; textbooks, 185–187; upside down, 191; vision therapy, 175–176
Recommended Web sites, 282–286
Record keeping, 163
Reinforcements, sending, 160
Repeated misbehavior, identifying the reason for, 151–152
Resources, 46; antibullying, 146
Respect, 14; self-, 33–37

Rewarding good behavior, 152
Right-brain dominance, 249–253; learning preferences, 252–253; Wacky Wordies activity, 251; word puzzles, 251
*Right-Brained Children in a Left-Brained World: Unlocking the Potential of Your ADD Child* (Freed/Parsons), 279
Rituals, establishing, 114–115
Roll sheet copies, 71
Rooms with a view, and test scores, 213
Routines, establishing, 114–115
Rules: for creating classroom rules, 143–145; for creating rules, 142–143; negatively stated, 144; of order, 65–67, 121; positively stated, 144–145; procedures vs., 142–143
Rules of order, 65–67, 121

## S

Safety needs, 128
schoolrack.com, 282
*ScienceDaily*, 226
Scientific support, for light sensitivity, 209–211
Scotopic (light) sensitivity syndrome (SSS), 174–175, 204, 206–209; connection between light and learning, 211–213; factors affecting, 207; and glare, 207; and grades, 213; and high-contrast print, 175, 207; and lighting, 207; scientific support, 209–211; signs/symptoms of, 209; study (Alberta, 212; and test scores, 212–213
Seating, 52–57, 52–59; alphabetical, 57; arrangements, 53; double semicircle, 55; double semicircle formation, 55; flexible, 53–54, 53–55; mobile classroom, 54; mobile classrooms, 56–57; modified U, 54; open, 57–59; open